Regional Input–Output Study: Recollections, Reflections, and Diverse Notes on the Philadelphia Experience

The Regional Science Studies Series edited by Walter Isard

Regional Input–Output Study: Recollections, Reflections, and Diverse Notes on the Philadelphia Experience

Walter Isard and Thomas W. Langford
Department of Regional Science
University of Pennsylvania
and
Regional Science Research Institute

The MIT Press Cambridge, Massachusetts, and London, England

339.23
I 76

This book is the tenth in the Regional Science Studies Series. For many of those who have recently perused the last two volumes, the highly abstract *General Theory: Social, Political, Economic, and Regional,* by myself and others, and the rather conceptual *An Analytical Framework for Regional Development Policy*, by Charles L. Leven, J. B. Legler, and P. Shapiro, the current study on regional input–output analysis will be welcomed as a book which brings regional science down to earth and firmly roots it in the world of reality. For the book and its associated table represent data laboriously culled from actual interview and contact with people who are responsible for data collection and record maintenance— data which describe probably better than any other set of data what a complex industrial metropolitan regional economy is, at a real point of time. On the other hand, the data collected are not any old set of random data. They represent materials, systematically collected and organized, to depict interdependence in an actual spatial setting. They are thus consistent with the interdependent focus of regional science and with that dimension of regional science which places emphasis on the orderly collection of comprehensive sets of data to test hypotheses on inter-dependence. These data have been collected having in mind the basic importance of theory and the development of proper concepts on the one hand, and the need for detailed thorough probing partial studies of particular sectors on the other hand.

This book demonstrates the feasibility of a highly detailed (500–600 sector) regional input–output study. This demonstration, together with the experiences it records and the lessons learned, should greatly facilitate the undertaking of the much needed multiregional studies which are disaggregated in character.

Finally, once again we have a study which points up the flexibility of the techniques and tools associated with the field of regional science. The study, initially conceived to explore the impact of NASA and other major federal activities and later extended to examine the impact of reduction in military expenditures, is shown to be not only applicable for such investigations, but also of basic significance for the new set of environmental problems which are emerging and which must be forcefully attacked.

Walter Isard

This book centers around procedures and methodology of regional input–output analysis. The discussion is primarily oriented to the experience in the construction of the most extensive and detailed regional input–output table completed to date. The table is the Philadelphia Region Input–Output Coefficient Table.* Elsewhere in four volumes of *Working Papers* [Isard, Langford, and Romanoff, 1966–1968], we have presented the detail of our procedures and methodology, with all their inadequacies and with all the computational errors which inevitably creep into any such extensive study. In contrast, in this book we wish to develop a series of general comments and discussion,[1] for the benefit of those who may undertake new input–output studies. We wish to record some of the mistakes we have made and report on the lessons we have learned. We wish to set down some of the thoughts we have had and now have on how to allocate the limited resources available for a study, how to use the table once it is constructed, and in general how to go about it. Put in another way, we write this book so as to make it easier for those who follow to evaluate more easily the costs and benefits of any proposed input–output study, to anticipate more adequately the difficulties, and to assess more accurately the gains. Also for those who have already made the decision to construct a regional input–output table, we hope to be able to help guide them through the host of problems that they will confront, and ease their resource allocation problem. Of course, those actively developing studies will want to read carefully the four volumes of *Working Papers*.

As is abundantly clear in the *Working Papers*, and in this book, we have made many mistakes in both judgment and calculation. Also there are many shortcomings of the data and our concepts. We would indeed be misleading if we were not to acknowledge these mistakes and shortcomings. But we must also add that it is in the nature of extensive, large-scale empirical investigations such as those involved in census-taking and tabulation, input–output analysis, and construction of regional accounts, that mistakes will be made, and that data shortcomings will exist. Too frequently, when government agencies have been the major producers of these large-scale empirical studies (because usually they alone have had the necessary resources), they have not found it possible to be entirely frank about the host of questionable procedures which must be employed in these studies. Nor have they been as free as we are to spell out in full

---

* The revised Philadelphia table of input-output coefficients covering 496 sectors and the final demand sectors can be purchased from the Regional Science Research Institute, G.P.O. 8776, Philadelphia, Pennsylvania 19101, U.S.A. at U.S. $4.75. Cash or check must accompany the order.

[1] Also in this book we do not present a systematic treatment, on the conceptual and mathematical level, of diverse regional input-output models. Such is available in Isard et al., 1960, Chapter 8.

the data inadequacies. Often, even when nongovernment agencies have undertaken large-scale empirical studies, there has been the usual pressure to complete the study by some deadline date. By that date the resources have been fully depleted, such that an unhurried, reflective evaluation of the methodology based upon hindsight is not possible.

Fortunately, because this particular study has had the good fortune to be conducted at a major university and a nonprofit research institute, we are in a position to reveal in full our errors, and the inadequacies of our procedures and data. Further, the authors have been able to find some free time to reflect on their experience, without undue pressure from other activities.

Such candor as ours should not be construed as implying that the findings and outcome of our study are not valuable. They are indeed valuable—and in fact more so than initially anticipated. We judge the final materials to be of a rather high order of accuracy for large-scale empirical studies, and we are finding them to be useful in many unexpected ways. Our candor should therefore not be construed as lending support to the narrow view that in the light of the many inadequacies of data and concepts, large-scale empirical investigations such as ours should be rejected for general theorizing. For the senior author, from his own experience with theory development, would assert that for every inadequacy of an empirical investigation there exist at least two questionable assumptions in a general theory.

The wise analyst and policy formulator recognizes, of course, the value of all kinds of studies, and knows how to evaluate and utilize findings from general theoretical studies, partial theoretical studies, small-scale empirical investigations, and large-scale investigations. He knows that the large-scale empirical investigations cannot substitute for the development of logical structures in terms of the insights the latter provide; he also knows that logical structures cannot substitute for the increased knowledge of relevant magnitudes which comes from such highly disaggregated empirical analysis as that which lies behind the Philadelphia study. Each type of study—theoretical, empirical, large-scale, and small-scale—has an important contribution to make to urban-regional analysis and to the understanding of basic social problems.

The subtitle of the book is to be emphasized, namely, *recollections, reflections, and diverse notes on the Philadelphia experience.* We wish to emphasize this subtitle because we really do not attempt any systematic development of a book on procedure and methodology for regional input–output study based on the Philadelphia experience. We are not able to do this, partly because the authors did not have that large amount of free time which would have allowed for the systematic development of such a book. Second, sometimes more informal statements are more useful than more formal ones. The former can often be much more revealing of the problems and the kinds of mistakes made. Hence, for these two reasons, the reader will have to put up with an "unsystematic" development of ideas.

The research for this study was initially undertaken by the Department of Regional Science, Wharton School of Finance and Commerce, University of Pennsylvania under a grant from the National Aeronautics and Space Administration (Grant NsG–497–39–010). The study was initiated in September 1962 under the direction of Walter Isard, in close association with Thomas W. Langford, Jr. and Eliahu Romanoff. At a later stage the research was carried on under the auspices of the Regional Science Research Institute through grants from the Federal Water Pollution Control Administration, U.S. Department of the Interior (Grant #WP–00938) and Resources for the Future, Inc.

Although Eliahu Romanoff was not able to join in the writing of this book, his contribution to the study was indeed a major one, and it is explicitly recognized in his joint authorship of Volume I of the *Working Papers*. At the early stages, Gerald J. Karaska contributed in an important way. Willis J. Winn, Dean of the Wharton School, generously made available the full facilities of the Wharton School. Sylvia Persky graciously handled the innumerable administrative problems. Many others were helpful at a number of places in the study. At the risk of failing to mention all who have helped, we wish to acknowledge our indebtedness to the following: David F. Bramhall, Stanislaw Czamanski, Henry Hertzfeld, Edward T. Horn, Susan Isard, Toni Isard, Eugene Jaffe, William Knapp, Robert MacDaniels, Daniel J. McNichols, John Riebman, Eugene Schooler, Mary Smith, Raymond Steben, Mary Sulena, Robert Thomas, Richard Wendell, and Caroline Whitney.

Finally, the authors gained much from the discussions of the informal ad hoc Regional Input–Output committee of the Regional Science Research Institute, comprising, among others, Professor W. Leontief, chairman, Harold Barnett, David Bramhall, John Cumberland, Edgar Dunn, Morris Goldman, Werner Hirsch, Charles Leven, William Miernyk, Leon Moses, Eliahu Romanoff, and Charles Tiebout; and Benjamin H. Stevens and Robert Coughlin, officers of the Regional Science Research Institute.

Of course, the authors alone are responsible for any of the shortcomings of this book.

W. I.
T. W. L.

References
Isard, Walter, et al. (1960). *Methods of Regional Analysis: An Introduction to Regional Science*. Cambridge, Mass.: M.I.T. Press.

———, Thomas W. Langford, Jr. and Eliahu Romanoff (1966–1968). *Philadelphia Region Input–Output Study, Working Papers*, Volumes 1–4. Philadelphia: Regional Science Research Institute.

1

2

3

4

10

11

12

13

14

15

Some New Directions: Environmental Quality Analysis and Standardization

Tables

Regional Input–Output Study: Recollections, Reflections, and Diverse Notes on the Philadelphia Experience

1.1 Introduction and Overview

The purpose of this chapter is to introduce the reader to the book by making a general survey of its contents. While the book is a rather unsystematic development of recollections, reflections, and diverse notes on an experience, nonetheless an overview and capsule summary of the materials covered are both possible and useful.

1.2 The Choice of a Region

Frequently, the first basic question in regional input–output studies concerns the choice of a region. Aside from cases in which the region of study is specified by a contract or grant, the need to avoid excessive data-collecting and processing costs requires that (1) the region chosen for the study *not* be changed during the course of the study; (2) there exist an abundance of usable secondary data for the region *when the region is large*; and (3) the region be of such a nature that the resulting input–output tables can be useful for the study of a number of problems—although on occasion a particular problem may be so important as to dictate the choice of region.

In the Philadelphia study, we decided to avoid the additional data-collecting and processing costs that would result if we chose a region that cut across county boundaries. We also decided to avoid the heterogeneity and complexities that would be encountered if we were to include in our study region the areas around Trenton, the state capital of New Jersey, and Wilmington, the primary industrial-metropolitan core of the state of Delaware.

We chose the Philadelphia Standard Metropolitan Statistical Area (SMSA)—a region with an abundance of usable secondary data and a homogeneous structure highly meaningful for analysis of economic interdependence. This region has a long and rich tradition as an urban area, a diversified economic base, and is subject to forces of population spread and suburban growth characteristic of current-day metropolitan regions of the United States.

1.3 The Choice of a Base Year

When the base year of the study is not specified by a contract, it is very desirable to choose a year for which an abundance of secondary data of quality are available from Census and other sources, through regular publications or special studies. Also, if extensive primary data are to be collected by interview, a year must be chosen which is not so recent as to result in negative responses by establishments in highly competitive industries that do not wish to disclose information on their recent operations; but at the same time the base year must not be so far in the past as to reduce significantly the ease with which respondents can find records in their files. Further, since it may take three to five years to complete a table of coefficients, the base year should be as recent as is consistent with the factors just mentioned in order to maximize the relevance of the derived technical production coefficients for evaluating impacts of present and future policies, and for other studies of a current nature.

Since the Philadelphia study was initiated in 1963, and since extensive Census data were available for 1958 and 1960 but not for 1961 and 1962, it would have been unwise to have selected a base year later than 1960. We chose 1959 as the base year because we had anticipated extensive use of 1959 data collected in the major Penn Jersey Transportation Study, which was in progress, and because this year was also relatively normal from the standpoint of business conditions.

1.4 The Selection of a Sector Classification System

When the Philadelphia study was initiated, our thinking was least crystalized on the issue of the proper sector classification system. Accordingly, we decided to conduct some exploratory work in order to let accumulating experience over time determine the final sector classification scheme to be adopted. Our initial explorations with schemes conforming to the 2- and 3-digit Standard Industrial Classification (SIC) codes led us to the conclusion that at such aggregate levels we would not be able to study relationships of significance for the region and at a depth that we would find stimulating. We therefore decided to develop a classification scheme comparable in detail to a 4-digit SIC system, despite the warnings of colleagues that we might never be able to complete the table on such a disaggregated basis. The final sectoring classification scheme used was 4-digit for manufacturing and most of the trade sectors; 3-digit for the rest of the trade sectors, the financial sectors and some service sectors; and 2-digit for the remaining endogenous sectors, with final demand disaggregated into 86 sectors.

Our sector classification system has shortcomings for at least several reasons. First, our system, as the SIC and others, probably does not reflect the proper mixture for input–output analysis of the three bases of classification—by process, by final product, and by raw material—that can be used. That this mixture should vary with the degree of disaggregation is clear, but what the mixture should be for any degree of disaggregation is yet to be determined through research.

Second, our sector classification system is undoubtedly too disaggregated at specific places; however, we feel that it is necessary in general to have disaggregation at least at a 4-digit sector breakdown in order to avoid errors from grouping together establishments with product mixes that differ greatly. Study of our Philadelphia establishments clearly demonstrate that the more detailed the sectoring scheme, the fewer the differences that exist among the production coefficients of the establishments of any given sector. Accordingly, the more detailed the sectoring scheme, at least up to a 4-digit level, the more accurate the impact analysis and projections when establishments are expected to grow and decline at different rates.

Third, our sector classification system should and could have been extended at certain places to a 5- or 7-digit basis. The electrical components industry, for example, should have been disaggregated at a finer detail than 4-digit. However, one must recognize that it may be exceedingly difficult for an establishment producing several 5- or 7-digit commodities to provide information on specific inputs associated with the production of each. Further, at such a detailed level there are questions regarding stability of coefficients and sensitivity to technological shift. Yet, it is better to err in the direction of overdisaggregation, because disaggregate data can always be aggregated at a relatively small cost, whereas aggregate data cannot always be disaggregated when desired.

A basic lesson that we learned from our Philadelphia study is that there can be considerable flexibility in setting up a sector classification system. A scheme may be comprised of 2-, 3-, 4-, 5-, and even 7-digit sectors. There are neither theoretical nor practical grounds to preclude this. Hence, the investigator can take into account the data sources, disclosure problems, and noncooperative attitudes unique to his region. He can develop the specific mix of sectors by the type-digit that is best suited to his region. On the other hand, when each investigator does develop his own unique sector classification scheme, it is desirable that he do so in ways that conflict least with the need for standardization for multiregional and interregional studies.

1.5 General Survey Procedures

When a big region like Philadelphia is the subject of an input–output study, cost considerations greatly restrict the amount of primary data that an investigator can seek. While he may be able to conduct a fairly complete census of government agencies, and of large financial, nonprofit, and other institutions, such as major insurance companies and universities, of necessity he can afford to interview only a sample of the numerous households and manufacturing and service establishments in his region. For each sector that is sampled, he must identify the point at which the marginal cost of obtaining additional information is equal to the marginal gains, and accordingly develop criteria that determine adequate coverage.

Although in theory the investigator should stratify the establishments in each sampled sector by size, output mix, capital vintage, and other major variables, in practice he seeks to obtain a certain percentage coverage of establishments and their employment, and frequently sacrifices sophistication of technique along the way because of numerous difficulties.

For example, in the Philadelphia study we generally defined adequate coverage for a sector as (1) when establishments accounting for 65 percent or more of a sector's employment had been successfully interviewed, and (2) when the number of these establishments was no less than three. For some sectors we were not able to meet these criteria; for others we raised them if we could expect a major improvement in the quality of its data by so doing. In general we tended to minimize the number of establishments to be interviewed by first interviewing the largest establishments in a sector. For cost and other reasons, we did not sample adequately establishments at New Jersey and suburban locations.

We learned many lessons. For example, when coefficients for all sectors, including manufacturing, transportation, and wholesale, are not to be calculated simultaneously, that is, when it is necessary to collect and process data and construct coefficients by sectors in some sequence, there are definite advantages in calculating the coefficients for the transportation and wholesale sectors first, so that when input purchases by manufacturing and other sectors are to be adjusted from purchasers' prices to producers' prices, the relevant margins are at hand. We consider justifiable our assumption that in an input–output survey, data on sales distribution are not to be preferred to data on input purchases. Although it is easier to obtain the data from establishments on distribution of their sales, particularly by 2-digit consuming sectors, the investigator is not able to check the quality of returns as effectively as he is when data are on input purchases. We judge that input purchase patterns are likely to be much more consistent among the establishments of a sector than their sales distribution data patterns are. We found that it is important to pretest questionnaires for content, at least by broad divisions of economic activity if not by group of sectors or sectors alone; and that it is desirable to have different size questionnaires for different sectors and for different sizes and kinds of establishments. Moreover, we should and could have collected much more basic information on nonmaterial inputs.

1.6 Secondary Production and Margins

Before coefficients can be constructed from the data on the completed questionnaires and in accord with the selected sector classification scheme, it is necessary to decide how to treat secondary production (output) and margins. There are advantages in transferring the secondary products and the inputs required for their production from each establishment's records to the sectors whose primary outputs correspond to the secondary products. By so doing the investigator can, for example, more easily and accurately reconcile the demands for any commodity with estimated supply. Offsetting this and other advantages are the major difficulties of identifying from an establishment's records the inputs associated with its

ORDER FORM

PHILADELPHIA REGION
INPUT-OUTPUT COEFFICIENT TABLE

9 panels covering 196 endogenous sectors and 86 final demand sectors

Mail this order to

Regional Science Research Institute
G.P.O. Box 8776
Philadelphia, Pennsylvania 19101, U.S.A.

Please send me _____ copies at $4.75 per copy of the Revised Philadelphia Region Input-Output Coefficient Table. Enclosed is a check of money order in the amount of $_____ U.S. (check or money order must accompany order).

Send Table(s) to:

_____

_____

_____

_____ Zip_____

production of any given secondary product. Further, there are certain questions concerning the validity of projections based on the coefficients that might subsequently be derived, although there are also questions concerning the use of coefficients constructed from an establishment's records when secondary products and associated inputs have not been transferred. Because the transfer of secondary production and associated inputs would have increased greatly the cost of the Philadelphia study, we decided not to effect such transfer except in a few unusual situations.

We chose to develop coefficients in terms of producers' (FOB) rather than purchasers' (delivered) prices. We judged that the use of producers' prices yields a more accurate set of technical production coefficients for a sector, because the derived coefficients remain unaffected by changes in the goods distribution pattern of a system. We therefore had to remove all transportation costs from outlays on inputs when these outlays were reported at purchasers' prices.

In the Philadelphia study we failed to obtain primary data from local and nonlocal transportation agencies. We used extensively the Office of Business Economics (OBE) national transport margins, defined by type of commodity. This was one of the least satisfactory procedures of our study. In retrospect, we should have derived transport margins directly from primary data, differentiated by transport mode, and we also should have obtained, at least for motor freight transportation, two margins, one for interregional shipments and one for intraregional shipments.

In the Philadelphia study we were successful in collecting quality primary data on wholesale services by 4-digit sectors and were able to derive an excellent set of wholesale margins. There are difficulties in the use of such margins, however. One difficulty arises because many manufacturers sell their output directly to other manufacturers, and the margins involved in these sales are in effect hidden payments for wholesale services produced as a secondary product of the selling manufacturer. Hence, wholesale margins should be applied explicitly only to fractions of the total intermediate sales recorded on a flow table. A second difficulty arises because there exist two types of independent wholesalers, merchant and nonmerchant, who generally incur different costs in operation because of differences in size and other factors. Therefore, for any given commodity two different margins may be applicable. To be able to apply these different margins, however, the investigator must have data from establishments on the percentage breakdown of purchases through each type of wholesaler—data that are exceedingly difficult to obtain.

For these and other reasons, it would have been difficult to apply the excellent wholesale margins we did derive. More pertinent, however, was the fact that once these margins were obtained, it was not feasible to go back to the edited coefficients for each manufacturing sector and adjust these coefficients for wholesale trade service expenditures. We now have learned that if wholesale margins are to be obtained from primary data, the interviewing of wholesale sectors must not come after that for manufacturing. It must precede or be simultaneous with the interviewing for manufacturing. And likewise, the interviewing of the transportation sectors should not come after that of the wholesale sectors, since the proper derivation of wholesale margins requires adjustment for and thus knowledge of transport costs.

In the Philadelphia study, primary data on retail operations were obtained directly, chiefly through mail survey. Although we were able to develop a good set of retail margins, we did not attempt to identify from primary sources that fraction of these margins which represents services provided by retailers who in effect export their services when nonresidents of the region purchase goods from them.

1.7 The Construction of Coefficients

Before the actual calculation of coefficients, the investigator must determine whether or not the data that he confronts for the establishments of each sector can and should be adjusted. He may judge that variations in the data primarily reflect scale economies or diseconomies, and he may decide to derive not average coefficients but rather coefficients relevant for a particular size of operation for use in making projections into the future and for impact analysis. On the other hand, he may judge that variations in the data primarily reflect differences in the specialization and efficiencies of the reporting establishments; he may wish to adjust them to or to use selectively the data on the returned questionnaires in order that his coefficients reflect a "standard" degree of specialization and efficiency. Or he may judge that variations in the data primarily reflect differences in technology and capital vintage and so may wish to use only returns of those establishments that follow best practice, thereby deriving coefficients to approximate for some future year average practice after allowance for technological change. Or he may judge that variations in the data primarily reflect the interplay of two or more of these factors and others as well, and accordingly may make adjustments and use the returns selectively. Whatever the case, it is important that the investigator be explicit as to what he assumes and what he does.

Additionally, the investigator must determine the number of coefficients he will calculate and, in particular, the cutoff point for each sector at which he stops calculating additional minor coefficients. This cutoff point generally must be determined on the basis of marginal costs and marginal gains. Further, the investigator must reach certain decisions on the actual calculation procedures themselves. While it is highly desirable to use electronic data processing when there exists a very large number of well-prepared questionnaires in which responses are complete and of excellent quality, there are, in practice, many reasons for not doing so. The responses the investigator receives usually turn out to be an unhealthy mixture of good and poor data. Some obvious outlays are often omitted by establishments. Other expenditures are wrongly classified by the respondent. Still others may be relevant, but this fact becomes evident only after all the responses have been studied. Moreover, the data often reflect different degrees of vertical integration among establishments and thus need to be adjusted. Too often the respondents provide approximate answers that are erroneous. Thus, for these and other reasons, the use of electronic data processing is often not practicable because it cannot substitute for good judgment and careful sifting of data by an alert analyst.

Another issue concerns the number of decimal digits to be carried in the computations. We chose six decimal digits in order to avoid the rounding to zero of coefficients pertaining to consumption of items that were small dollarwise in terms of the output of any given consuming sector but that cumulatively could not be ignored if there was to be an accounting for the total output of the sectors producing these items. Also, although in theory it is most efficient to perform certain computations simultaneously for all sectors, such as margin adjustments, there is also a great advantage in using slack resources of research staff and director as they become available and thus doing many of the calculations on an establishment-by-establishment basis, with no particular schedule in mind. In this way bottlenecks are avoided and a more careful sifting of the data is possible.

In general, although there is no single best procedure for editing the data, filling in gaps, ironing out inconsistencies, and upgrading the data of poor returns, the extensive use of visual inspection, balance techniques, and comparison with other sources of data can eliminate most if not all the serious errors in the calculation of the coefficients.

1.8 Output Estimation and Control Totals

The estimation of gross output by sector, to serve as control totals, is frequently a major source of error in input–output work because of inconsistencies in definitions and inadequacies of the secondary data utilized. Output may be measured either in physical or money units. The use of physical units avoids spurious changes in output because of fluctuations in prices, and spurious differences in output when the same homogeneous unit is sold at different prices. On the other hand, the use of money units is much more in keeping with the records maintained by establishments and greatly facilitates checking questionnaire returns for consistency, establishment by establishment and sector by sector.

Sector output, whether in physical or money units, can be viewed from the standpoint of (1) production, (2) shipments, or (3) sales. Serious errors can arise in input–output analysis from the inappropriate use of any one or more of these bases for measuring outputs of the several sectors. For example, during the course of a year certain establishments may perform much work on large units of products that are not yet finished and therefore would not be registered as output when shipments or sales are used as the measure. Also, *indirect* measurement of output in terms of value added or employment can give rise to still other major errors.

A piecemeal approach to the estimation of gross output by sector has often been considered to be inferior to the approach that would carefully construct a relevant set of social accounts. From such a set, a highly aggregate input–output table can be constructed, providing control totals for each of a few major economic divisions, from which estimated output can be obtained by sectors through disaggregation. Aside from the fact that a carefully constructed set of social accounts is not likely to be available for the study region, it is to be recognized that social accounts are really secondary data, and their allocation among economic divisions and then sectors is again keyed to secondary data by means of indices. Frequently, such multiple use of secondary data leads to large errors in the estimate of the output finally determined for a given sector.

In the Philadelphia study we eschewed the approach that would construct a consistent set of social accounts, and built up in piecemeal fashion a set of output control totals for 4-digit sectors. For the manufacturing sectors we used as guidelines the value-of-shipments data from the 1958 Census of Manufactures, even though we found many errors in the Census classification of large establishments and suspected errors of the same order of magnitude in the Census classification of small and medium-sized establishments. We had to update the 1958 Census material by means of employment indices that have many shortcomings, and we had to multiply employment estimates of each sector by an appropriate estimated value of output per employee—where this value, based on a variety of materials, was also subject to error. We realize now that we should have used more extensively the data from the local Pennsylvania sources and from our own survey returns to derive value of output per employee. We should have recognized more pointedly that censuses tend to use rather outdated classification schemes—for example, with regard to ordnance, electronics, and research and development sectors—reflecting the fact that governmental bureaucratic practice generally can change only slowly with time. Lastly, we and many other analysts would profit greatly were the Census and other sources of data able to provide information on air and water pollutants, and solid waste, noise, and other noneconomic commodities that we will have to project in future studies for evaluation of alternative comprehensive pollution control schemes.

1.9 Final Demand Sectors

Regional input–output analysts can and should define the set of final demand sectors in a much more flexible way than national input–output analysts do. The regional analyst can cut the circle of interdependence at different places than the national analyst can, and he should do so, since the traditional final demand sectors—households, government, capital formation, and exports—play quite different roles in the functioning of a regional economy. Parts of these sectors may well be placed in the structural matrix; also, parts or even the whole of certain basic industry sectors may be placed among the final demand sectors.

In the Philadelphia study, the households sector was treated as a single sector. It should have been disaggregated to recognize at least different expenditure vectors of several different income classes, and we should have collected primary data on factor payments by type and on wages and salaries by type of occupation. Such disaggregation, or other disaggregation, such as that on migrant and nonmigrant population, can help correct some of the imbalance in a sector classification scheme; and it enables the investigator to capture more accurately different income multiplier effects and their repercussions upon the diverse sectors of the economy.

In our study, we did not make any attempt to collect data on inventory and inventory changes, because most input–output studies have had unsatisfactory experiences in attempting to account for inventory change. While we might have assumed that inventory changes of smaller firms are on net unimportant, and accordingly might have confined our attention to the collection of inventory data for the larger firms for 1959, this year was a year of rather normal conditions, for which we would judge that there were no major inventory changes, except with regard to steel items, for which we were able to adjust anyway.

In the Philadelphia study we did not directly question establishments on their capital expenditures on plant and equipment; we now realize these questions easily could have been placed at the end of the questionnaire. Rather, we developed total capital expenditures by sector on the basis of data available for the five Pennsylvania counties, and then derived capital coefficients for each of 45 sectors on the basis of Census of Manufactures and National Planning Association data. For purposes of dynamic regional input–output analysis, the capital coefficients that were derived are perhaps as useful for projection as any set of capital coefficients that could have been derived from data reported by establishments for one, two, or more years in the past. Modernization of equipment and technological change make obsolete very rapidly the data from which capital coefficients are derived.

While the capital coefficients in the study are perhaps some of the most relevant available, the difficult problems in using such coefficients in dynamic regional models should be fully appreciated. Among engineers, among economists, and between engineers and economists, there are significant differences on key issues such as what existing capacity is, what if any piecemeal additions of plant and equipment can effect expansion of capacity, and what rates of wear and tear and obsolescence are appropriate for dynamic investment programming.

In the treatment of government sectors, not only must the investigator maintain a distinction among federal, state, local, and other levels, but also, where possible, he should develop government sectors in terms of programs, rather than solely by agencies or units. In this way the program mix (product mix) problem is partly avoided and it becomes possible to use input–output analysis more effectively for policy evaluation. For similar reasons, it is also important to keep a full record of all transfers of funds among government agencies and to disaggregate the tax receipts (revenues) row so that revenues from specific taxes pinpointed for particular programs can be projected and contrasted with planned levels of expenditures on these programs.

The final demand sectors of the Philadelphia study embody perhaps the most comprehensive and extensive coverage of expenditures by federal establishments yet developed for a large metropolitan region. The state government activities of New Jersey and Pennsylvania were largely outside the region; hence, only the relevant parts of these activities were covered. Most of the important activities of the many local governments were covered and in typical fashion placed within the structural matrix.

1.10 The Estimation of Imports, Exports, and Interregional Flows

The critical importance for regional analyses of data on imports and exports has been clearly recognized. In regional input–output work it is now almost a *sine qua non* to obtain total imports and total exports, both disaggregated by commodity. The key issue in current work is whether to seek data on sales distribution by commodity and region of destination, or data on purchases of each input by region of origin, or both. We judge it is better to attempt to collect and develop one good set of data than two sets of poor or mediocre data; and that it is best to focus on input purchases data by region of origin, even though this focus may lead to higher data-collection and processing costs.

A second issue concerns the choice of an appropriate set of regions to use in the collection of imports and exports data. While it is highly desirable to choose that set of regions which may also be used in other regional input–output studies, and while it is desirable to define regions in terms of areas such as states and even counties, rather than larger areas such as multistate units, practical considerations of costs and the fact that few other regional input–output studies may be concomitantly under way suggest that in his choice the investigator had better give more weight to the set of regions most suitable for the immediate purposes and objectives on hand than to the set that is likely to make his data most useful for future input–output studies.

In the Philadelphia study, each sector's exports to the rest of the world were estimated directly from sales distribution data provided by establishments, with the use of location and marketing theory and other knowledge that we possessed. Often this task involved the adjustment of technical coefficients to yield more reasonable estimates of intermediate demand in order to satisfy the equation: *regional production plus imports (total supply)* = *intermediate demand plus exports plus other final demand (total demand)*. Imports by sector were estimated almost entirely indirectly as a residual from the equation just stated. When the residual was such as to suggest a *negative* amount of imports for a sector, the technical production coefficients along the sector's row generally were adjusted upward to increase the estimate of intermediate demand so that estimated imports were no longer negative.

Looking to the future, we hope for (1) interregional data from the Census of Transportation that will be more suitable for multiregional input–output studies, (2) collection by public agencies of more data on multicounty units smaller than states, and (3) the implementation of one or more multiregional studies. Now that the detailed Philadelphia region coefficient table is completed, we believe it feasible to attempt a pure interregional input–output study in which primary data from wholesalers on their sales distribution by regions and commodity purchases by region would be used to estimate the sales distribution and input purchase patterns of establishments that sell and buy through wholesalers. It is also feasible to implement a multiregional Moses-Chenery type study, whose data requirements are less severe, and a Leontief balanced regional input–output model, whose data requirements are least stringent of all. However, the strong assumptions of the Leontief model, e.g., that national coefficients approximately characterize conditions of production in each of the several regions of a system, limit its application to an examination of the impact of alternative national policies when it is desirable to consider regional implications *and* when it is not possible to consider each region in and of itself together with its interrelations with the rest of the world.

1.11 Reconciliation and the Undistributed and Dummy Sectors

In the construction of an input–output table, there always comes that day of reckoning when the various magnitudes recorded must be examined for consistency. For each commodity viewed as primary output of a sector, the sum of the purchases listed by sectors, including the final demand sectors and estimated exports, must equal the sum of local production, estimated imports, and change in inventories. Further, the coefficients in any column must add to unity. Invariably, many inconsistencies exist in the table as first constructed. To eliminate some of these inconsistencies, dummy sectors may be introduced. Such sectors can be used, for example, to receive that output of any given sector which we know was sold locally to various establishments that failed to record their purchases of such output because each of these purchases was minor— as in the case of office supplies and lubricating oils. Dummy sectors are also used to receive the very significant output of sectors such as maintenance and repair construction, and transportation services, purchases of which are almost invariably reported inadequately by establishments. The outputs of the dummy sectors are then allocated to different using sectors in a way that the investigator judges to be most appropriate. The investigator may also develop modules pertaining to the consumption of certain output items (e.g., office supplies) in a fixed-proportions pattern in assigning the total output of these items (as listed in the dummy sector) to diverse consuming sectors.

Often, however, a full allocation is difficult to make, as in the case of newspaper advertising. This situation then requires the establishment of an undistributed demand column, which serves as a place at which the investigator may set down local output that cannot be allocated meaningfully to other sectors. In this column he may also set down other output that he judges would be too costly in time and effort to assign to consuming sectors. Further, he may place in the undistributed demand column the secondary products of a sector—output often unaccounted for because establishments tend to list their inputs by commodity and assign a sector classification to any given commodity corresponding to the sector producing it as primary product.

In the Philadelphia study we found that many of the items placed in the unallocated demand column were outputs from nonmanufacturing sectors. This situation reflected our failure to ask manufacturing establishments properly for their purchases of service inputs. Hence, if we were to do the study again, we would ask a more detailed set of questions and thereby reduce the items in the undistributed demand column in both number and magnitude.

We frequently made across-the-board increases in technical coefficients to account for the failure of establishments to report minor purchases, or to record properly some major purchases. Sometimes we were able to adjust the coefficients selectively on the basis of our knowledge, or to review carefully the allocation of certain inputs, as was done for textile inputs into the apparel industry.

To match the undistributed demand column, we constructed an undistributed inputs row, and in order to have the coefficients in each column add to unity, we developed an "unspecified import" row, which was not included in the structural matrix.

1.12 Subarea Analysis: Bucks County

Early in the Philadelphia study we decided that it would be desirable to explore intraregional analysis within a regional input–output framework. We chose Bucks County as the subarea to be studied within the Philadelphia region. We particularly desired to cast light upon the strategic importance of imports and exports for a subarea of a metropolitan region, and the differences in technology that generally might be associated with differences in size and spatial positions of establishments within the metropolitan region.

Although it was not possible to complete this part of the study, we did learn many valuable lessons. One was that it is feasible to construct an interregional table for three regions when one is a subarea of a metropolitan region, the second is the rest of the metropolitan region, and the third is the rest of the nation. Second, we learned that when data are available for a subarea on a 4-digit basis, they should not be aggregated to a 3-digit basis. Generally speaking, the investigator cannot find the appropriate weights so that an aggregate sector emerges with the proper product mix and relevant technical production coefficients. Moreover, he cannot develop accurate trade coefficients for aggregate sectors, since the relevant trade patterns for the different commodities of an aggregate sector can be so different that lumping them together introduces serious errors in projected flows, especially when the production of the subarea is highly specialized. In fact, our preliminary analysis suggests that for small subareas it is desirable to move in the direction of further sector disaggregation, by 5- or 7-digit commodities, so as to obtain more useful trade coefficients.

We also learned that it is absolutely essential to conduct a careful survey of households when the subarea is a suburban area that yields, at the minimum, a breakdown of each household subsector in terms of goods purchased in the subarea and goods purchased in the rest of the region. Also, the investigator should obtain employment data disaggregated by occupation and place of employment.

Finally, there is no simple answer to the question of whether the investigator should (1) collect comprehensively and process systematically primary data on a subarea, or (2) impute relationships on the basis of a good set of primary data for the larger region supplemented with secondary data for the subarea and responses to a few key questions on the expenditures of the subarea's households and on input purchases and sales distribution of its establishments. Our Bucks County experience suggests that we can effectively obtain the necessary primary data in at least 4-digit detail for a suburban area and the metropolitan region, and that it is not too bold to move ahead to develop a pure interregional model for improvement of intrametropolitan analysis and greater understanding of internal interdependencies.

1.13 The Measurement of Indirect Effects and the Use of the Inverse

In regional input–output study there always arises the basic question of whether or not the investigator should use an inverse based on full technical coefficients or on such coefficients reduced by the percent by which each of the inputs corresponding to a coefficient was provided through imports. On first thought the investigator tends to use an inverse based on *reduced coefficients*, so that he avoids the overestimate, from his use of full technical production coefficients, of impact of changes upon local production and consumption. However, when the impact upon a region is generated by a change in a national program, such as the Vietnam War program, that also has direct impacts on all other regions of the nation, it is more appropriate to use an inverse based on full technical production coefficients. Otherwise the investigator's estimate of national impacts indirectly derived as a sum of regional impacts tends to be considerably smaller sector by sector than when he chooses to estimate national impacts directly with the inverse of a national input–output table. Therefore, in the Philadelphia study we chose to invert the table of full technical production coefficients, which provides us with an inverse that is useful when regional impacts of changes in other national programs, such as housing and social welfare, are to be examined.

There are two sources of serious error in the use of the Philadelphia inverse based on full coefficients. One arises from the fact that we are not able to adjust the Philadelphia exports vector for changes stemming from different demands by other regions for Philadelphia products because of the direct impact of a changed national program upon them. The second source of error arises because of the tendency to overestimate changes in the production of local sectors that produce products that are imported in significant quantity. It would be highly desirable if two inverses—one based on full technical coefficients, the other based on reduced coefficients—could be developed and used in order to gain further insight into the repercussions of both nationally and regionally generated changes.

Sometimes it is possible to triangularize an input–output table. By so doing the investigator can make computations directly and avoid the use of an inverse. Triangularization also makes possible additional insight into the way in which sectors do and do not cluster and helps isolate meaningful industrial complexes.

A more basic issue concerns the relative merits of the inverse and the round-by-round iteration procedure. When the investigator plans to use the technical production coefficients many times without changes in them, it is far cheaper for him to do so with an inverse. In contrast, when he plans to use these coefficients without change only a few times, he may find a round-by-round iteration much less costly. The round-by-round iteration, of course, has the further advantage that it allows the investigator to check more effectively the reasonableness of his assumptions and the consistency of magnitudes as they are being projected. A first-round computation can be performed and changes in assumptions and coefficients can be made easily if it becomes apparent that unreasonable projections and inconsistencies are being generated. The same is true for the second-round and subsequent computations.

There are many other arguments for and against each procedure. In general, neither one is optimal, and the procedure to be chosen for a study largely depends on the particulars of that study. In the case of the Philadelphia region we have developed and used an inverse, and we are likely to use the inverse many times; however, we have already found it useful to employ a round-by-round computation procedure for numerous small problems.

Finally, there is the question of the stability of the coefficients. This question can be reported upon only after the results from a number of applications of the Philadelphia table have been studied, preferably against a background of results from the application of other regional input–output tables after the sectoring systems of these tables and the Philadelphia table have been made comparable.

1.14 An Application of the Inverse: The Impact of Vietnam War Expenditures on the Philadelphia Economy

In making an application of the Philadelphia coefficients table and its inverse, we chose to examine what the impact of Vietnam War expenditures had been on the Philadelphia economy in the year 1968, assuming that the structural matrix of 1959 was relevant in its entirety. We further chose to examine possible offset programs that might have effectively utilized resources in 1968 that would have been available had there been no Vietnam War effort.

In this application we fully exploited the systematic coverage of the federal government activities that we had been able to develop in disaggregated form in the construction of the final demand sectors for the Philadelphia economy. These activities numbered 36; the data for them had been obtained from special questionnaires conforming to the accounting technology and classification used by the agencies.

Since Philadelphia is a major procurement center for defense needs, it was important to distinguish between federal agency expenditures for the goods and services procured for usage by other units of the military services and those expenditures for goods and services directly consumed by the agency in Philadelphia in the achievement of its mission. These two expenditure patterns are very different.

To estimate the impact of the Vietnam War expenditures, we projected for each federal agency what its level of operations would have been in 1968 had there been no war. The difference between the agency's actual 1968 level and its projected level represented the direct impact of the war on this agency. Over all 36 sectors, this direct impact amounted to $0.28 billion in terms of goods that were purchased from local establishments only. The total impact, direct plus indirect, was estimated through the use of the inverse to be $1.28 billion. This impact was also detailed in terms of each of Philadelphia's 496 sectors. For example, the total impact on Philadelphia's construction activity was estimated to be approximately $13.9 million. In this application we also examined the direct and indirect impacts of each federal agency on each of the 496 sectors. Thus we were in a position to estimate the impact of a 50 percent cutback in the operations of the U.S. Naval Shipyard, where we also extended the impact analysis to cover employment as well as reduction in the wages and salaries generated.

If there had been no Vietnam War, the Philadelphia economy would have been considerably different in structure. The resources that were consumed by the military effort would not have been idle but would have been absorbed by a host of peacetime activities, some of which would have been federal government programs. To illustrate the kinds of changes that might have taken place in the Philadelphia economy, we supposed that the $0.28 billion of resources spent by the federal agencies on goods and services from Philadelphia establishments to support the Vietnam War had been used alternatively in 1968 to support social welfare programs consisting of elementary and secondary education (to an amount of $170 million), institutions of higher education (to an amount of $57 million), and low-income-housing construction (to an amount of $57 million). Using the coefficients of the Philadelphia table to determine what the composition of expenditures would have been for each of these programs, and the inverse to obtain the direct and indirect impacts of the changes in the final demand sectors consistent with this alternative expenditure program for the $0.28 billion, we identified the changes that would have been manifested in each of Philadelphia's 496 sectors. For example, the output of the apparel sector would have been smaller by $17 million and the electrical machinery sector by $59 million. On the other hand, there would have been favorable effects on agriculture, local government, and household sectors. The total aggregate output of Philadelphia would have been somewhat smaller but not significantly so.

One clear lesson learned from this application is that when any federal government program, military or nonmilitary, is changed in magnitude, whether contracted or expanded, there must be concomitant changes in other government programs as well, whether they be tax programs, social welfare programs, or environmental conservation programs. Such concomitant change is necessitated by the accounting identity that must be made explicit and checked for when we treat such a huge behaving unit as the federal government. We also came to appreciate from this application that the impact of a Vietnam War program or other programs of national and multiregional dimensions goes beyond the nation and affects other parts of the world. In particular, important impacts may fall upon smaller nations of the world whose export trade is closely linked to the United States economy and whose production may become disrupted easily by changes in our federal government programs.

1.15 Some New Directions: Environmental Quality Analysis and Standardization

Looking into the future, we see a number of new directions for profitable research. One would be concerned with the application of input–output methodology to problems relating to environmental quality. Here the input–output framework is easily extended to cover concomitantly the economic and ecologic systems. The set of rows of an input–output table can be extended to cover ecologic commodities such as biological oxygen demand (BOD [5-day]), sulfur dioxide (SO_2), and water of specified content. Parallel to these commodities the set of columns can be extended to cover ecologic processes such as photosynthesis, replenishment of oxygen supply in water, and cod production. In effect, the inputs and outputs for any economic sector are extended to cover the inputs from the ecologic systems and the outputs to the ecologic systems—inputs being water of specified content, outputs being BOD (5-day) and SO_2. Similarly, the inputs and outputs of each ecologic process cover commodities that are not only ecologic but also those commodities, such as codfish, corn, and grass, that have come to be designated economic commodities. In short, the Philadelphia 496 order table is to be extended to cover many more commodities and processes, and thereby to expose basic interrelations between the economic and ecologic subsystems. This step forward requires, as well, the systematic classification of ecologic commodities, such as the diverse water pollutants and air pollutants, in detail comparable to that of economic commodities. It also necessitates a systematic classification of natural production processes comparable to the SIC classification scheme for economic production processes. To demonstrate the necessary procedures to achieve this advance, we set down a preliminary classification scheme for water and water pollutants as ecologic commodities. We also set down in an extended table some of the main inputs for the processes involved in the basic food chain that produces both herring and cod as final products and begins with the photosynthesis process in marine areas. It also becomes clear that as we extend the set of relevant commodities and processes to include the ecologic, we must also include new sets of regions—namely, environmental regions such as AIR, WATER, and LAND. The Philadelphia region then functions as a subregion of each of these major regions, and as an integrated subsystem of the total ecologic-economic system.

Another new direction which has been probed somewhat but never effectively explored and implemented would involve the development of a central information facility and standardization procedures for input–output analysis. A central information facility should function (1) to develop a comprehensive and accurate inventory of input–output and related efforts; (2) to compile, edit, and consolidate information from particular studies to a common format; and (3) to serve as an archive of input–output information.

The development of standardized research procedures would complement the work of a central information facility and permit major external economies in input–output studies. Useful activities in this context would entail (1) the development of (a) several sector classification systems generally useful in input–output investigations, (b) one or more representative input–output structures for each of many sectors, and (c) one or more consistent sets of regions usable for many studies and suitable for effective classification and spatial disaggregation of imports and exports; and (2) the integration and reintegration of regional input–output data with other regional and national social accounts.

Standardization is no easy task, however. As yet, no suitable similarity index or other effective measure or technique has been developed by which to compare sets of coefficients for the same sector in different regions.

Finally, it is clear that with the greater abundance of relevant data that we can expect in the future for more meaningful areas, and with the conduct of multiregion input–output studies and the development of regional capital coefficients, the investigator will be in a much better position to simulate his region of study within an input–output framework. He will be in a still more effective position to do this when a central information facility has been established and standardization practices have been defined and employed in diverse studies.

2.1 General Considerations

One of the first questions that a regional scientist may confront in under-taking an input–output study is the choice of the region to be studied.[1] We explicitly stress "may confront," because on a number of occasions the region may be prechosen. That is, a contract or research grant or other source of funds for a study may also specify the region (such as a state, a cluster of states, or even a nation) to be considered—as was the case for the Washington State input–output study [Bourque, et al., 1967]. Very often, however, the region may be unspecified, with boundaries and other aspects to be determined by the regional scientist, as was the case in the Philadelphia Region Input–Output Study.

Ideally, the analyst does not need to specify the region at the start. He can "build up" to the region finally decided upon. He can begin collecting and processing data for the establishments in a subarea (set of sites). He can then add to his sample the establishments in a second subarea, a third subarea, and so forth. He can continue this step-by-step procedure until his investigation encompasses a set of subareas (not necessarily all contiguous) that satisfies his conception of a region. This set should be appropriate for the one or more problems explicitly (or implicitly) in his mind, and for the depiction and analysis of the interrelations of relevance for him.

Alternatively, the analyst may begin with an area (a core and some surrounding territory) that he views as a preliminary region. As the col-lection and processing of data proceeds, he may, at one or more points in the study, add to or subtract from the region subareas of one type or another—until he achieves what he considers to be an "appropriate", region.[2]

In practice, neither of the two procedures just described is feasible. Initial indecision in the specification of the study region leads in general to large increases in the cost of an input–output study. This consequence arises from the fact that the choice of sectoring, survey procedures, and the specification of other elements of the study are dependent in large part on the particular characteristics of the total region to be studied. Thus, changes in the physical extent of the study region while the investi-gation is under way must lead to changes in the set of establishments to be surveyed, the questions to be asked, the sectors to be examined, and so forth. Such change is costly.

The factors governing the definition of the region for study can be

[1] We take it for granted that simultaneous with this choice is a clear *identification* and *demarcation* of the geographic area that corresponds to any region considered for study.

[2] In this paragraph, we speak of subareas. Other investigators, such as those concerned with flow analysis, may prefer to speak of cores and surrounding territory, with less emphasis (implicit or explicit) on the property of boundary.

many, including (1) the areal units for which data are available; (2) the set of problems to which the investigator wishes to address himself; (3) the relevance of particular problems vis-à-vis the general planning problem; (4) the existence of other studies, completed or in progress; (5) the scope and nature of possible future studies; and (6) the availability of financial resources and skilled research personnel.

It is clear that to conduct an input–output study we need an abundance of the proper kinds of data. What may be characterized as abundant and proper kinds of data in turn depends on the purposes of the study, the sectoring scheme, the survey procedure to be used, and a number of other factors. These factors will become evident in Section 2.2, where we discuss the specific choice of the Philadelphia region. The point to be made here is that the practical consideration of *current* or *potential* data availability must be given considerable weight.

As is well recognized, there are many specific problems on which an input–output analyst might wish to concentrate, including, among others, water quality management, air pollution, sonic pollution, sold waste disposal, airport location, transport system redesign, land-use control, industry location, shopping center location, fiscal interdependence among governmental units such as suburbs and central cities, crime and juvenile delinquency, housing and new town design, disarmament and conversion, social welfare program evaluation, open space, capital budgeting, unemployment and job opportunities, educational system reorganization, metropolitan government, and slum clearance. Associated with each problem may be a "best" region. However, when more than a single specific problem is to be attacked in a study, a conflict often arises in the definition of the relevant region. For example, the water management problem in the Philadelphia area clearly requires a definite region for analysis—namely, one that gives appropriate consideration to the Delaware River watershed—which at least in part would be radically different from that region relevant for transportation planning purposes.

When such a conflict exists, it must be resolved by the use of some "compromise" region if the two problems are to be examined by the same study. Too frequently, however, the "compromise" region is so inappropriate for any one of the two (or more) problems to be studied that an analyst must reject it. He may then insist on not trying to cover more than one particular problem with any given input–output study. Otherwise, we can define neither a proper region nor, as we shall see later on, a proper sector classification, appropriate survey procedures, and so forth.[3]

---

[3] For example, unless the problem is identified beforehand, one cannot know (1) the sectors that are likely to be impacted most in a *direct* manner, and (2) the associated sectors with which these sectors are closely linked and which are likely to be impacted most in an *indirect* manner.

This point of view, however, is an extreme one. At times it is justified, but at many other times it is not. It is clear that in metropolitan regional planning it is usually financially impossible to undertake an input–output study merely to attack one small or moderate-size problem alone. Practical considerations require that such an involved and expensive study be used to attack more than one problem, and in general that it should be useful for a large number of problems. This situation then means that the investigator must see to it that the input–output study is not applied to those problems that it is unsuited to attack because of the particular region, base year, or sector classification chosen.

Also, in regional planning it is not always possible to anticipate the set of problems that may have priority at the time at which the study will be completed and in subsequent years. Existing problems constantly change in importance, and new ones emerge. Therefore, at best, an investigator can only specify a region that, from experience and intuition, he expects to be relevant for the set of problems to be attacked once the study is completed.[4]

Other factors also govern the definition of a region. The areal coverage and, as will be discussed in subsequent chapters, the detail sought and the survey procedures used are all obviously dependent on the financial resources and research personnel available. A larger region can always be covered, provided that a sufficient amount of these resources exist. Other factors relate to the possibilities for implementation of recommendations and to the perspectives or space and time horizons of present and future decision-makers. Clearly, in a study contract let by political leaders, the investigator does not adopt a region that is meaningless to these leaders or remains so after attempts at their education.

Finally, the choice of region may be affected by the desirability of and possibilities for investigating interregional linkages, that is, the relation of the region to the nation as a whole and to other regions within a multiregion system. When these questions are to be examined, there may arise a problem of defining the region for study such that it forms, together with other regions in the system, both an exhaustive and disjoint set of regions—exhaustive in the sense that all the areas of a nation or other bounded unit are covered, and disjoint in the sense that there is no overlap among the regions. This question of the definition of a region suitable for interregional and/or multiregional research will be taken up in Chapter 10, which deals with imports and exports.

[4] When an input–output study is designed primarily to facilitate an attack on one and only one major problem—for example, the impact upon the surrounding area of the NASA Electronics Facility once planned for Cambridge, Massachusetts—there is the danger that when the study is completed, the problem will no longer exist, at least in the form in which it was initially conceived and/or perceived.

2.2 Possible Definitions of the Study Region

In the Philadelphia study, several alternative definitions of the Philadelphia region were considered. Some of these definitions were oriented
to the Census definitions of standard metropolitan statistical areas, which
are depicted in Figure 2.1. Others were not.

One region to which we gave very serious consideration was that
employed by the Penn Jersey Transportation Study. This region (study

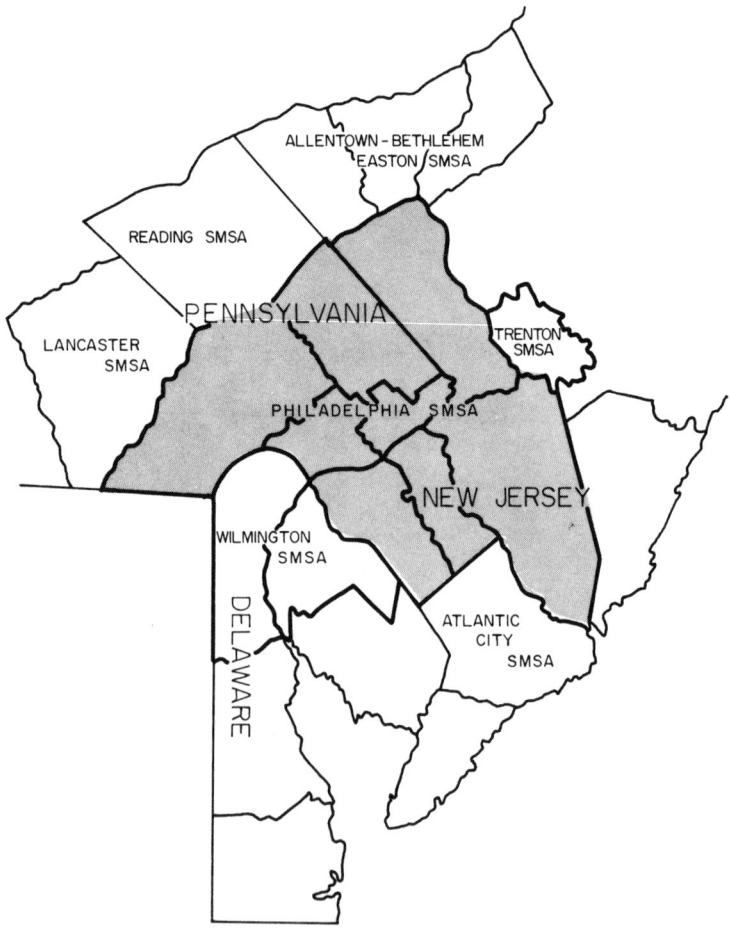

Figure 2.1. Selected Standard Metropolitan Statistical Areas, Pennsylvania, New
Jersey, and Delaware

area) was of considerable interest because of the extensive data that had been collected on the movement of goods and people, detailed by origin and destination. As depicted in Figure 2.2, the Penn Jersey region cuts across most of the counties centering around the County of Philadelphia. (The counties relevant for our choice of region, together with certain of their characteristics, are listed in Table 2.1.) Just because the Penn Jersey study area did cut across these counties, the adoption of that region as our study region would have led to unmanageable problems in the establishment of control totals, the utilization of the Census and many other secondary sources of data, and the specifications for primary data. The cost of our study would have increased substantially.

Further, there existed a serious question as to how appropriate the Penn Jersey study area was for the study of the very problem that it was

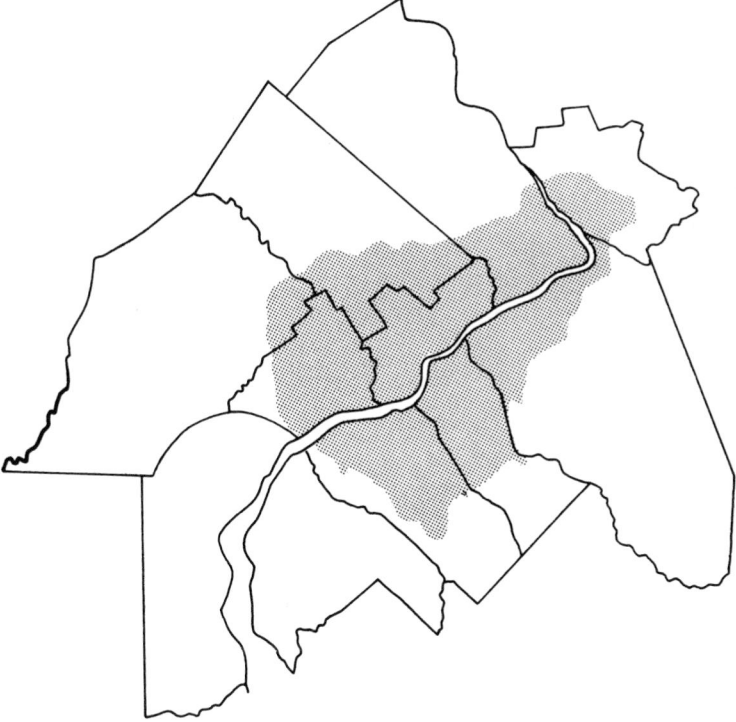

Figure 2.2. Penn Jersey Transportation Study, Cordon Area. From Thomas W. Langford, Jr., "Area Data Service—Secondary Data Utilization Center," in Wroe Alderson and Stanley J. Shapiro, eds., *An Area Data Service Feasibility Study*, Philadelphia: Pennsylvania–New Jersey–Delaware Metropolitan Project, Inc., 1962.

Table 2.1. Selected Characteristics of Counties Relevant for the Choice of Region

County	SMSA	Population 1960	Area (sq. m.)	% Urban Population
Pennsylvania				
Berks	Reading	275,414	864	64.3
Bucks	Philadelphia (pt.)	308,567	617	75.3
Chester	Philadelphia (pt.)	210,608	760	43.8
Delaware	Philadelphia (pt.)	553,154	185	96.0
Lancaster	Lancaster	278,359	944	49.5
Lehigh	Allentown-Bethlehem-Easton (pt.)	227,536	347	79.4
Montgomery	Philadelphia (pt.)	516,682	492	79.5
Northampton	Allentown-Bethlehem-Easton (pt.)	201,412	374	68.7
Philadelphia	Philadelphia (pt.)	2,002,509	127	100.0
New Jersey				
Atlantic	Atlantic City	160,880	575	83.8
Burlington	Philadelphia (pt.)	225,129	819	71.3
Camden	Philadelphia (pt)	392,035	221	95.4
Cape May	—	48,555	267	54.0
Cumberland	—	106,850	503	72.8
Gloucester	Philadelphia (pt.)	134,840	329	68.0
Mercer	Trenton	226,392	228	89.2
Ocean	—	108,241	639	35.7
Salem	Wilmington (pt.)	58,711	350	49.8
Warren	Allentown-Bethlehem-Easton (pt.)	62,220	362	
Delaware				
Kent	—	65,651	595	19.4
Newcastle	Wilmington (pt.)	307,446	437	86.6
Sussex	—	73,195	946	18.7

designed to attack. We also questioned the validity and usefulness of this study area for future studies of problems of the Philadelphia region in the light of suburban expansion. We therefore decided not to adopt the Penn Jersey study area. Concomitantly, we decided to use counties as the building blocks for our study region.

The Penn Jersey study area was only one of several possible definitions of our region that did not conform to the Census definitions of metropolitan areas. Other areas were considered as possibilities for the study region, but only briefly. For example, we considered the area defined by the five southeastern counties of Pennsylvania—Philadelphia County and the four counties surrounding it. To have adopted this set of counties as our study region would have meant that we would have ignored the substantial commutation that takes place between Philadelphia and the New Jersey counties. It would also have meant that we would have ignored the New Jersey counties within which major growth in the region was occurring. As with the Penn Jersey study area, we would have confronted major difficulty in using the Census data on standard metropolitan statistical areas, although there was an abundance of secondary data from the Commonwealth of Pennsylvania.

Also, we could have chosen the single county of Philadelphia as our study region. To have done so, however, would have meant that we would have failed to examine most of the critical interdependence relations in which we were interested. Our findings would have been of very limited interest to decision-makers and political leaders, since most, if not all, the critical problems of the Philadelphia region go beyond the city boundaries.

Another area, the Delaware River Basin, might have been selected as the study region. While this choice would have led to findings that would have been illuminating for water management, upon which we will comment later, such findings would not have had much significance for studying problems arising from interdependence. Moreover, such a choice would have made the utilization of secondary data extremely difficult.

Other areas that we examined as possibilities for our study region were oriented to the Census definitions of standard metropolitan statistical areas. Of those rejected, the one that was considered most seriously was that of the Penjerdel (Pennsylvania–New Jersey–Delaware) Study. This region consists of 11 counties in three states and constitutes the core of the Delaware basin. It includes Mercer County, New Jersey, which contains Trenton, the capital of the State of New Jersey. Hence, the incorporation of Mercer county in our study region would have meant that the state government operations of the State of New Jersey would have had to be included in detail in the study. We judged that the inclusion of these activities, oriented as they are to the entire New Jersey population and economy, would have distorted the results of the study.

Additionally, the Penjerdel region includes both New Castle County, Delaware, and Salem County, New Jersey, which in 1959 constituted the Wilmington Standard Metropolitan Statistical Area. If our region were to have covered both these counties, certain difficulties would have been introduced into the study, for within these counties are located E. I. duPont de Nemours and Company and other major chemical producers (e.g., Hercules Powder Company and Atlas Powder Company). These companies form an exceedingly intricate complex that is difficult to unravel in terms of intersectoral flows. From whatever data these corporations might have had on their various plants, not to mention what they would have made available, clear distinctions between their several units producing alkalies and chlorine, cyclic crudes, dyes and organic pigments, inorganic pigments, synthetic fibers, plastics, and other specific chemical products would not have been possible.

Of course, one way to have looked at this complex would have been to consider it as a category of its own, say a 3-digit category, with an industry mix quite different from anything that we knew of. But such a sectoral treatment would not have been consistent with the detail desired.

Hence, for these reasons, and also because it was questionable whether the chemical complex and the Wilmington area in 1960 were an organic part of the Philadelphia region, we chose to exclude New Castle and Salem Counties from our region and to reject the use of the Penjerdel study area. This rejection meant that we also rejected as possible study regions still larger regions, which would have included the Lancaster-Reading area, the Atlantic City metropolitan area, and the Allentown-Bethlehem-Easton metropolitan area. It is unlikely that we would have given any serious attention to the inclusion of these additional metropolitan areas as part of our study region even if the objections to the use of the Penjerdel study area did not exist, because these metropolitan areas are not strongly oriented to the Philadelphia core. They appear to have orientations to other major areas, such as the Greater New York metropolitan region. Further, to have included them would have greatly increased the cost of collecting primary data, and this cost would have far exceeded the resources that were available for our study.

By this process of considering and excluding various alternatives, we narrowed down the eligible alternatives to one, the Philadelphia Standard Metropolitan Statistical Area. As defined by the United States Bureau of the Budget in 1960, this area contains the following eight counties: Bucks, Chester, Delaware, Montgomery, and Philadelphia in Pennsylvania; and Burlington, Camden, and Gloucester in New Jersey. This region is well defined and strongly oriented to a core, and it allows us to study the major intraregional interdependencies in which we were interested in 1963.

There is no question that our definition of the region is not ideal. The northeast section of Bucks County, for example, is clearly oriented to the Allentown-Bethlehem-Easton area; the extreme eastern sections of Burlington County are not oriented to the Philadelphia core, but rather to what might be considered a generalized New Jersey coastal region; and so forth. Yet despite these and other shortcomings of the definition, given the problem of collecting large amounts of data and the need to use the extensive secondary data wherever possible, the choice was found to be appropriate—even after the study was completed. Given the experience we had and the knowledge we now possess, it is doubtful that we would select a different region if we had to make the choice again.

One question that we might examine briefly is whether our choice of a region would have been different, or would now be different, if we were to use a 2- or 3-digit instead of a 4-digit SIC classification. Whereas for some input–output studies an investigator might vary his region according to the level of disaggregation of his sectors, in the case of the Philadelphia study we would probably choose the same region. Again, this choice would be likely because of (1) the cost of collecting and processing large amounts of data, (2) the consequent need to exploit all available secondary data, and (3) our judgment that the eight-county aggregation in 1960 was best from the standpoint of capturing for analysis most if not all of the basic intraregional flows associated with the Philadelphia economy. However, if we were to follow a two-digit classification, we might be more easily induced to include in our region the Wilmington SMSA (New Castle County, Delaware, and Salem County, New Jersey), for the chemical complex could have been wholly included within SIC 28; however, including the Wilmington area would have required that we develop more adequate procedures for handling the agricultural sectors. Our treatment of the agricultural sectors of the Philadelphia economy, while adequate perhaps for a highly urbanized area, was indeed rather crude.

Another interesting question is whether we would have defined our region differently had we been more alert, at the start, to the major environmental problems that now exist in the region and could have been forecasted. Two basic considerations are relevant here. First, the model underlying the Philadelphia input–output study is primarily economic in nature. A controlling factor in the choice of the region, therefore, must be the extent to which basic economic and technical relationships and intraregional flows can be identified and subjected to analysis. Since the Philadelphia SMSA constituted for 1960 not only a viable but also the most relevant *economic* unit, the choice was correct. To the extent that the physical areas associated with the maintenance of environmental quality—for example, the watersheds, airsheds, and solid waste disposal districts—differ significantly from the physical area of the most relevant economic unit, that is, the Philadelphia SMSA (Standard Metropolitan Statistical Area), it becomes necessary to adjust the region, or to adapt the analytical framework, or both. Such a modification is necessary if we are interested in the water management problem in the Philadelphia region, for which the relevant physical area might be defined as the Delaware River system and with which is associated the operating administrative unit, INCODEL (the Interstate Compact of the Delaware Basin), a cooperative undertaking of the states of Pennsylvania, New Jersey, Delaware, and New York, and the federal government.

It may be contended that a type of problem such as water management requires concomitant analysis of two or more different types of regions. One type of region relates to the economic activities based on the use of a resource, e.g., water, and the generation of pollution and related effects.

This is the economic region. (In some cases it may be a socioeconomic or politicoeconomic region.) The second type of region relates to the environmental activities associated with the physical production of the resource and absorption of outputs from the economic system to the ecologic system. This is the environmental region. For example, the Delaware River system would constitute such a region, where the supply areas of fresh water are included as well as the areas of use and pollution. In addition to these two types of regions, a third type may also be identified and considered relevant for study—the region of effective political-administrative action, such as the counties, states, and other relevant authorities included within INCODEL. Thus, an effective attack on the problem may require interrelated analysis at two or more different levels of regions. Accordingly, a proper definition of a region in an input–output study may consider the need not only to depict technical economic interrelations and the full array of major intraregional flows, but also to coordinate analysis of the economic inputs and outputs (inclusive of pollutants) and of both environmental and political processes in the context of regions properly defined for such analysis.[5] Such consideration can lead to the development of more sophisticated policy-oriented regional input–output analysis. This kind of analysis provides additional justification for the construction and development of general-purpose regional input–output tables designed to capture the basic interrelationships of an economic-type region but flexible as to use in connection with different problems and with different political-type environmental-type regions. There still remains the point that no general-purpose table can be adjusted to provide detailed sectoring and classification appropriate to all types of problems.

While the Philadelphia study relates to a large population and a highly industrialized urbanized area, there exists a need for studies that relate to smaller economic areas. Such areas may be agricultural or semiurban counties, or small units such as the Boulder economy.[6] In such studies the need to have recourse to secondary sources of data may be less intense. The investigator often may be able to obtain the necessary data almost entirely by interview and survey. Accordingly, the existing political units, such as counties and minor civil divisions for which official data are published, need not exert much influence on the determination of the boundaries of the region to be studied. In the case of the Boulder study, boundaries of the economy were identified on the basis of indicators of

[5] See Chapter 15 for other relevant discussion concerning regions for environmental quality problems.
[6] See Miernyk et al., 1967. Another illustration is the Downington subarea of the Philadelphia region, for which an independent informal study was made.

social, political, and economic interactions such as telephone exchange areas, travel patterns, local newspaper circulation, and utility services areas. For such a study, usually a more satisfactory definition of the region is obtainable than when boundaries are largely governed by the availability of secondary sources of data.

2.3 Characteristics of Our Study Region

Having chosen the area to serve as our study region, it is desirable briefly to describe the region in order to understand better some of the decisions made concerning base year, sectoring plan, data sources used, and a number of other basic questions. We shall touch upon the region's main characteristics, its position relative to other large urban regions, and its internal composition—as seen from the data available when the basic decisions regarding the study were made.

The Philadelphia region was one of the first urban regions to develop in this country. It contains one of the oldest cities in the United States, Philadelphia, and includes other early settlements that have contributed to the advanced urbanization of the area. With the growth of the Eastern seaboard and of the nation over the years, the region has become a highly diversified area wherein almost all kinds of enterprise known to exist in advanced metropolitan regions are represented. This characteristic makes the region an ideal laboratory for the testing and application of new and improved techniques of regional analysis. The large size of the region is particularly important for a detailed input–output study. Its size makes possible the disaggregation of economic activity into many sectors, for most of which a satisfactory sample can be obtained. The region, while covering five counties in the Commonwealth of Pennsylvania and three in the State of New Jersey, and straddling the Delaware River, which forms the boundary between the two states, is a well-defined nodal region.[7] Its activities tend to cluster in and around the central city, and constitute a large enough base with sufficient interdependence in its structure to permit meaningful examination of the impacts of diverse exogenous forces.

The relative importance of the Philadelphia region in the national economy can be seen from Table 2.2, which ranks the population of the ten largest Standard Metropolitan Statistical Areas as of 1960.

The changes in the spatial distribution of population within the Philadelphia SMSA during the 1950–1960 period can be seen in Table 2.3. This table shows that the region, as most metropolitan areas, experienced a declining population in the central city and a growing suburban population.

---

[7] For definition of a nodal region, see Isard et al., 1960, pp. 322–324; Isard, 1956; and Teitz, 1962.

Table 2.2. Population of the Ten Largest Metropolitan Regions, 1960

SMSA	Population (000)	% U.S. Population
New York–N.W. New Jersey*	14,759	8.1
Chicago–N.W. Indiana*	6,794	3.7
Los Angeles–Long Beach, California	6,743	3.6
PHILADELPHIA–New Jersey	4,343	2.4
Detroit, Michigan	3,762	2.0
San Francisco–Oakland, California	2,783	1.6
Boston, Massachusetts	2,589	1.4
Pittsburgh, Pennsylvania	2,405	1.3
St. Louis, Missouri–Illinois	2,060	1.1
Washington, D.C.–Maryland–Virginia	2,001	1.0

* Standard Consolidated Area.
Source: Bureau of the Budget, *Standard Metropolitan Statistical Areas, 1960*. Washington, D.C.: U.S. Government Printing Office, 1961.

Table 2.3. Changes in Population Distribution by County, Philadelphia, Pa.–N.J. SMSA, 1950–1960

County	Population (000) 1950	1960	% Change, 1950–1960
Bucks	145	309	113.4
Chester	159	211	32.3
Delaware	414	553	33.5
Montgomery	353	517	46.3
Philadelphia	2,072	2,003	− 3.3
Pa. Part	3,143	3,592	14.3
Burlington	136	224	65.2
Camden	301	392	30.4
Gloucester	92	135	47.0
N.J. Part	528	751	42.2
Philadelphia SMSA	3,671	4,343	25.1

Data may not add to totals due to rounding.
Source: U.S. Bureau of the Census, *U.S. Census of Population: 1960*. Washington, D.C.: U.S. Government Printing Office, 1962.

The share of the five Pennsylvania counties in the region's population has continued to decline over the years. While in 1900 these counties accounted for 89.6 percent of the region's population, by 1920 their share had declined to 88.2 percent, and by 1940 to 87.5 percent. During the 1950–1960 period the five counties' share declined from 85.6 to 82.3 percent. This point is important to keep in mind, because, due to limited information on a disaggregated level for the New Jersey part of the region, data for the five Pennsylvania counties were used in estimating changes over time for the region as a whole.[8]

[8] See Chapter 6 for discussion of methodology for estimating detailed control totals for the manufacturing and other producing industries.

Table 2.4. Distribution of Population and Employment by County, Philadelphia, Pa.–N.J. SMSA, 1960

	Population		Employment	
	Persons (000)	% of Region	Employees (000)	% Region
Bucks	309	7.1	110	6.7
Chester	211	4.8	78	4.7
Delaware	553	12.7	207	12.6
Montgomery	517	11.9	201	12.2
Philadelphia	2,003	46.1	789	47.9
Pa. Part	3,592	82.7	1,384	84.1
Burlington	224	5.2	66	4.0
Camden	392	9.0	146	8.9
Gloucester	135	3.1	49	3.0
N.J. Part	751	17.3	261	15.9
Philadelphia SMSA	4,343	100.0	1,645	100.0

Data may not add to totals due to rounding.
Source: U.S. Bureau of the Census, *U.S. Census of Population: 1960, General Social and Economic Characteristics, Pennsylvania and New Jersey.* Washington, D.C.: U.S. Government Printing Office, 1962.

Table 2.5. Employment Distribution by Economic Divisions, Philadelphia, Pa.–N.J. SMSA, 1960

Economic Division	Employment (000)	% Total
Agriculture, Forestry, and Fisheries	20.2	1.2
Mining	1.8	0.1
Construction	82.8	5.0
Manufacturing	588.5	35.8
Transportation, Communications, and Utilities	109.9	6.6
Wholesale and Retail Trade	291.3	17.7
Finance, Insurance, and Real Estate	76.8	4.7
Services	319.0	19.4
Government	80.0	4.9
Not Classified	74.8	4.6
Total	1,645.1	100.0

Source: U.S. Bureau of the Census, *U.S. Census of Population: 1960, General Social and Economic Characteristics, Pennsylvania and New Jersey.* Washington, D.C.: U.S. Government Printing Office, 1962.

The employment characteristics of the region are also of interest. Table 2.4 summarizes the distribution of employment by place of residence in the eight counties of the SMSA. The high degree of concentration in the core county, Philadelphia, is clear. Table 2.5 summarizes the total employment of the area's residents by major industry groups. The domination by manufacturing is consistent with the long history and economic diversity of the region.

Finally, data on output of the Philadelphia SMSA by economic division are pertinent. They are presented in Table 2.6 for the year 1959. The composition of output of the region for 1959 is compared with that of the nation for 1958 in Table 2.7. Although there are minor differences in the definitions of the sectors even at this level of aggregation, and although the United States data are for an earlier year, nonetheless the comparison appears meaningful. It shows the differences one would expect to find between a major metropolitan area and the nation; for example, agricultural activity is smaller and manufacturing is larger in the metropolitan area than in the nation.

Table 2.6. Estimated Output of the Private Sectors by Economic Division, Philadelphia, Pa.–N.J. SMSA, 1959

Economic Division	Output ($000)	% Total
Agriculture, Forestry, and Fisheries	134,709	0.59
Mining	30,922	0.14
Contract Construction (incl. SIC 656)	1,771,985	7.80
Manufacturing	11,475,776	50.50
Ordnance (SIC 19)	16,411	0.07
Manufacturing (SIC 20–39)	11,459,365	50.43
Transportation, Communication and Utilities	1,641,392	7.22
Transportation	775,765	3.41
Communication	370,937	1.63
Electricity, Gas, and Sanitation Services	494,690	2.18
Wholesale and Retail Trade	3,457,665	15.21
Wholesale	1,655,219	7.28
Retail	1,802,446	7.93
Finance, Insurance, and Real Estate	1,571,264	6.91
Finance	623,887	2.75
Insurance	833,989	3.67
Real Estate	113,388	0.50
Services	2,640,367	11.62
Services	1,293,811	5.69
Medical	411,758	1.81
Educational	611,573	2.69
Other	323,225	1.42
Total	22,724,080	100.00

Data may not add to totals due to rounding.

Table 2.7. Percentage Distribution of Private Sector Output by Economic Division, United States, 1958 and Philadelphia, Pa.–N.J. SMSA, 1959

Economic Division	% Total U.S., 1958	% Total Philadelphia SMSA, 1959
Agriculture, Forestry, and Fisheries	6.21	0.59
Mining	2.42	0.14
Construction	8.41	7.80
Manufacturing	42.29	50.50
Transportation, Communication, and Utilities	7.92	7.22
Wholesale and Retail Trade	11.55	15.21
Finance, Insurance, and Real Estate	10.72	6.91
Services	9.48	11.62
Total Private Sector (%)	100.00	100.00
Output ($ million)	824,330	22,724

Source: U.S. Department of Commerce, National Economics Division, Office of Business Economics, "The Transactions Table of the 1958 Input–Output Study, Revised Direct and Total Requirements Data," *Survey of Current Business*, 45: 9 (September 1965), Table 1. The outputs of the three dummy industries, Sector 81, *Business, Travel, Entertainment and Gifts*, Sector 82, *Office Supplies*, and Sector 83, *Scrap, Used and Secondhand Goods*, were excluded from the tabulation. Their combined output was calculated as 1.14 percent of total private sector output. The private sectors consist of OBE industries 1 to 77. At this level of aggregation, these sectors do not correspond exactly to the Philadelphia study sectors.

References

Bourque, Philip J., et al. (1967). *The Washington Economy: An Input–Output Study* (Business Study No. 3). Seattle: University of Washington.

Isard, Walter (1956). "Regional Science, the Concept of Region and Regional Structure," *Papers and Proceedings of the Regional Science Association*, 2: 13–26.

———, et al. (1960). *Methods of Regional Analysis: An Introduction to Regional Science*. Cambridge, Mass.: The M.I.T. Press.

Miernyk, William H., et al. (1967). *Impact of the Space Program on a Local Economy: An Input–Output Analysis*. Morgantown, W. Va.: West Virginia Library.

Teitz, Michael B. (1962). "Regional Theory and Regional Models," *Papers and Proceedings of the Regional Science Association*, 9: 35–50.

In any regional input–output study it is necessary to determine the base year for which interindustry relations are to be explicitly depicted and examined. At times the base year may be determined by a contract or research grant, or by the existence of some unusual source of data, such as a special national or regional survey. However, in the Philadelphia input–output study it was possible to select the base year.

A key factor relevant in the selection process is the availability of secondary data. Perhaps for most regions the most important sources of secondary data are the federal Censuses. For regional input–output studies in the United States the Censuses of Manufactures, Business, Selected Services, Trades, and Transportation are most useful. They are taken or are generally planned to be taken roughly every five years. For example, there was a Census of Manufactures in 1958, another in 1963, and still another in 1967. Less important but still very valuable are the Censuses of Population and Housing. These are taken decennially in the first year of each decade.

Additionally, there may be various censuses conducted by states. For example, the Commonwealth of Pennsylvania takes an industrial census annually; so does Massachusetts. Finally, major studies such as the national consumer surveys of the Bureau of Labor Statistics, and the Penn Jersey Transportation Study for the area in and around Philadelphia, may be important sources of data.

Clearly, the dates for which the data of the censuses and other studies pertain are important for the choice of the base year of an input–output study. However, just as important as the quantity of secondary data is the quality of those data and their relevance to the needs of a study.

A second factor in the selection of a base year relates to the implications of the selection for the collection of primary data by interview and questionnaire. From one standpoint, the investigator may reason that he can maximize both the quantity and quality of data from interviews and questionnaires by his choosing as base year the last calendar (or fiscal) year. This reasoning is especially valid if the last year is also a year for which census data had been collected. Respondents often can find most quickly and with least trouble their most recent financial report; and if they also can obtain from their files a recently completed census questionnaire, they are in a position to answer most of the questions posed by the interviewer. However, the request for data only one year old raises the problem of disclosure. Respondents are considerably more reluctant to release data on their most recent operations than data that are five or more years old. Hence, especially for the highly competitive industrial sectors—such as steel and chemicals—it may not be possible to obtain adequate responses to questions on operations for a recent year. However, for other sectors—for example, utilities, financial institutions, governmental agencies—recent financial data may be procured easily.

A third factor relates to the "up-to-dateness" of the study. Any decision to seek data for not the latest but a previous year confronts problems in the conduct of extensive empirical studies, such as an input–output study, because by the time the data have been fully processed and developed they may describe an economic structure of some years ago. The long time necessary for the completion of a study—as much as five years —is a result of (1) the vast amount of work to be done; (2) the time it takes to train skilled interviewers and research personnel, which often can be done only on a limited scale; and (3) the fact that funds may be available on just a year-to-year basis and at an inadequate level. Consequently, questionnaires may still be in the process of completion three years after the beginning of a study. Thus, to avoid having coefficients and other findings that are outdated, the investigator is tempted to select a base year as close as possible to the time when the interviewing for a study is initiated.

Of course, the investigator may partly avoid outdated coefficients by placing greater weight on the most efficient establishments from which responses have been received and smaller weights on the less efficient establishments; this procedure supposedly adjusts for "gradual" technological improvement in production within a sector. Also, if a table is highly detailed, certain post hoc adjustments can be made to bring coefficients up-to-date. In general, however, during the construction of the coefficients of a table these procedures are not to be recommended because of the subjective elements they introduce.

Another consideration pertaining to the "up-to-dateness" of a study is based upon our experience in the Philadelphia survey and later in the Boston study. Although the investigator requests from an establishment its data for the base year, he must be content with whatever data the firm is willing and able to furnish. Too frequently such data will not be for the base year. The data may be for a more recent year, perhaps the most recent year, since as previously noted such data may be the most accessible to the busy executive. Or the data may be for some other year for which the respondent had previously completed another questionnaire. Thus, while an input–output study is designed for a base year, frequently coefficients are derived from a mixture of data for several years—usually years subsequent to the base year;[1] somehow the investigator adjusts and forces this conglomerate of information into the mold of the base year.

---

[1] This factor tends to minimize the costs of changing the base year to a *later* year once a study has been undertaken, and once it is determined that the initial choice of a base year is not suitable. These costs obviously arise because the data already

Although it is difficult to generalize, and although the base year selection depends on the specifics of a study and dates of Census and other publications, some analysts might suggest that an investigator associated with a nongovernmental agency should set a base year at least two years previous to the year of the initiation of the interviewing. However, other analysts might consider it feasible to choose the last calendar year as base year. If in the Philadelphia study we had chosen a base year later than 1960, we probably would have encountered serious nonresponse from the manufacturing sectors—despite the excellent relations we had with the business community through the Wharton School. Since 1960 was a census year, and 1961 and 1962 were not, and since we began our study in 1963, it would have been unwise to have chosen a year later than 1960.

A fourth set of factors, generally much less significant than those just noted, relate to the general business conditions during the year considered as a possible base year. If the year is either a boom or recession year, the data reported by establishments are not likely to reflect "normal" production conditions. For example, in a boom year relatively unproductive labor may be employed temporarily, and quality of output may be below average. Purchases of inventories, maintenance and repair work, and capital expenditures may be abnormal. In a downturn there may be an overstatement of the labor coefficients; in an upturn, an understatement. Generally speaking, the investigator searches for a base year that represents normal business conditions; thus he avoids making special adjustments to the data because of "unusual" production and marketing conditions.[2]

In the case of the Philadelphia study, 1959 was the year selected as base. The data for the Penn Jersey Transportation Study were available for this year, and initially it was thought that these data could be used extensively in the study. It turned out, however, that the Penn Jersey

---

collected must be either properly adjusted or replaced entirely by new interview data. (It may even be that the possibility of reinterview may not exist, or may be dim, since many firms will refuse to fill out a second questionnaire.)

[2] One other small consideration relates to the question of whether the choice of a calendar year is better than that of some fiscal year—e.g., the fiscal year beginning July 1 and ending June 30. Usually, the calendar year is to be much preferred. Generally speaking, data are more available by calendar year. Moreover, the case studies by the Internal Revenue Service show that corporate fiscal years tend to average about the calendar year. In our study, when data were available only for the fiscal year, especially for a fiscal year beginning July 1, we chose to ask for information for fiscal year 1960 (July 1, 1959, through June 30, 1960) rather than fiscal year 1959. Not only were the former data more recent, but also we felt that for most establishments the first half of 1960 involved operations similar to those of the first half of calendar year 1959.

data did not provide the amount of usable data originally expected. There were difficulties in using their definitions and interpreting the responses they received. Much of the data was for the year 1960, and some for 1961. Further, it developed that their data were not sufficiently detailed; our need was for data disaggregated on a 4-digit rather than a 2- or 3-digit SIC basis. Had we been able to foresee the limited usefulness of the Penn Jersey data, we probably would have chosen as base year either 1958 or 1960. For 1958, the national input–output table was being prepared by the Office of Business Economics (OBE) of the U.S. Department of Commerce, and the Census of Manufactures, the Census of Mineral Industries, and the Census of Business had been completed. For 1960, the Censuses of Population and Housing had been completed.

Our experience in this regard suggests that whenever an investigator does expect to rely heavily upon some set of data, even census data, he should examine these data very carefully before allowing their availability to affect any basic decisions. He should also be thoroughly aware of the interview technique used to obtain the data in order to know their strengths and weaknesses.

The choice of 1959 as the base year, however, was not a bad choice. Although we were not able to use directly census control totals available for years 1958 and 1960, it was possible to adjust the census data to obtain reasonable estimates for the intervening year. Obtaining control totals is of course extremely important for any input–output study. As will be discussed in Chapter 5 it is impractical to interview 100 percent of the relevant establishments, institutions, and other behaving units, thereby to obtain total output, total employment, and so on, by the simple addition of data provided on completed questionnaires. Hence, a base year is to be chosen for which control estimates are available or can be satisfactorily derived from reliable data.

From the standpoint of business conditions the year 1959 was rather appropriate for our input–output work. For the Philadelphia region, 1959 was a normal year. Boom forces had spent themselves by early 1958 and recession elements did not appear until mid-1960. There was, however, a steel strike in 1959 which did result in abnormal purchasing patterns for stock steel items, and for which we had to adjust the reported data.

As already suggested, the selection of 1959 as base made it relatively easy to obtain access to business information in the first year or two of the study. Many of the large manufacturers interviewed during these years did not consider data on operations in 1959 as highly confidential. The difficulty with the choice of 1959 as base year arose as the study progressed and when we made the decision, two to three years later, to interview intensively establishments in the service and trade sectors. By then, the records of some establishments were no longer easily available, and in certain cases had even been destroyed.

Subsequent to the initiation of the Philadelphia study, input–output work was undertaken on the Boston region beginning in 1965. In accord with the considerations just discussed, 1963 was chosen as base year for the Boston study. It was judged that interviewing in the years 1966 and thereafter would not incur disclosure problems in highly competitive industries. Further, 1963 was a year for which the Census of Manufactures had been carried out, and is the year for which another national input–output table was being constructed by the Office of Business Economics.

4.1 Background

Of all decisions initially made in the Philadelphia study, perhaps those relating to sectoring were the ones most changed. Of all the questions we confronted when we began the study, we were least clear as to how the issue of an appropriate sectoring scheme would be resolved. We had some notion of what the region would be and what the base year would be. We also knew, as will be indicated in later chapters, the likely sources of secondary information on control totals and knew that we would seek data primarily on inputs purchased rather than on distribution of sales. But we had no good idea of how disaggregated our sectors should be.[1]

In one sense, indecision on this question was to be anticipated. The location of our research activity made clear the great advantages we could derive from doing a study for the Philadelphia region. The existence of secondary data and our actual knowledge of the structure of the region pointed out the gains from choosing the Philadelphia Standard Metropolitan Statistical Area (SMSA) as our region. Our choice of base year was clearly restricted to 1958, 1959, or 1960 if we wanted to use effectively the available secondary data while avoiding a small response rate in survey work because of our seeking data for too recent a year. Finally, the director of the project had no question whatsoever of the much greater value of data collected on input structures rather than on sales distribution, and he was of the strong opinion that it is best to concentrate one's efforts in obtaining one set of good reliable data rather than to spread them too thinly. But there was really no previous knowledge or experience as to what would be the "best" sectoring scheme for our study.

Perhaps we could have followed some formal procedures and thought processes in order to reach a decision on what would be the best sectoring scheme. On the other hand, we were not under the obligation to produce a final report by some deadline date, we had no specific client to serve but rather were serving society in general, and we were in a position to seek additional sources of funds should our initial grant run out. Further, the director strongly believed that the existing knowledge on how to determine a "best" sectoring scheme was too flimsy for reaching any decision on this question at the time we began the study. He took the position that our work was as much exploratory as to final application as

---

[1] As will be suggested later, a sector may be defined ideally as a category of one or more establishments having common input, process, and output characteristics. In practice, establishments cannot be found that are homogeneous in all these respects; and typically, a sector turns out to be a grouping of one or more establishments that are heterogeneous in at least one basic characteristic. This consequence results from the actual lack of homogeneity in outputs and production processes, and such factors as disclosure rules and incomplete data, which force a grouping of establishments that are not strictly homogeneous.

the primary work of our initial sponsor, the National Aeronautics and Space Administration (NASA), and he decided that we would let accumulating experience determine in time the final sectoring scheme. The director felt strongly that considerable exploratory work had yet to be done in the field of regional input–output analysis and that at least some key aspects of our research probe should be left flexible so that creative thinking could be introduced more easily as we gained experience and understanding of regional structure.

We began the study with a rough, preliminary consideration of some 2-digit SIC sectors. This represented an initial probe into the feasibility of a scheme based largely on the 2-digit SIC system. Obviously, such a scheme was to be consistent with that used in the Office of Business Economics (OBE) sectoring plan for the 1958 interindustry sales and purchases study,[2] and hopefully with other studies based on Census data. However, as we began a careful search for meaningful relationships from two-digit data—such as those relating to SIC 20, *Food and Kindred Products*, and SIC 23, *Apparel and Other Finished Products Made from Fabrics and Similar Materials*—we soon discovered that we would not uncover relationships that would be of regional significance. Two-digit data were too gross to identify what we perceived to be vital relationships within the Philadelphia economy, and to demonstrate how the input–output technique could be productively used in impact studies and in attacking the problems confronting the Philadelphia economy.

We therefore moved on to the consideration of the feasibility of a scheme based largely on a 3-digit SIC system—again one that would be able to be converted to the OBE sectoring plan. We proceeded with such a scheme for some time; but once more, as we looked at and evaluated the coefficients derived for the initial 3-digit sectors examined, we perceived many inadequacies in terms of their potential use. We were once again unhappy with the prospects. We judged that a scheme oriented to a 3-digit SIC code was still much too aggregated to provide the data considered necessary for the studies in depth that we would find stimulating. Accordingly, the director made the bold decision that we should pursue detail comparable to the level of a 4-digit SIC system. This decision was taken despite the warnings of many colleagues that we would be getting into such deep water that we would never come to realize the goal of completing the input–output table. Nonetheless, we proceeded, the director having in mind the possibility that if resources did run out and/or if we did have poor response in interviewing and on other counts, we would complete the interindustry study for the manufacturing sectors

[2] In particular, the scheme was consistent with the OBE plan reflecting revisions as of November 1961.

only. As it transpired, we were able to complete the study for the manufacturing sectors and most of the trade sectors on a 4-digit basis; we were
able to treat the rest of the trade, the financial, and some service sectors,
which we had initially anticipated doing at a 2-digit level, on an approximately 3-digit basis; and we were able to disaggregate final demand by
86 sectors. We did have to devote a tremendous amount of time and
effort to the study, but it is now clear that 4-digit SIC sectors for input–
output studies are feasible both for regions and for the nation. Reliable
data and more stable coefficients can be obtained with such detail. It is
not an impossible task, as so many thought.

4.2 The Standard Industrial Classification (SIC) System and Its Basis

As is well known, there exists in the United States a Standard Industrial
Classification (SIC) system that has been and is now used extensively in
many economic and regional studies.[3] This system takes into account
three different possible bases for grouping establishments. At times, it is
most meaningful to classify establishments by *type of process used*. For
example, the system recognizes that an establishment producing steel by
a blast furnace operation should be classified differently than an establishment putting out steel solely with an electric process. At other times, it
is meaningful to classify establishments by *type of dominant raw materials
used*. For example, all woven fabric mills using cotton are grouped in one
sector, while those using wool are grouped in another. And still other
times, it is most meaningful to classify establishments by *type of final
product or service*. For example, establishments producing dairy products
are placed in one sector, while those producing meat products are in
another. Because of these different possible bases for classification, it
becomes difficult to state the level of detail that is most desirable. When
process alone is used, one level of detail may be most appropriate. When
final product or *raw material* alone is used, still other levels of detail may
be most appropriate.

Because of changing technology, data needs, and diverse other factors,
including practical considerations, the SIC system has evolved over time
using all three bases of classification in different degrees at the various
levels of detail in its system. At the single-digit level—0, 1, 2, . . . , 9—the
system is based on major economic divisions: agriculture, mining, manufacturing, and so forth. At the two-digit level—. . . 20, 21, 22, . . . ,
35, 36, 37, . . .—the system is based primarily on a commodity basis. At
the three-digit level—011, 012, . . . , 224, . . . , 371, . . . , 899—the system

[3] See Bureau of the Budget [1957, 1963, and 1967]. When the Philadelphia study was
initiated, the latest SIC manual was the 1957 edition. Since then SIC manuals for
1963 and 1967 have been published that contain revisions and reformulations representing improvements in the classification scheme.

is still based predominantly on a commodity basis, but the process classification is used increasingly. At the 4-digit level, the system is based for certain industries on a commodity basis and for other industries on a process basis—depending on the structure of the industry. At the 5- and 7-digit level, the system is once again oriented primarily to a commodity basis.

Since the assumption of constant production coefficients plays a key role for the input–output analyst, one can expect that he would generally prefer classification of establishments by process. He would like to avoid putting into any one industrial sector establishments that produce the same commodity but by highly different production processes; for when technology stays the same and the relative importance of establishments changes, so will the average coefficients for the sector—this is inconsistent with their constancy assumption. The analyst would also like to avoid the formation of sectors on the basis of inputs used; for again, when technology stays the same and there is a change in the relative importance of two establishments processing one and the same raw material to yield quite different products, the average coefficients will change. Again, this is inconsistent with a constancy assumption. On the other hand, the analyst must also recognize that when sectors arc specified wholly on the basis of process similarities (i.e., input structure), output homogeneity will not be preserved for those sectors whose establishments produce quite different outputs when the relative levels of operation of these establishments change.

4.3 Lessons Learned

4.3.1 The Question of Insufficient Aggregation In Section 4.1 we presented a brief historical account of how the sectoring scheme evolved. Now that the Philadelphia study is completed, it is relevant to ask whether it would have been better to have made different choices with regard to sectoring, and further, what general lessons we have learned that are applicable to sectoring problems for input–output studies that may be undertaken in the future.

First, consider the question of whether it would have been appropriate to have used a more aggregate classification, say 2- or 3-digit systems, or some combination of these two. Our general reply is *no*. The reason for this position is that almost every input–output sector must represent an implied product-mix. This point does not raise a problem if the investigator is concerned with pure description of "what is" or "what has been." The difference between a 2-digit sectoring scheme and a 4-digit sectoring scheme is then simply one of detail. A 4-digit scheme yields considerably greater detail and thus significantly increases the number and types of hypotheses and models that might be tested. However, such detail does involve additional cost; and the investigator must weigh the gains against these costs.

The real problems emerge when an investigator wants to employ his input–output data for impact and projection purposes. Here he must allow for changing product mix of different sectors. However, the use of constant production coefficients and other input–output data for a sector *generally* implies constant product mix. We say "*generally* implies" because if it were the case that the different establishments in a sector produce with the same constant production coefficients even though they produce different products, then the use of the average production coefficients for a sector as constant production coefficients would be valid, however much the relative outputs of the establishments producing the different products were to change. But in most cases the establishments yielding different products use different sets of inputs, which then are averaged to yield the sector's set of production coefficients, in which typically each establishment's coefficients are weighted by its output. Therefore, it follows that if the relative outputs of these establishments were to change significantly, so would the sector's production coefficients. Then it becomes less and less valid to use as constants the production coefficients that were derived for that sector for a base year, because that base year's product mix is no longer relevant.

In general, it is clear that the more detailed the sectoring scheme, the fewer the differences among the production coefficients of the establishments in any given sector, and therefore the fewer the errors involved in using a sector's production coefficients for a base year as constants. Put another way, when an aggregated sector is disaggregated, the analyst explicitly allows, at least in part, for changes in product mix of the aggregate sector by requiring the specification of the changes in the output of each of several disaggregate sectors. Presumably, a good sectoring scheme does differentiate the products, at least in part, in terms of the different subgroups of products or processes with respect to whose output direct and indirect impacts are to be examined.

In support of the statements of the previous paragraph we may now report on some of the variations found to exist in the coefficients actually derived for the Philadelphia establishments, and for sectors at different levels of aggregation. Karaska [1968] examined variations in the Philadelphia establishments in a paper that drew heavily upon his work with us. As he noted, the variation in input coefficients among establishments within any given sector may reflect many factors: different accounting procedures; existence of imperfect competition; differences in entrepreneurship; differences in restrictions imposed on production; differences in climate and other exogenous factors within the natural environment;

differences in capital vintage and response to technological risks; and differences in size of firm and product mix. He examined the *total materials* coefficient for the 4-digit sectors of each 2-digit SIC sector, for the 3-digit SIC sectors in each 2-digit SIC sector, and finally for the 2-digit sector itself. That is, he considered all the establishments in any given 2-digit SIC sector, and using the standard "coefficient of variation" as the appropriate measure, he estimated the variation among these establishments in their total materials coefficient. Then he considered the establishments that fell in each of the 3-digit SIC sectors contained in the given 2-digit SIC sectors and estimated the variation in the total materials coefficient for the establishments that fell in each 3-digit SIC sector. Finally, he considered the establishments falling in each 4-digit classification contained within each 3-digit SIC of the given 2-digit SIC sector and calculated the variation in the total materials coefficient among the establishments of each of these 4-digit sectors. He concluded that variation of this coefficient among the establishments within a sector increased with the level of aggregation of the sector. Some of his findings are illustrated in Tables 4.1 and 4.2.

Table 4.1. Coefficients of Variation for Total-Materials Technological Coefficients Aggregated at the 4-Digit Level and Summarized by 2-Digit SIC, Philadelphia Manufacturing, 1960

SIC Number and Name	Coefficient of Variation	Number of 4-Digit Industries
29 Petroleum	0.1116	2
31 Leather	0.1198	2
24 Lumber and Wood	0.1224	2
20 Food	0.1246	5
28 Chemicals	0.1993	5
39 Miscellaneous	0.2424	10
37 Transportation	0.2630	1
26 Paper	0.2648	6
22 Textiles	0.2663	10
36 Electrical Machinery	0.2695	7
32 Stone, Clay, and Glass	0.2845	6
34 Fabricated Metals	0.2882	14
25 Furniture	0.2885	5
35 Machinery, except electrical	0.2954	18
33 Primary Metals	0.3168	5
27 Printing and Publishing	0.4000	10
30 Rubber and Plastics	0.4032	2
38 Instruments	0.5150	5
23 Apparel	0.5582	11
TOTAL	0.3076	126

Source: Gerald Karaska (1968). "Variation of Input–Output Coefficients for Different Levels of Aggregation," *Journal of Regional Science*, 8, 219.

Table 4.2. Coefficients of Variation for Total-Materials Technological Coefficients Aggregated at the 3-Digit and 2-Digit Levels and Summarized by 2-Digit SIC, Philadelphia Manufacturing, 1960

3-Digit Level			2-Digit Level		
SIC Number	Coefficient of Variation	Number of 3-Digit Industries	SIC Number	Coefficient of Variation	Number of Firms
29	0.1747	2	29	0.2230	11
20	0.2318	8	24	0.2849	10
24	0.2547	2	28	0.3238	38
28	0.2749	6	26	0.3144	32
31	0.2766	3	20	0.3433	48
26	0.2796	3	25	0.3483	30
25	0.2851	4	37	0.3708	11
37	0.3155	2	31	0.3894	18
22	0.3275	8	34	0.4132	77
34	0.3347	8	39	0.4284	53
35	0.3627	8	22	0.4377	67
36	0.3656	7	35	0.4509	110
33	0.3673	6	30	0.4537	15
39	0.3992	6	33	0.4804	38
30	0.4032	2	32	0.5249	44
27	0.4471	6	27	0.5336	49
32	0.4959	4	36	0.5357	36
38	0.5075	4	38	0.6035	24
23	0.6309	7	23	0.6373	73
Total	0.3654	96		0.4262	784

Source: Gerald Karaska (1968). "Variation of Input–Output Coefficients for Different Levels of Aggregation," *Journal of Regional Science*, 8, 219.

While there can be many differences among scholars as to how variation among coefficients should be rigorously measured and which coefficients ought to be examined, there is no question, from the data developed by Karaska, that there is significant variation among the establishments of sectors in general and that this variation decreases significantly as the classification of sectors proceeds from 2-digit to 3-digit and then to 4-digit.

In short, it seems to us that a disaggregated scheme, at least to a 4-digit level in manufacturing, is more consistent with constant production coefficients than a 2-digit scheme. Further, it is to be expected that the accuracy of impact analysis and projections in general also will increase significantly with the increase in the detail of classification.

Actually, the choice of the sectors of the Philadelphia tables was governed in part by hard realities of data collection. In the manufacturing sectors, the basic data were collected for establishments that were initially classified by industrial directories and other listings on a 4-digit SIC basis; and further, secondary data for output estimates were available on a 4-digit SIC basis. Hence, it was generally easiest to sample at the 4-digit SIC level. Thus, the data were in a sense already there by 4-digit sectors. We could have weighted the coefficients or data for each 4-digit sector to have obtained appropriate coefficients for 2- or 3-digit sectors. Our weighting might have been based on the employment or output of each 4-digit sector. However, to have done so would have meant the loss of considerable information. Further, it is not certain whether we could have saved any significant amount of resources by doing so. On the one hand, to have aggregated would have incurred the costs of aggregation; on the other hand, we would have achieved subsequent cost savings in constructing the table because we would have had fewer sectors and the problem of reconciling data would have been eased. In sum, we judge that our decision to retain data by the 4-digit level in the manufacturing sectors was a wise one.

The preceding remarks relate primarily to the manufacturing sectors of the table. In practice we did not obtain a similar amount of detail for the nonmanufacturing sectors. Time-cost constraints that were imposed on the construction of the nonmanufacturing sectors precluded a complete delineation by 4-digit sectors. While our experience indicates that for the wholesale services sectors a 4-digit breakdown does not yield coefficients much different than a 3-digit breakdown, and for the retail service sectors a 4-digit breakdown appears only slightly more advantageous than a 3-digit breakdown or even a 2-digit breakdown, clearly for business and personal and other service sectors, it would have been highly advantageous to have developed coefficients by 4-digit sectors. That is, had we had the resources to do a complete job on the nonmanufacturing sectors, we would have disaggregated a number of activities *at least* to a 4-digit detail. It is worthwhile to point out that generally speaking, a proper disaggregation of nonmanufacturing sectors in input–output studies has usually been assigned a lower priority than the proper disaggregation of manufacturing sectors. One must guard against this tendency. It is valid to seek fine detail on certain nonmanufacturing sectors. And clearly, if we are to understand our evolving metropolitan regions more thoroughly as their nonmanufacturing sectors become increasingly important over the years, we must seek at least 4-digit detail on a number of these sectors.

4.3.2 The Question of Insufficient Disaggregation Having concluded that at least a 4-digit classification is desirable for most of the sectors for the general type of study comparable to our Philadelphia region study, we might now ask the question whether still finer detail should have been or should be sought for certain activities. If we were to redo the study, we would still begin with the manufacturing establishments as classified in industrial directories on the 4-digit basis, but we definitely would place together establishments with good responses in terms of certain specific 5- and even 7-digit classifications. We know now that we could have done so in our Philadelphia study without causing subsequent problems in reconciling the data of the table or in obtaining an inverse.

There are a number of specific points to be made here, however. First, in some instances the data in the Philadelphia table already reflect specific 5-digit sectors in that all the establishments within a given 4-digit sector also all lie in a specific 5-digit sector. For example, the several aircraft manufacturers that exist in Philadelphia all are of the rotary-wing (helicopter) type and should be classified in an appropriate subgroup of SIC 3721.

More important, we explicitly did consider for certain sectors a classification finer than 4-digit. We did disaggregate the sectors within the needle trades into manufacturers, jobbers, and contractors. Since our sample for each of these three subsectors did not appear adequate, and since we had been warned of the great difficulties in dealing with a 4-digit system, not to mention a system with some 5-digit sectors, and since we had not completed or inverted a coefficient table on a 4-digit basis, we judged that it would be wise not to risk additional problems by disaggregating parts of our 4-digit scheme. In retrospect, however, we easily could have obtained an improved sample for each of the parts of the needle trade sectors, and easily could have employed three sectors instead of one sector to represent each of the needle trade sectors.

A general problem arises, however, when one pushes into a 5- or 7-digit classification scheme. This problem is related to one that we shall mention several times, a problem that comes to exist when mergers lead to the establishment of firms engaged in activities representing more than one SIC category. In such a situation, it becomes increasingly difficult to obtain from the firm the detailed input data relevant to *each* of its 4-digit SIC products.[4] When the investigator starts to use 5- to 7-digit classifications, the problem is magnified because it exists at the establishment level. Most manufacturing establishments engage in the production of more than one 5- or 7-digit commodity. From each of these establishments information is required on input purchases by the 5- or 7-digit commodity produced. Few establishments have cost accounting systems that can yield such information.

It is hardly necessary to state that the investigator must not seek disaggregation in and for itself. For example, there appears little if any basis for employing a finely disaggregated set of sectors that might distinguish

---

[4] Perhaps the recent Securities and Exchange Commission rulings requiring disclosure of information on product lines may aid in obtaining at least a limited amount of such information.

between regular wrapping paper, gift wrapping paper, Christmas wrapping paper, and all other "special occasions" wrapping paper. Disaggregation should be meaningful. It should increase the validity of the technical coefficients, or make possible more significant policy analysis, and so on. Further, the investigator should keep in mind that a very fine sectoring scheme (as reflected, for example, in a 7-or-more-digit SIC classification), yields coefficients highly sensitive to the normal ongoing processes of change in technology and improvement in production operations with existing technology. In this sense, the coefficients for such a finely disaggregated classification system may tend to be unstable. On the other hand, they would be extremely valuable for estimating and projecting the impact of technological change. Thus, the investigator must make a choice here. Usually, if the resources are available, he will choose the more finely disaggregated sectoring, since detailed data can always be aggregated at a cost, whereas more aggregate data cannot always be disaggregated when desired.

4.3.3 The Proper Mix of Aggregation and Disaggregation Increasingly, as the study progressed, we came to recognize explicitly an important point. For an input–output study, there is much more flexibility in the procedure for developing an appropriate classification system than we had originally been aware of, or had allowed ourselves to think about. Against the background of the SIC system or any other classification system, there is no reason why an investigator cannot take the establishments in his region and develop a scheme that includes some 2-digit sectors, some 3-digit sectors, and some 4-, 5-, and even 7-digit sectors. He can also split SIC sectors that have the same or different number of digits and combine the parts to form new sectors.

Now, of course, the investigator confronts, pragmatically, a number of constraints on the choice of a proper mix of 2- to 7-digit sectors. For example, some 4-digit sectors may include too few establishments to permit disaggregation. Or because of an inadequate number of responding establishments in one or more closely related 4-digit sectors, it may be necessary to aggregate these sectors to a 2- or 3-digit level; the inadequate number may result because of disclosure rules, or because respondents may refuse to furnish data or may in fact be unable to respond adequately, or both. Further, the 3-digit or 4- or 5-digit sectors themselves may not be important enough to justify the high cost of gathering the data for them—especially when these sectors may use the same sources of raw materials and may face similar market situations. Moreover, because two or more sectors may represent successive stages in the production of a single output by vertically integrated firms that account for a large fraction of the outputs of the sectors, it may not pay to try to disaggregate by these sectors. The significance of these points will obviously become more evident as we consider survey and other problems discussed in the chapters to follow.

It is also clear now that in a study of a major metropolitan region such as Philadelphia, the investigator can develop the specific mix of sector detail that is best suited to his region; and where appropriate, he can even define and construct anew certain sectors. After all, each metropolitan region is unique in some respects. The subpopulations of its establishments are different from those of other regions, as are its resources and needs for input–output studies. Therefore, to some extent at least, each region needs its own sectoring scheme.

Note that this last statement runs counter to a recommendation made by the Ad Hoc Committee on Classifications for Regional Input–Output Studies of the Regional Science Research Institute. At its February 10, 1964, meeting, that committee recommended (p. 2) that "there should be one common classification into which all regional studies' classifications are capable of being translated in a simple way—whatever their level of aggregation, and that this must be the Standard Industrial Classification. One simple working rule which might be proposed is that anyone working at, let us say, the 3-digit industry level should never split a 4-digit industry among several of his sectors. In all cases, where possible, the sectors for an input–output study should correspond in general to a four digit SIC level."

Clearly, the recommendation of the Ad Hoc Committee is much too severe. To reiterate, the input–output study must be oriented to the important peculiarities and needs of a region. Such may dictate the formation of a new sector when (1) a large establishment engages in activities that cut across each of several SIC categories, (2) the data are obtainable on only the establishment basis, and (3) the resulting coefficients may have considerable stability. For example, the objectives of the Boulder input–output study made it necessary to define two new sectors, the space sector and the space-related sector [Miernyk, et al., 1967]. To illustrate in another way, if one is studying the past and the present, a classification system that ignores a one-man new establishment just starting off is acceptable. If, however, the points of time are today and 15 years from now, then a classification system must be very sensitive to one-employee new establishments that may possibly provide the driving force for a metropolitan region 15 years hence.

Clearly, we encounter a conflict at this point. A classification system that is optimal for an input–output study of a particular single region is not likely to be the same as the one that is optimal for the study of another particular region and, more important, for the study of a system of regions to which the given region belongs. At this point we cannot suggest any general procedure to resolve this conflict. The investigator needs to be knowledgeable on the specifics of the conflict. We can recommend, however, that the investigator who conducts a single region input–output study keep in mind the needs of interrregional and multiregional studies. He, as well as others, should look forward to development of the capability to use the results of an input–output study for one region in the conduct of input–output studies in all other regions. He has much to profit from such a capability. We therefore recommend that he try to develop a classification scheme for his region in such a way that its sectors can be easily recombined to yield sectors that are standard, e.g., the SIC sectors. Further, when it does become necessary for him to introduce new and different sectors, we urge that he fully document his work and clearly indicate the parts of the existing SIC system or other types of sectors that were put together to form the new sector. He should do this in such a way that his results can be unscrambled so as to yield data by standard sectors.

4.4 Summary

From our general experience with regard to sectoring, we may state that the detail we sought and accomplished within the resource constraints was appropriate for the Philadelphia region. The final sectoring scheme is shown in Table 14.A1 on pp. 176–193. We have been relatively satisfied with the outcome. We now find that we can conduct a wide range of interesting studies for the Philadelphia region that we had not anticipated. It is possible, for example, to ask what the closing and relocation of the Frankford Arsenal might mean for the Philadelphia economy. We can quickly, and at minor cost, obtain and project an impact in great detail and aggregate the detail quickly into the categories we desire for policy purposes. It is possible to complete studies for other regions (e.g., Baltimore and Dallas), where the data of the Philadelphia study are useful to fill in existing major gaps in their stocks of data. We can set up a relevant matrix for each of these regions, examine impacts of developments, and quickly obtain results that can be aggregated to the categories relevant for decision-makers.

With our wealth of detail, we can effectively play around with the notion of industrial complexes, testing whether they exist by trying out all kinds of linkages and forms of aggregation. Different kinds of correlations and regressions can be pursued to determine and detect different kinds of linkages. We can study impact on particular sectors in fine detail. We can look at the intraregional markets for these sectors and relate them to production and investment policies of the firms in that sector.

In short, we find that we can do many things that we never would have dreamed of doing if the details were not right in front of us.

References

Bureau of the Budget (1957, 1963, 1967). *Standard Industrial Classification Manual*. Washington, D.C.: U.S. Government Printing Office.

Karaska, Gerald (1968). "Variation of Input–Output Coefficients for Different Levels of Aggregation," *Journal of Regional Science*, 8: 215–227.

Miernyk, William H., et al. (1967). *Impact of the Space Program on a Local Economy: An Input–Output Analysis*. Morgantown, W. Va.: West Virginia Library.

Regional Science Research Institute, Ad Hoc Committee on Regional Input–Output Studies, *Recommendations*, Cambridge, Mass., February 1964, p. 2.

5.1 Introduction: Census Versus Sample

Input–output studies are without question among the most data-ravenous economic models that have been developed. Vast quantities of information must be obtained in order to produce the desired tables. To obtain this information it is usually necessary to collect extensive primary data to supplement such secondary data as may be available from various sources. Two alternative procedures are available for the collection of the data. One involves a complete census of establishments, such as was used in the Kalamazoo study [Smith, 1960]. The other uses data from a sample survey of establishments by sector. In the latter case, many survey designs are possible depending on the size of the region, the nature and characteristics of the industries, the objectives of the study, and the available resources.[1]

There are, of course, advantages and disadvantages of a complete census relative to a sample. Some of the advantages are (1) that the investigator obtains output estimates simultaneously with input estimates, thus avoiding the problems of deriving control totals, as will be discussed in the next chapter; (2) that the data as they are finally processed are of a somewhat higher degree of accuracy; and (3) that the investigator may be able to construct a flow table that is "inherently" in balance and internally consistent—that is, he may be able to avoid imputing magnitudes and forcing and stretching the data by a variety of procedures, which also will be discussed in subsequent chapters. On the other hand, there is one major and overpowering disadvantage. For a large region such as Philadelphia, the cost of obtaining a complete census as well as editing and processing all the responses would be tremendous. For example, consider that in food retail operations alone, a complete coverage would encompass 10,429 grocery stores, chain stores, and supermarkets. Without question, the small advantage of having a firmer basis for calculating coefficients by utilizing the data from the completed questionnaires of the last few percent of this population is more than offset by the increase in cost. Clearly, for this and many other sectors, the loss of accuracy from additional information is not commensurate with the increase in cost of collection and processing data after a certain point is reached in the coverage of its establishments.

5.2 Sampling Technique and Coverage Criteria

In the Philadelphia study the limited resources relative to the size of the region made it absolutely necessary to sample establishments by sector.

---

[1] In particular, two broad categories of survey designs can be distinguished: (1) the sampling of specific industries particularly important to a region, as in the Utah Study [Moore and Peterson, 1955]; and (2) the sampling of each sector in the region, as in the Washington Study [Bourque et al., 1967].

From both general and formal standpoints, sampling techniques and survey methods have been discussed extensively in the published literature. This chapter therefore concerns itself only with the experience we gained in the application and nonapplication of these techniques and methods in our regional input-output study.

Clearly, a first step in any study is to identify with reasonable accuracy the population to be sampled. For regional input–output analysis, the population comprises the establishments in the diverse economic sectors, including nonprofit-type institutions, the agencies of government, and the household units. The family or household units can be sampled and surveyed with procedures that are well developed; for example, see the Boulder study [Miernyk et al., 1967].[2]

The number of government agencies in a region is usually small. Therefore, it is often feasible to obtain complete coverage in a survey. Occasionally, minor civil governmental units, such as a local field office of the U.S. Department of Justice, may not be sampled; and its inputs may simply be estimated on the basis of its employment. Likewise, where there are a relatively few large nonprofit institutions in a sector, as with universities, 100 percent coverage should be sought.

The difficult sampling problem arises with the economic establishments associated with manufacturing, trades, services, and all other profit-making activities.[3] How can we identify that point for each sector at which the marginal cost of obtaining additional coverage is equal to the marginal gains? Or how can we identify that point at which the coverage of establishments in a sector allows the investigator to estimate coefficients with sufficient reliability? In input–output work, this problem has very special features. Within any given sector, the establishments usually will differ greatly in size, output mix, capital vintage, and complexity of administrative structure. Theoretically, the investigator may stratify the establishments in each sector by these characteristics and then proceed to sample randomly each stratum for establishments to be interviewed, replacing establishments that refuse to respond with other establishments, again chosen randomly. However, the population in each stratum is often too small for application of formal statistical sampling techniques. There may be, for example, only two or three firms (if not just one) in any single stratum. Moreover, if one stratum contains three firms, each with fewer than ten employees, and another has two firms, each with more than a

---

[2] Often the data for a survey of households may be supplemented with data from national consumer surveys such as the Bureau of Labor Statistics, Wharton School, and University of Michigan studies.

[3] A difficult problem may also be encountered in the survey of a number of different types of nonprofit institutions, such as religious units, in which the bookkeeping is most diverse in character, if at all appropriate.

thousand employees, is it appropriate for the investigator to spread his resources evenly among these two strata by interviewing one firm from each? Or, alternatively, is it more appropriate for him to interview the two firms with a thousand or more employees and ignore those firms having fewer than ten employees? From the standpoint of deriving co-efficients that truly reflect the sector's structure, perhaps the former procedure is more desirable. However, from the standpoint of studying impact of major developments on the economy, it would appear more desirable to have the data for a second firm employing one thousand or more than to obtain data for a firm with fewer than ten employees.

Practical considerations such as these guided the Philadelphia study. There was much less attention paid to formal statistical sampling techniques than several scholars on the project felt desirable. In particular, the director of the project was aware of how quickly resources can be dissipated on refinements without obtaining the necessary final results, and of the large number of input–output studies initiated but never completed because of poor allocation of funds and attempts at undue refinement. He often overruled his associates who would have preferred the use of more satisfactory sampling techniques, taking the position that we first must ensure that there be results, however crude.[4] He therefore insisted that we first concentrate on obtaining data from firms with large numbers of employees and then fill in with firms that might be sampled with known probabilities from different strata if appropriate and *if possible*.

It was necessary to develop some workable definitions of "adequate coverage" for any sector, by which to be guided and, in practice, from which to deviate when the "going got hard." An adequate coverage for a sector was taken to be achieved when (1) establishments accounting for 65 percent or more of a sector's employment had been successfully interviewed, and (2) the number of these establishments was no less than three. (Obviously, where there were fewer than three firms engaged in the sector, this second criteria was dropped.) In general, as indicated, we tended to minimize the number of establishments to be interviewed. Thus, we tended to begin interviewing with the largest of the establishments in any given sector until the 65 percent employment criterion was met. We

---

[4] This mundane, nonscholarly approach is often necessary, especially for those sectors in which one initially can expect little if any cooperation from establishments. For these sectors, the investigator takes the data whenever and however they can be obtained, and is happy when he is able to obtain any at all. If there are relatively few firms that possibly may cooperate and provide the full set of data, he tends to interview these firms at the start, especially if they are large, in order to ease the problem of getting sufficient returns to satisfy his percent employment criterion for adequate coverage. There were a few important sectors in the Philadelphia study in which data were obtained only because of close personal relationships.

realized that this procedure yields a sample that does not represent the "in-fact" technology of a sector. The smaller firms tend to be omitted. In a number of sectors, these smaller firms operate with technology somewhat less advanced than the larger firms. In some sectors, however, such as some of those including diverse electronics, instruments, and research and development operations, the smaller firms tend to be more innovative and, in fact, to have the more advanced production techniques.

There is still another question: Should an investigator allow his criteria of adequate coverage to vary among sectors, particularly since the rate of technological change as well as other important elements differ among them? The answer is *yes*, especially when the investigator uses a highly disaggregated classification system, and when the total number of establishments in any given sector is small. For example, where sectors with relatively small firms were judged to be undergoing rapid change, we interviewed a larger number of firms, with emphasis on obtaining more coverage of smaller firms and with some tendency to increase the percent coverage of employment in that sector. Such was the case in the apparel industries, where subsamples were constructed for manufacturers, jobbers, and contractors, and in the wholesale sectors, which were stratified with regard to merchant and nonmerchant wholesalers. Similarly, where the general quality of responses was not high, we tended to increase coverage in terms of percent-of-sector employment and the number of firms. Responses that were not "reasonably" complete usually were not counted in meeting the criteria.

Also, where a sector had many small establishments of a similar character, such as textiles, we recognized that a lower coverage, such as 50 percent, might be adequate. In contrast, where a sector had only a few large establishments, such as steel mills, we judged that a higher coverage, such as 75 percent, was necessary. Also we allowed coverage criteria to reflect the composition of a sector's output mix. We judged that sectors that produce only one or a few products with a limited number of similar processes can be surveyed with a lower coverage than heterogeneous sectors that have a wide variety of processes.

There were also other considerations that we kept in mind. When a base year is normal in all respects for a particular sector, the adequacy criteria need not be changed. When that year is atypical for a sector, because of recession or boom conditions or other factors, the adequacy criteria should be raised. Alternatively, for atypical periods it may be relevant to obtain data for one or more years other than the base year to use with base year data to estimate "normal" coefficients for the base year. Further, it may very well be that for establishments producing a few large units, such as turbine systems or ships, the data for several years centering around the base year should be obtained and averaged in order to derive meaningful input–output coefficients.

Another basic problem peculiar to input–output work for metropolitan regions concerns the adequacy of a sample in terms of intrametropolitan location. Ideally, data should be collected from firms representative of operations at central city, suburban, and nonurban locations. This point is particularly relevant since suburban plants tend to be newer plants using newer technology and having different input structures than the generally older central city plants. Yet from the standpoint of utilizing the resources most effectively, an investigator must deviate, at least to some extent, from good sampling practice. Consider the situation in which there is a compact and tight agglomeration of many small and medium-sized firms in and about the central business districts, and there is a diffuse distribution of firms in the suburbs. In the course of a single day an interviewer may be able to interview four to six firms in the central business district but only two or three in suburban areas. Hence, with limited resources, a proper spatial distribution of firms in the sample may be achieved only at the expense of the number of firms covered in a sample. That is, there usually must be some tradeoff reached in the study between the spatial representativeness of a sample and its coverage.

Frankly, in the Philadelphia study establishments in the city of Phila-delphia were oversampled vis-à-vis establishments in the other seven counties because the former were more compactly located and accessible. Also, establishments within the five counties in Pennsylvania were over-sampled relative to establishments in the three counties in New Jersey because they were more accessible and more easily identified from secon-dary data, and because we had greater rapport with them.

One other relevant factor to bear in mind on this problem is a psy-chological one. Input–output work is unpleasant work—often tedious in terms of the routine of correcting questionnaires, setting down the data, eliminating inconsistencies, computing coefficients, and so forth, and often frustrating in terms of the many negative responses received during the interviewing process. From a very practical standpoint, it is important to keep up morale when the going gets tough—as it often does in the inter-mediate and later stages of a project after the initial excitement of starting something big and new wears off. In the mind of the senior author, during these stages there is no question of the importance for an interviewer's morale of obtaining at least one positive response during the course of a day. Therefore, whether consciously or not, we often chose to interview in the course of a day a set of establishments at a central-city location so that a large number could be contacted. By so doing, the probability of receiving at least one positive response was higher rather than lower.

5.3 Conducting the Survey

As with any study involving the collection of large quantities of primary data, there is the question of whether to interview in person, conduct a mail survey, or use some combination of the two methods. Without question, personal interviews are the only method of collecting *quality* data. However, personal interviews are expensive, and frequently because of limited funds the investigator must employ mail survey for supplementary purposes. It was our general practice to begin the collection of data for any sector through personal interview with a long, detailed questionnaire, except for retail trades.[5] Once a good response was obtained for a sufficiently large number of establishments in a given sector, we would then conduct a limited survey intended either to augment the data obtained from the long questionnaires or to obtain some data from some of the small firms that were not sampled by the more expensive method. In the limited survey, we used short questionnaires and relied heavily on mail service. However, in using returns from a mail survey, an investigator must be more careful. Checks on the reliability of the response cannot be established so effectively as through personal interview. It was our practice that when we had already obtained good coverage through personal interview, we would use the additional data from mail survey only when such data could be established to be of high quality.

The primary data from interviews and mail survey were augmented by data on the returns of the Regional Economic Survey of the Penn Jersey Transportation Study, by data from local secondary sources, mostly available in published form, and by information obtained from interviews with knowledgeable persons in an industry. Frequently, when a specific piece of information was lacking or when the quality of data gathered on a particular input was questionable, we sought further information through a series of telephone calls.

Conducting personal interviews effectively is not a simple matter. In the Philadelphia study we learned much from our mistakes. In the beginning we often found that our interviewers were improperly prepared in that they had insufficient knowledge of the establishment to be interviewed and of manufacturing processes in general; and that our questionnaires for many establishments were improperly structured. Our experience confirmed the principle that a senior staff member should participate in the early interviews to identify some of the more difficult problems of the sectors under study. In effect, the use of senior staff is often the least costly path to the desired information, despite the high cost of their time.

[5] Among the retail sectors personal interviews were completed for only the two largest: department stores and chain food stores.

Ideally, prior to interview it is desirable to review the existing knowledge on the production function of the sector to be interviewed so that the interviewer can suggest input items that might be forgotten by the respondent. It is advisable for the interviewer to avail himself of any offer to tour the facilities of an establishment in the sector to gain firsthand knowledge, although this procedure takes time. Also, it was found that both graduate and undergraduate business school students, particularly those from the fields of marketing and accounting, were generally more effective as interviewers than students from such other fields as economics, city planning, geography, political science, or sociology. Business school students are better acquainted with the realities of business operations rather than with theory.

In addition to properly trained and informed interviewers, it is very desirable to have the proper letters of introduction. One letter should be from a high public official enthusiastically spelling out the importance of this study for evaluating possible ways of dealing with a current governmental problem. Another should be from a top university administrator ensuring the integrity and scientific conduct of the study. A third should be from a leading business official (for example, the president of a Federal Reserve Bank or a respected executive of the Chamber of Commerce) assuring the respondent of the importance of the study in attacking the problems confronting the business community.

These letters of introduction should be accompanied by a personal letter from the director of the study (1) pointing up the objectives of the study, (2) repeating its specific contribution to an effective attack on the particular regional problems that are of concern to the establishment to be interviewed, and (3) indicating the potential value to the establishment of the data to be obtained. Finally, after the introductory letters have been mailed and sufficient time (perhaps 5 to 7 days) has been allowed to elapse for the letter to be received and read, there should be a request by telephone for a staff appointment with the appropriate executive of the establishment.

The interview, which may take more than half an hour but customarily not more than an hour, should further acquaint the respondent with the study and its purposes, and attempt to complete the questionnaire as far as possible at that time. In cases where all the requested information cannot be furnished during the interview, a copy of the partially completed questionnaire, together with a set of printed instructions and a return mail envelope, should be left for the respondent to mail upon completion.

In the Philadelphia study, if the questionnaire was not returned within four to six weeks after the interview, the respondent was contacted by mail. If the questionnaire was not received within 30 days after the reminder letter, a telephone call was made to inquire if further assistance was desired in answering the questions, and to urge the respondent to complete the questionnaire.

It is important, of course, to be prompt in keeping appointments, to be courteous and neat in appearance, and to follow the customary business procedures and formalities in interaction. A thank-you letter should always be mailed out upon receipt of a questionnaire.

There are several other practices that can be extremely helpful in increasing the response rate. One is to guarantee explicitly the confidentiality of the response, and to make clear the steps taken to ensure confidentiality. We found it useful also to stamp the word CONFIDENTIAL prominently in red ink over the first page of the questionnaire. Another good practice is to list questions in order of importance to the study, *ceteris paribus*. The first questions are generally answered with greater care and in greater detail. Also, where possible it is wise to place at the beginning of the questionnaire those questions that are easiest to answer. If the first questions are difficult to answer, or are likely to be confusing, the respondent may become discouraged and not provide any information at all.

When major parts of a study are completed, it may be useful to circulate these with the questionnaires that are subsequently distributed so that respondents have a better perspective of the kind of scientific and technical knowledge that is to be the outcome of the study. This practice helps reduce anxiety concerning possible misuse of data that may be provided. It is also well to bear in mind that in certain sectors it is necessary to "break the ice." For example, in some sectors, such as electronics, the investigator does not obtain an adequate response merely by sending out questionnaires or arranging for interviews. By some means or other, the investigator must make effective contact with a leading establishment or individual within the sector. Once the basic cooperation of a leading establishment of a sector has been obtained, and this contact is made known, it becomes possible to induce other firms to follow suit and complete the questionnaire with equal detail.

5.4 The Temporal Sequence of Interview, by Sector

Another major issue concerns the temporal sequence in which sectors are to be interviewed. If the research procedure is first to collect the data for all the sectors of the economy rather than to collect, process, and develop coefficients for each sector or subgroup of sectors one at a time, then the choice of which major industry division to probe first is not so important. On the other hand, if an investigator must proceed on a piecemeal basis and treat sectors or major industry divisions one at a time, as was done in the Philadelphia study, then this question is a very real one. In the Philadelphia study we began with manufacturing. At the start, we were not certain how much of an input–output study we would be able to complete. Therefore, since by the terms of the research grant it was most important for us to complete the coefficients for the manufacturing sectors as a minimum, we began with manufacturing. We completed most of our interviewing of manufacturing establishments and did extensive work on the calculation of input–output coefficients for manufacturing sectors prior to interviewing the nonmanufacturing sectors. However, had we known that we would be able to complete a table as extensive as the current Philadelphia table, and given our decision to develop coefficients on the basis of producers' prices rather than purchasers' prices, we would have found it more efficient to have begun our interviewing with the transportation and wholesale sectors. Such a plan would have permitted us to calculate transportation and wholesale trade margins first, and would have allowed us to adjust manufacturing purchases to a producers' price basis more accurately. Alternatively, had we decided to build the table at purchasers' prices and then to revalue the table to producers' prices during the reconciliation phase, the accuracy of our adjustments would not have depended on which interviewing sequence we had chosen.

Experience also suggests that within the manufacturing industries, interviewing should commence with primary industries that process raw materials into intermediate products. This procedure enables the interviewing staff to become familiar with such products and to ask more knowledgeable questions later, when these products are encountered as inputs into establishments operating at a more advanced stage in the overall production process.

5.5 Input Purchases Data Versus Sales Distribution Data

The large quantity of detailed data required for the construction of an input–output table may be obtained in two basic ways. By one method the investigator seeks data on input purchases by producing sectors. In the second, he seeks data on the distribution of sales by consuming sectors.[6] Ideally, he should seek both sets of data, because with both sets he can doublecheck his estimated coefficients and maximize consistency and accuracy. However, when the resources of a study are limited, as is almost invariably the case when we deal with a very large region like Philadelphia, the investigator must make a choice.[7] Generally, it is much better to have one complete set of data than two incomplete sets.

---

[6] For examples of input–output tables built from output data, see Coughlin and Isard, 1963, and Hansen and Tiebout, 1963.

[7] See, however, the state of Washington study [Bourque et al., 1967], in which both sets of data were estimated. When inconsistencies did arise between sales data and purchases data, the principal investigators met over the kitchen table, shared their knowledge on the items in question, and when necessary arrived at some compromise to eliminate the inconsistency. A real question arises, however, as to the scientific legitimacy of this procedure.

If we are to collect and process one set of data, which set should we choose? No simple answer to this question would be applicable to all studies. Much depends on the level of detail desired.

Suppose for the moment that we seek to collect and process data by 2-digit sectors. To obtain data from an establishment on its percentage distribution of sales by 2-digit consuming sectors probably would be easier than to obtain data from it on its purchases by 2-digit sectors. As already noted, several studies have chosen the former course of action. However, this course does encounter a number of substantial problems.

One basic problem concerns the checks and balances that the investigator is able to apply to the data. When data are collected on the input structure of a given establishment of a sector, these data can be compared with data provided by other establishments. Major discrepancies can be identified, the data can be verified for reasonableness with engineers, major gaps can be identified through knowledge of technology, and so forth. In contrast, the sales distribution data of any single establishment in a sector are much less subject to verification. Compared to input data, they can vary much more widely among the establishments of a sector because the markets of these establishments can differ so much with reference to both industries and areas served. The sales data can only be edited in accordance with known marketing relationships, since our data on shipments between sectors via diverse transport modes are poor. In short, when we seek sales distribution data, we are much less able to sift out poor data and to manufacture good data when there are gaps. This is one major reason why, in our Philadelphia study, we chose to seek information on input structures.

When we seek detail by 4-digit sectors, additional factors become significant. In highly competitive industries the investigator cannot expect to obtain a full set of an establishment's data on sales, even though he requests only the percentage distribution by consuming sectors. The establishment would consider that such data would reveal too much information on its markets. On the other hand, the establishment may be quite willing to provide 4-digit detail on its purchases, since such data are less likely to reveal information that might be of interest to and improve the positions of its competitors.

Another factor that complicates the problem when a study is for a region as large and diverse as Philadelphia is that many establishments may sell or market their output through merchant wholesalers. Many manufacturers, therefore, are not fully aware of the exact identity of the consuming sectors to which their products are sold. This problem becomes more severe as the sector classification becomes more detailed. To circumvent this problem it is possible, of course, to seek the data from the merchant wholesalers. Unfortunately, the merchant wholesalers do not keep records in the detail necessary for an adequate response—that is, data on the percentage distribution of sales to sectors purchasing the output of the establishments that the merchant wholesalers market.

Finally, we observe that in a regional input–output study, the investigator is tempted to seek detail not only on sales and purchases between establishments in the region but also on (1) exports to the different consuming sectors of several regions, and (2) imports from the different supplying sectors of several regions. He is therefore tempted to ask a question that concerns (1) the distribution of an establishment's output by consuming sectors by regions, (2) the sources of each of its inputs by regions, or (3) both of these items. From our experience, we have learned that this question is difficult and time-consuming to answer adequately and correctly, and can involve considerable waste of funds if not posed correctly or if insufficient returns are received. We shall discuss this matter at length in Chapter 10, in which we are concerned explicitly with exports and imports.

5.6 Size and Content of Questionnaires

The experience of the Philadelphia study has indicated that there are many fine points that are desirable to know concerning the size and content of questionnaires. Many of these points are not fully appreciated until the interviewing process is fairly well along.

For example, we realized early that we did not follow a sufficiently rigorous procedure with regard to the pretesting of questionnaires. We started off with a questionnaire that we thought to be adequate based on our knowledge of questionnaires used in other input–output studies. We subsequently revised our questionnaires as we identified ways of improving and obtaining a more satisfactory response. We should and could have tested several survey forms and evaluated the results prior to the final choice of questionnaire form.[8] Pretesting should be done for each of the major sectors of the broad divisions of economic activity—wholesale and retail trade, services, manufacturing, and so forth. We also have found in connection with our Boston study that when the typical establishment was interviewed, a prelisting of input items considered relevant for its sector on the basis of the Philadelphia materials facilitated the process of response by the establishment. Such prelisting indicated both the kinds of information of likely relevance in its operations and the degree of detail at which information was being sought.

[8] At times such pretesting will suggest that inputs be specified not only in dollar terms but also in physical quantities, especially when the respondent is in a position to provide much better data on the physical quantities involved.

Even within the manufacturing division it may be desirable to pretest questionnaires for firms whose operations fall within a single SIC sector only, and for those whose operations cut across several sectors. Pretesting of questionnaires for this latter type of firm will assume increasing importance for input–output work, since the tendency of United States firms is to merge and consolidate in conglomerate form over many different kinds of production operations. As already indicated, such conglomerate mergers make the problem of obtaining satisfactory response at the establishment level much more difficult.[9]

Pretesting questionnaires throws considerable light on basic questions concerning their design. One issue that confronted us at the start was the length of the questionnaire. We were aware of the inadequate response to the Penn Jersey Transportation Study questionnaire, which ran in excess of 19 pages. Also, we wondered whether a private university had enough leverage in the business community and whether we ourselves had sufficient backing to obtain adequate response even to a relatively short questionnaire. Accordingly, we tended to err by developing a somewhat shorter questionnaire than we might otherwise have done. The questionnaires that we actually employed are presented in the appendixes of the volumes of the *Working Papers* [Isard, Langford, and Romanoff, 1966–1968].

From experience we learned that different sizes and structures of questionnaires were appropriate for different kinds of establishments. When an establishment had a computerized accounting system, it was relatively easy to obtain information and answers to detailed purchases and sales questions. When an establishment did not have such a system but was relatively large, again a considerable amount of detailed information was rather easily obtained. However, smaller establishments with less formal accounting operations were highly sensitive to the length of the questionnaire. The shorter the questionnaire with which they were confronted, the higher the response rate. For the smaller establishments with little or no formal accounting procedures, we found it very important to request total dollar value of materials consumed by the establishment as an item separate from the dollar values of detailed material inputs. The difference between the total value of materials, which was specified separately, and the sum of the value of the detailed items yielded an approximate value for the unspecified material inputs. On occasion, when this residual appeared unreasonable, our pointing this out to the respondent made possible a second interview from which more consistent information was obtained.

[9] In fact this tendency may require restructuring of what we currently conceive to be an adequate input–output sectoring procedure and framework.

We learned other lessons. As with many input–output studies, we underestimated the importance of nonmaterial inputs and overestimated the difficulties in obtaining data on them.[10] Accordingly, we asked too few questions regarding them in our first questionnaires. We did not find as useful as we had hoped the data on major material items consumed, which are listed by SIC sector in Table 7A of the U.S. Census of Manufactures [1958]. We found that the outputs of the establishments of any sector tend to be rather heterogeneous and specialized, reflecting the fact that many small establishments tend to concentrate in the production of a limited number of goods. In their production, inputs other than the relatively small number listed by the Census may be basic.

Establishments with computerized accounting systems often responded to our questionnaire by providing us with an EDP (electronic data processing) tabulation of purchases, coded by type of commodity on a highly disaggregated basis. The interviewer is of course delighted with such a wealth of data; but his delight is not shared by all workers on a project, for if the data are more disaggregated than the sectoring scheme used, they must be aggregated into the proper 4-digit SIC or other classification. This process can be extremely costly and time-consuming. Therefore, it is wise to be explicit at the start of an interview, to indicate to the respondent the classification system being used, and to request that to the extent possible the data furnished conform to this classification system. Although in input–output work the analyst can use all the data that can be provided in the proper form, no matter how detailed, he should avoid to the extent possible unnecessarily detailed data.

References

Bourque, Philip J., et al. (1967). *The Washington Economy: An Input–Output Study* (Business Study No. 3). Seattle: University of Washington.

Coughlin, Robert E., and Walter Isard (1963). *Planning Efficient Hospital Systems* (Discussion Paper Series No. 1). Philadelphia: Regional Science Research Institute.

Hansen, Lee, and Charles M. Tiebout (1963). "An Intersectoral Flows Analysis of the California Economy," *Review of Economics and Statistics*, vol. 45.

[10] Also, on a number of occasions the justification for not obtaining information relating to certain nonmaterial inputs has been the instability of the coefficients associated with these inputs. Because of the nature of the specialization of firms in providing business services, we find that establishments in one year will have purchased certain engineering, advertising, accounting, and computing services outside the establishment, and perhaps in a previous or subsequent year will have obtained them from within some unit of the establishment, where they are produced. Thus, with proper adjustments of intra- and intercompany transfer and purchase data, the instability of the coefficients associated with these services can be removed and stable coefficients can be obtained.

Isard, Walter, Thomas W. Langford, and Eliahu Romanoff (1966–1968). *Philadelphia Region Input–Output Study, Working Papers*, Volumes 1–4. Philadelphia: Regional Science Research Institute.

Miernyk, William H., et al. (1967). *Impact of the Space Program on a Local Economy: An Input–Output Analysis.* Morgantown, W. Va.: West Virginia Library.

Moore, Frederick T., and James W. Peterson (1955). "Regional Analysis: An Interindustry Model of Utah," *Review of Economics and Statistics*, 37: 368–383.

Smith, Harold T. (1960). *The Kalamazoo County Economy.* Kalamazoo, Mich.: The W. E. Upjohn Institute for Employment Research.

Once we began to receive the responses from questionnaires, we had to start thinking about when and how to construct technical coefficients for any sector to serve as its estimated production function. Yet, before we could actually begin calculations, we had to confront and resolve a number of basic conceptual questions. Among these questions were the treatment of (1) secondary production[1] and (2) margins (transportation, wholesale, and retail).

6.1 The Treatment of Secondary Production

Typically, the output of an establishment cannot be said to be 100 percent homogeneous. If an establishment, for example a blast furnace unit, does not produce two or more distinct products (say pig iron, BTU in the form of flue gas, and road fill in the form of slag), it produces several closely related products (such as a dairy producing milk, chocolate milk, fruit drinks, and ice cream) or different qualities of a single product (such as No. 1 pencils, No. 2 pencils, and No. 3 pencils). While it is unlikely that an input–output analyst will seek a sectoring scheme that distinguishes between production operations yielding No. 1 pencils and those yielding No. 2 pencils, he may well want his scheme to distinguish between such operations as those yielding milk and other dairy products and those yielding orange and other nondairy drinks.

There are several reasons why he may seek this distinction. First, if there are different production functions for each of these two sets of products, he may want to know the production functions for each of these sets rather than their weighted average. (If an establishment's data are edited without effecting this distinction, the resulting data for the establishment are implicitly a simple weighted average of the two functions.) He therefore wants to take out of the establishment's reported data the output of the secondary products (nondairy drinks) and the inputs required for their production, and transfer such output and inputs to the sector for which nondairy products represents the primary output (or to establish a new sector pertaining to nondairy products if there are no establishments in his region for which these products are primary output).

More important, if the investigator desires to make projections and study impacts of various developments or programs, and if these projections and impacts imply different relative changes in the demand for these two sets of products, then his estimates of indirect effects are much more accurate if he separates these two sets of products in two sectors (provided that each set has stable production coefficients). It can be very

[1] Secondary products of an establishment include the miscellaneous receipts from contract and commission work, repair work, scrap and salable refuse, and non-associated service activities (including retail, wholesale, transport, and auxiliary business services), as well as the production of products other than those of the primary classification (including research and development).

important for him to have accurate estimates of such indirect effects, as, for example, when the inputs into dairy operations come from local agricultural sectors whose levels of production are declining, while the inputs for soft drinks, except for water, are imported.

Moreover, the investigator may wish to make an allocation of the several sets of products among their different sets of consuming sectors. (He may want to do so in order to supplement his input data or to reconcile conflicting estimates and reports). This point is well illustrated when we consider meat packing establishments that also produce hides for leather. If meat products go to one set of consuming sectors and the hides to another, then the investigator can achieve a much more accurate impact analysis if he allocates each of these two sets of products independently to the two different sets of consuming sectors than if he allocates a simple weighted average of these two sets of products to some combined set of consuming sectors.

In sum, by transferring out secondary production and its associated inputs and placing them in an appropriate sector, the investigator obtains (1) sectors whose outputs are more homogeneous; (2) estimated production functions that are more relevant; and (3) a framework that is easier to balance.

On the other hand, there are major disadvantages to transferring out secondary production and its associated inputs. If establishments reporting data do not keep separate records on inputs for the production of each output, and hence may not be able to furnish relevant input data, then the investigator must impute such data. He can do this, perhaps fairly easily, with respect to dairy products and nondairy products. But where the secondary product is not so independently produced, then numerous arbitrary factors appear in allocating inputs to secondary production. These arbitrary elements reach their maximum when the secondary product is strictly a by-product, such as slag and blast furnace gas, whose output has negligible, if any, effect on the set of inputs used.

Further, from the standpoint of projection analysis, such transfer of, for example, blast furnace gas into another sector can be misleading; for if we project an increase in demand for blast furnace gas, which is a primary product of the sector *blast furnace and similar gases*, and if concomitantly we project a decrease in demand for pig iron, we cannot expect the economy to meet the increase in demand for blast furnace gas. In fact, we would expect a decrease in the supply of blast furnace gas because of the decrease in demand for pig iron. But when blast furnace gas is placed in an independent sector that is built up from outputs and inputs transferred to it from blast furnace and other establishments, then it is easy for the investigator, particularly when he is using an inverse, to project in inconsistent fashion an increase in blast furnace gas production concomitant with a decrease in pig iron production.

Perhaps the most telling reason for not transferring a secondary product and its inputs to the sector that produces this product as primary output is a pragmatic one. By not doing so, the investigator avoids the major effort and cost involved in differentiating the various inputs associated with the output of any specific secondary product from those of the primary product of an establishment. However, if secondary products are not removed from recorded sales of an establishment, it is desirable to have information on the percentage distribution of the total sales of that establishment (and of all establishments of its sector) among all the products yielded by the establishments in its sector. Such a percentage distribution provides some light on the validity of the derived input coefficients.

Another practice regarding secondary products has been used on occasion by OBE in the development of the national input–output tables. This practice transfers the output of an establishment's secondary product from the sector to which the establishment is assigned to the sector whose primary output corresponds to that product; however, this practice does not concomitantly transfer the inputs required to produce such product. From certain standpoints there are advantages to this procedure. For example, it does permit a more accurate allocation of commodities to consuming sectors, and a reconciliation of the demands for a commodity with the supply of the commodity from the sector producing the commodity as primary output. On the other hand, not to transfer the associated input expenditures on secondary commodities results in input coefficients that are distorted and therefore not usable per se for projection and impact analysis purposes.

Let us return to the question of the extent to which the practice of not removing secondary products and their associated inputs leads to errors in projection and impact studies. There are certain additional points to be made. First, consider the case of a small region where a few establishments account for a substantial portion of the region's output, and where each of these establishments is engaged in the manufacture of more than one commodity. To suggest that each establishment's output is dependent upon the demand for only its primary product, and is not affected by changes in demand for its secondary products, may do violence to reasonable projections. Hence, in such a situation a strong case can be made for secondary product transfers in order to make explicit the effect of change in secondary product demand upon regional activity. The case for secondary product transfer also may become of increasing importance with the growth of conglomerate mergers and horizontal integration in many industries. But as already noted, multiestablishment firms, in general, are not willing to provide information on individual plant units and their outputs of single commodities. Thus, while the argument for secondary product transfers may become stronger with time, it may become correspondingly more difficult to effect such transfers accurately.

Next consider the situation for a large region like the Philadelphia SMSA. Is it less justifiable in the study of such a region than in a study of the nation not to transfer out secondary products and their associated inputs? Alternatively put, in the case of a projection for a large region like Philadelphia when compared with a national projection, is it less legitimate to assume that the average establishment in the average sector will expand or contract its production equally among all its outputs?

One may argue that the nation is much larger than the region and that national change is an average over many more establishments than regional change. Hence, within any given sector there is likely to be less percentage variation among establishments when all the nation's establishments are covered than when only a region's establishments are covered. Moreover, the analyst may contend that the variation in the degree of specialization by type of product (primary or secondary) is likely to be less for the nation's establishments on the average than for a region's establishments. Thus, he might argue that to achieve any given degree of accuracy of projection or impact analysis, there is less need for secondary product transfer in the case of the nation than in the case of the region. However, the question is much more complex than is implied by this discussion, and it is not at all clear that any answer can be reached.

The reasons just given for removing or not removing secondary products are in terms of the objectives of a single isolated regional input–output study. However, the analyst may also wish to compare his derived co-efficients with those of other studies. If so, then to achieve effective comparison he must follow the practice with regard to secondary products that has been pursued in these other studies.

In the Philadelphia study, we decided that in general we should not attempt to separate secondary products from the primary output of establishments. This decision was based on several factors: (1) we did not have unlimited resources; (2) our staff was not eager to undertake any more work than was necessary; and (3) as we weighed all the arguments pro and con, we found no clear-cut net advantage or disadvantage with regard to separating out secondary production.

Moreover, we did not wish to follow the particular OBE practice noted above. We judged that it would lead to coefficients that would yield distorted results in our projections and impact analyses, and we had little reason to develop two different sets of tables, one to serve for nonprojection and nonimpact studies, the other for projection and impact analyses. Thus, our input coefficients for each sector correspond to production of both primary and secondary products. Despite the fact that the input coefficients pertain to a specific product mix, we believe that except perhaps for one or two sectors, the distortions in the derived coefficients are only minor.

There were a few sectors for which we did make exceptions in order to preserve the reasonableness of the derived coefficients. Where a commodity was produced almost entirely as secondary product by one or more establishments, such output together with its estimated inputs were removed from the data for those establishments and put into the sector whose primary output corresponded to the specific commodity. To illustrate, one of the largest producers of licorice paste in the United States is in the Philadelphia region and produces a greater dollar value of output in paperboard than in licorice paste. Hence, we removed the secondary products and associated production expenses from that establishment and put them in the sector whose primary product includes licorice paste (SIC 2087, *Flavoring Extracts and Syrups not elsewhere classified*).

The practice of separating out secondary production must, of course, be followed to a larger extent in other kinds of studies. In the Boulder study, whose objective was to examine the impact of space and space-related activities, it was necessary to effect product separation in the case of two government agencies and in establishments in the space and space-related sectors. In these cases, all space and space-related activities were assigned to one of the two sectors set up to cover these activities while all other activities were assigned to one of the other industry groups or government sectors [Miernyk et al., 1967, pp. 56–60].

6.2 Margins

As goods flow through the marketing system from producer to consumer, they may be subject to three basic margins: the transport, wholesale trade, and retail trade margins. The price that the purchaser pays may be derived as follows:

Producer's Price		$ _____
Plus Transport Cost	$ _____	
Plus Wholesale Margin	$ _____	
Plus Retail Margin	$ _____	
Purchaser's Price		$ _____

Although these margins are involved in virtually all transactions, they are not always explicit. In the normal marketing channel, goods flow from the final producer to a wholesaler, then to a retailer, and then finally to the household consumer. Similarly, goods may flow from an intermediate producer to another producer via a merchant wholesaler. However, a manufacturer may sell directly to another manufacturer without the intervention of an identifiable wholesaler. In this case, the wholesaling function is performed by the first manufacturer; and to identify the margin associated with his sales, it is necessary to determine from his operating costs the value of the secondary product (wholesale trade) that he provides. Also, a wholesaler may in fact sell directly to household consumers; his delivered price should therefore cover both wholesale and retail margins, as well as transport cost, rather than just the wholesale margin and transport cost when he sells directly to retailers and manufacturers.

It is clear that trade margins are involved in virtually *all* transactions. Theoretically, they are identifiable from the operating costs of the establishment providing the trade service(s), being a function of *both* the nature of the buyer *and* the seller. In practice, the *explicit* determination of these trade margins is extremely difficult.

Associated with the margins of an economic system are several sets of prices. The two most relevant sets, however, are the prices at the door of the factory and the prices at the location of the user, that is, the beginning point and the end point of a commodity flow. While either producers' or purchasers' prices can be incorporated into an input–output format, it generally is more desirable to have the transactions in the input–output flow table recorded at producers' prices rather than at purchasers' prices. Such a procedure tends to yield a much more accurate representation of the technical requirements of production for the establishments within a sector. It ensures that the estimates of technical production coefficients (except those relating to the trade and transport inputs) are unaffected by changes in the goods distribution pattern of the system.

6.2.1 Transport Cost Margins Consider, first, the transportation cost margin. This margin is applied to the producer's price of the good specified at the factory (i.e., the FOB price) to yield the delivered price to the consumer at his location. The estimation of this margin is difficult in actuality because of the great variety of practices and customs that establishments use to account for transportation cost.

In the derivation of appropriate transport cost margins, it must first be recognized that different transportation modes can be employed in the shipment of a commodity. Because major differences do exist in transportation costs by truck, rail, air, water, and pipeline for different commodities being shipped different distances, it is desirable to obtain transport cost margins by modes. Moreover, the specification of mode(s) of shipment is important when it is desirable to disaggregate the transportation industry and to obtain estimates of the output of each of the sectors of this industry.

Beyond differentiation by mode it is desirable, as we learned from our Philadelphia experience, to have at least two different sets of transport margins for each mode. This is particularly important in the motor freight sector. One set should be local transport margins to be applied to intraregional shipments. The second should be nonlocal or interregional transport margins to be applied to interregional shipments. These two types of margins are important not only for adjusting the data reported by establishments, but also for allocating reported and imputed transportation expenditures between local transport agencies and those transport agencies outside the region who export their services to the region of study.[2]

In the Philadelphia study, in theory, we should have interviewed transportation agencies in order to obtain primary data for constructing transport cost margins. In practice, we recognized that it would be extremely difficult for us to obtain such data given the complicated structure of the transportation agencies in the region. We therefore decided to use the OBE aggregate transportation cost margins employed in the development of the 1958 national table.[3] When an establishment reported outlays in purchasers' prices, these outlays were accordingly reduced by the amounts corresponding to the OBE transport cost margins,

---

[2] On this point the Ad Hoc Committee once recommended the following: All transportation expenditures by the enterprises and consuming units of a region should be treated as local purchases when the total of transportation expenditures does not exceed the output of the local transport industry. When total transportation expenditures do exceed this output, then the difference should be viewed as the cost of imported transport inputs and should be evenly distributed percentagewise over all local sectors incurring transport cost. Clearly, this procedure is inadequate.

Conceptually, the investigator can carry the differentiation among margins farther than noted in the text. He can differentiate among (1) intraregional transport cost margins when the transport inputs are furnished by local agencies; (2) interregional transport cost margins on exported goods when transport inputs are furnished by local agencies; (3) interregional transport cost margins on exported goods when transport inputs are furnished by nonlocal agencies; (4) interregional transport cost margins on imported goods when transport inputs are provided by nonlocal agencies; and (5) interregional cost margins on imported goods when transport inputs are provided by local agencies. However, such a distinction would in the usual case be much too fine, given some of the crude estimates one must employ in input–output study. Further, common carriers subject to ICC regulations must charge the same rate in moving a commodity from one region to another regardless of the location of the head office of the carrier. And often, in practice, the most important distinction is between carriers subject to ICC regulations and those subject to regulations of a state authority.

[3] Unpublished data prepared by OBE.

and these amounts were added to whatever transportation outlays the establishment reported.[4]

There were at least two major difficulties, however, in the use of the OBE margins. One difficulty related to the fact that the commodity classification employed by OBE was much too gross when compared to our sector classification. (Recall that the OBE study has a significantly smaller number of sectors than our Philadelphia study.) Second, the OBE margins are transportation cost margins relevant for the nation as a whole, and thus not necessarily representative of the distribution pattern associated with the Philadelphia transactions. Thus, if we were to do the Philadelphia study over again, we would probably not use the OBE margins without major change. More specifically, although we might use the OBE margins on all purchases from nonlocal sources, we would not use these margins on intraregional shipments. We would apply to such shipments margins that were smaller and that at the minimum would cover terminal (loading and unloading) charges and some assessment for line-haul cost that might be associated with intraregional shipments. This assessment probably would be estimated from interview of local transportation establishments, and might be either a flat sum differentiated by commodity or a percentage of terminal cost.[5]

6.2.2 Wholesale Margins Margins of wholesale establishments are usually defined as the gross sales less the cost of goods purchased for resale. They are usually included in all sales of goods to retailers, industrial, commercial, institutional, and professional users, and other wholesalers. They are involved primarily in intermediate transactions.

There are at least two basic factors that complicate the proper determination and application of wholesale margins in input–output analysis. One is that in practice not all producers sell their outputs through independent wholesalers. A manufacturer may sell a good directly to

---

[4] Frequently, we obtained a response that did not indicate whether the input expenditures were at producers' prices or at purchasers' prices. We then assumed that the input expenditures were at purchasers' prices and accordingly removed our estimate of transportation cost from them. We had no way to check the legitimacy of this procedure. Also, it is important to recognize that some manufacturers who provide their own transportation services—on goods purchased or sold, or both—do not properly record expenditures for the production of these services as transport expenditures, but rather record them as fuel expenditures, labor expenditures, and so forth, which cannot be separated out from expenditures on manufacturing account. Our inability to separate these expenditures leads to distortion in the coefficients that are derived.

[5] With the 1963 OBE input–output study for the United States, it now becomes possible to calculate sector- and mode-specific transportation rates. The rates derived in this manner coupled with data from the new transportation census promise to provide a firmer basis in the future for the estimation of relevant transport cost margins.

another manufacturer. Such a sale does not incur a merchant wholesale margin; however, it should be interpreted as involving a wholesale margin, in which the selling manufacturer is viewed as supplying the wholesale service as a secondary product, and the corresponding margin is implicitly included in the selling price. Since wholesale trade services are a secondary product of the manufacturer, in theory the value of the wholesale service he performs together with the associated inputs ought to be transferred to the wholesale trade column. In practice, an attempt to do this is only feasible in rare cases; it is much better to leave such output and inputs in the sector corresponding to the primary output of the manufacturer.

Such, in fact, was the practice adopted by OBE in the 1958 inter-industry table for the United States. OBE defined the output of the trade sectors so as to exclude the gross margin of any sales office of a manu-facturer on the assumption that these margins were included in the value of the manufacturer's shipments as reported in the Census of Manu-factures.[6]

Because direct sales of one establishment to another without the intervention of an independent wholesaler are very large in magnitude, and because there is no effective way to identify and treat such sales, it is not desirable to apply wholesale margins across the board to all inter-mediate sales. Theoretically, they should be applied only to fractions of these intermediate sales; and of course margins should be differentiated by using sectors. In practice, in the OBE study and in most, if not all, other input–output studies, such is not done. The procedure that seems to be generally followed involves the uniform application of wholesale margins by commodity groups to *all* transactions, with application of a few particular margins on certain types of sales to selected using sectors, or groups of using sectors, when appropriate data are available.[7]

A second complicating factor in determining wholesale margins relates to the fact that there are two groups of independent wholesalers to be treated. One group comprises merchant wholesalers, defined as establish-ments that engage in buying and selling merchandise on their own account, including farm products. Included as merchant wholesalers are those generally known as merchant distributors, importers, exporters,

---

[6] However, OBE did not include in its estimated output of trade sectors the receipts of the trade establishments from nontrade services performed and manufacturing conducted; such receipts were transferred to the appropriate sectors. Concomitantly, OBE transferred into the trade sectors the gross margins of sales of merchandise by establishments classified in the service industries and the value added by resales of goods in manufacturing establishments.

[7] It should be noted that in input–output work it is rare that a clear statement is given on the specific procedures used in the application of wholesale margins.

terminal grain operators, and wagon and truck distributors. The second group comprises nonmerchant wholesalers, including those independent wholesalers not previously defined, and usually includes manufacturers' sales representatives and agents.

Clearly, it is desirable to distinguish between merchant and nonmerchant wholesalers of the same commodity. Merchant wholesalers may operate, generally speaking, at larger scales than nonmerchant wholesalers; they incur different costs and set different margins. Therefore, different margins should be applied to commodities according to the type of wholesaler involved in the specific transaction.

Aside from the involvement with collection and processing of more data, however, the application of the two different wholesale margins to a specific commodity, one margin when the commodity passes through merchant wholesalers and a second when it passes through nonmerchant wholesalers, runs into empirical difficulties. Such application requires information as to whether independent wholesaling services were performed in any transaction, and if so, whether these were merchant or nonmerchant. In most cases the respondent does not have this information. Hence, the investigator may be forced to use some type of simple weighted average margin.

Beyond differentiation between merchant and nonmerchant wholesalers, there can be differentiation between local wholesalers and nonlocal wholesalers. As with transport margins, there is the question of whether the same margins are to be applied to inputs from both wholesalers outside the region and wholesalers inside the region. When we use the procedure of applying one and only one set of wholesale margins, we are in effect assuming that the margins of wholesalers located outside the region selling products in the region are identical with the margins of wholesalers located within the region. In the Philadelphia study, for which most of the wholesalers serving Philadelphia consumers lie largely within the northeastern United States, this procedure is reasonable, especially since as a metropolitan region Philadelphia contains a full range of wholesalers. However, this procedure might not be relevant for smaller and less urbanized areas; thus, for these areas there may arise the problem of obtaining relevant margin values for wholesalers not located within the region. This problem is intensified by the fact that wholesaling is a very complex process, one that differs greatly among the types of commodities handled. Wholesalers have different customs in different regions. Some may engage in substantial formal commercial lending service, while others may engage in institutional break-bulk packaging and/or warehousing. Some wholesalers—for example, SIC 5091, *Metals and Minerals, Wholesalers*—effect substantial changes in the product and provide specialized production services, as in the forming, bending, coating, and so on, of metal shapes and sheets. Consequently, differences in wholesaling activities among regions and by commodity make it difficult to develop the appropriate wholesale margins.

Yet in input–output studies for areas less urbanized and smaller than the Philadelphia region, it is clear that because of regional differences in labor, power, and other input costs, and differences in scale and diversity of operations, the investigator may wish to distinguish crudely among (1) the wholesale services and margins applied by small local wholesalers to commodities purchased from producers within the region; (2) the wholesale services and margins applied to goods that are shipped into the region and incur wholesale services by wholesalers outside the region (assuming that the purchases of such commodities are to be recorded not in terms of purchasers' prices but in terms of producers' prices plus transport cost plus wholesale margins); and (3) wholesale services and margins applied by any large local wholesalers who might be located in the area and who engage in extensive import-export as well as local trade.[8]

In the Philadelphia study we were able to attack effectively the problem of determining appropriate margins to be applied to sales that passed through the hands of independent wholesalers. We were able to develop a reliable set of wholesale trade margins by 4-digit sectors through the collection of primary data from interviews.

Unfortunately, we were not able to put to effective use the derived set of wholesale margins. As already indicated, we had decided at the start of the study to attack the manufacturing sectors first. At the time we did not know whether we would have any resources remaining to attack the wholesale sectors also; and if we were to have any remaining resources, we did not know how deeply we would be able to probe into these sectors and what kinds of margins we would ultimately derive. Accordingly, we decided to postpone adjusting our edited data and coefficients for manufacturing with regard to wholesale margins. As it turned out, we were able to interview extensively the wholesale sectors. However, once this was done, it was not feasible to go back to the edited coefficients for each manufacturing sector and adjust them for expenditures on wholesale services.[9]

One major difficulty stemmed from our inability to distinguish between those transactions in the structural matrix that in fact entailed independent wholesale services and those that did not. As already indicated, where

---

[8] In a number of actual cases, the margins of both small and large local wholesalers may not be sufficiently different to justify this distinction.

[9] However, OBE wholesale margins were applied to scrap goods in the intermediate sector matrix, and to all transactions in the final demand sectors.

independent wholesalers are involved, the investigator with relative ease can identify the sales on which the appropriate wholesale margins are to be applied. However, in the many cases where the producer performs the wholesale function when he sells his product directly to an intermediate producer, the identification of the value of wholesale services provided and the realized cost is extremely difficult. Thus, we found ourselves in a position in which we were not able to adjust the coefficients for wholesale margins without substantial imputation of unknown wholesale service margins and, hence, without lowering the quality of the coefficients.

Even if we had been able to effect such imputation, however, we would have faced an inconsistency. When producers do provide wholesale services in the sales of their product directly to other producers, they are in fact providing wholesale services as a secondary product. But the convention adopted in the Philadelphia study was not to separate out secondary products but rather to retain them as part of the total output of an establishment in its corresponding sector. Hence, it would have been inconsistent to have identified these wholesale services and shifted them to wholesale sectors.

As a consequence of these factors, the material input coefficients shown in the Philadelphia coefficient table include the wholesale margins associated with each transaction. Consequently, the transportation input coefficients derived are overstated in that the base to which the transport cost margins were applied improperly included the costs of the wholesale function. This last comment points up the obvious need constantly to exercise care that all margins are accounted for at the proper point in the expenditure adjustment process.

Our experience leads us to pose a fundamental question, to which we have already alluded. In conducting an input–output study, is it desirable to interview first those wholesale, retail, and other sectors that charge margins so that we have on hand at least rough estimates of the proper margins to be applied to the material input costs reported by manufacturing establishments? Or at least, should those sectors be interviewed concomitantly with the manufacturing sectors?

One can well argue that a proper plan for an input–output study should be explicit as to the sequence in which establishments in the different sectors are to be interviewed—at least so that some of the shortcomings of our Philadelphia study can be avoided. Such a specification might properly extend to the point that a complete sectoring scheme and a proper method for deriving coefficients be decided upon early in the study, since otherwise the study may not evolve in a most efficient manner. Yet also recall that the insistence of the director in the Philadelphia study *not* to preplan did yield some very fruitful outcomes. Clearly, if we had preplanned the sectoring scheme for a comprehensive coverage of the Philadelphia region, and a corresponding method for constructing coefficients, we would have had to confine ourselves to no more than 200 sectors. We could not have risked a 500-sector study, given the initial resources at our command; and in fact, the shortcoming of our study in being unable to use fully the good wholesale margins we did obtain would not have arisen, for we would not have derived these margins. So one of the major outcomes of the refusal to preplan was that we were able to avoid any initial straitjacketing that a well-laid preplan would have imposed.

Moreover, recall that an appropriate hedge in an input–output study often involves beginning a probe into interdependence with the examination of the export sectors of a region—the sectors often of greatest initial interest to those who support the study. These sectors frequently lie within the manufacturing division. However, as nonmanufacturing sectors become increasingly basic to a regional economy, beginning the interviewing with establishments in nonmanufacturing sectors increasingly will provide the desired hedge and also will tend to obviate the shortcoming just noted for the Philadelphia study.

In developing a strategy for an input–output study, another point is to be considered. Since, in general, the wholesalers and retailers actually pay transportation costs, and so are affected by transport margins, it follows that the transport margins and thus the necessary materials on transport costs ought to be collected and processed before (or at least simultaneously with) the collection and processing of materials to determine wholesale and retail costs and margins. To do so necessarily implies that in the collection of the data on wholesale and retail establishments, considerable care is exercised in the detailing of the information on transportation services that the wholesalers and retailers themselves provide so that this information can be used to remove transportation services in the calculation of the wholesale and retail margins.[10]

6.2.3 Retail Margins Margins of retail establishments are customarily defined as the gross sales less the cost of goods purchased for resale. They are usually included in or assigned to all sales for personal, household, or farm consumption. They are usually not applied to any sales to consumers who are intermediate producers, primarily because such sales

---

[10] We recognize that, in practice, the sequencing of margin costs often proceeds in reverse order. That is, given the purchasers' price, the retail margins may first be removed, then the wholesale margins, and finally, the transport margins in order to arrive at producers' price. But on the other hand, as in the Philadelphia study, where it was decided that the retail margins were to be allocated wholly to personal consumption expenditures, the investigator can delay the determination and removal of these retail margins until final demands are specified.

are usually in larger quantities and are subject to different pricing arrangements. Yet there are certain items that may be purchased by intermediate producers directly from retail establishments in very limited quantities and are accordingly legitimately subject to retail margins. In the usual input–output study, however, the identification of such items and the application of retail margins to them involve more refinement than can be justified when resources are limited.

Ideally, personal and household expenditures on goods should be broken down into those purchases directly from retailers within the region and those from retailers outside the region. This breakdown permits the application of local retail margins only to those purchases made within the region, the purchases from retailers outside the region being imports of both the goods (at producers' prices plus any transport cost and wholesale costs) and the services of the retailers located outside the region.

In the Philadelphia study primary data on retail operations were directly obtained, chiefly through mail survey. Interviews were confined to a few major retail operations, such as department stores. Because of a good response to our survey, the retail margins appear to have been adequately developed. Except for sales to nonresidents of the Philadelphia region, the output of the retail trade sectors was wholly confined to estimated purchases of retail services by the Philadelphia household sector. We did not attempt to apply retail margins to the retail purchases of institutions, producers, and other nonhousehold units. Also, we did not seek the additional refinement that would involve breaking down retail margins into (1) purchases of services of retailers outside the region and (2) purchases of services of retailers inside the region.

References

Miernyk, William H., et al. (1967). *Impact of the Space Program on a Local Economy: An Input–Output Analysis.* Morgantown, W. Va.: West Virginia Library.

————, et al. (1969). *Simulating Regional Economic Development: An Interindustry Analysis of the West Virginia Economy.* Morgantown, W. Va.: Regional Research Institute, West Virginia University.

7.1 Questions of Character and Number of Coefficients

We have specified in Chapter 6 the practices adopted in our Philadelphia region input–output study with respect to the treatment of (1) secondary production; and (2) transport, wholesale, and retail margins. However, before we could proceed to edit and process the data from the questionnaires for the derivation of technical production coefficients, we had to reach decisions on a few more important issues.

Recall that the discussion in Chapter 5 indicated some of the relevant factors for defining a proper sample of firms. One factor is size of establishment. This factor is important since there may or may not exist scale economies or diseconomies in the production of the primary product (or product mix) of a sector. A second factor is the technology and capital vintage of the establishment. This factor is pertinent because very different input structures may be associated with different technologies and capital vintages. A third factor is the efficiency of the establishment; and a fourth factor is the product mix of the establishment. These last two factors may also give rise to significant differences in input structures.

Once the data are collected, however, the problem of taking these factors into account is not a simple one. First, the data that the investigator has in front of him are usually not entirely what he had anticipated. For example, the set of establishments that has in fact responded may be very different from the set that the investigator initially may have desired to have successfully interviewed. Further, the frequency distribution of responses in terms of different levels of quality of response may be very different from what was anticipated. The large firms may have turned in relatively poor data; the small, better data; and so forth. The actual set of data that the investigator has then influences the next steps he takes and may lead to significant changes in the set of procedures he initially had outlined.

More important, the data that the investigator has in front of him may not reflect in any simple way the play of each of the four factors just mentioned. They may reflect instead a net result of a complex interplay of these and other factors. Hence, the investigator may not be able to normalize in any simple way for efficiency, or capital vintage, or size, or product mix, if there are reasons for him to do so.

Nonetheless, despite the fact that a complex interaction of various factors may be reflected in the data which the investigator confronts, he needs to make decisions concerning whether each of these four and other factors are significant for any sector being examined; and if they are significant, whether or not to make any adjustments of the data for the sector. It is also important that he be explicit about these decisions.

7.1.1 Adjustments for Size of Establishment Consider the case in which the investigator faces a set of responses and judges that scale economies or diseconomies, and only these economies and diseconomies, account for the observed differences in the production functions of the establishments in the sector being examined. He recognizes that whereas an input–output model does not admit scale economies or diseconomies, that is, whereas it does explicitly assume constant production coefficients, it is well known that scale economies do exist in production. (We accept the unrealistic assumption of constant production coefficients chiefly because it leads to a more operational model for certain impact studies.)

If the investigator is to advance the hypothesis that the data for a sector do reflect scale economies or diseconomies and only these in the operation of the establishments of that sector, he in effect assumes away the operation of other factors leading to differences in input structures. He in effect assumes that the establishments of a sector that have provided the data have the same technology, or if not, that the effect of the technology factor is negligible. He in effect assumes that all establishments are operating at the same level of efficiency, or if not, that the differences in efficiency among them leads to negligible differences in their input structures. He in effect assumes that if the product mixes of the establishments are not the same, differences among them lead to negligible differences in input structures.

On the basis of such assumptions as these, the investigator may hypothesize that the differences in input structures that he observes are a result of scale economies or diseconomies. If so, he may still not allow this hypothesis to affect the construction of the coefficients that he is to derive. If the goal of the study is to present what exists on average, he may do nothing other than weight the input structures of reporting establishments by employment or output. Or he may follow this practice if he considers that the size distribution of the reporting establishments may also characterize the size distribution of producing establishments in the year for which projections are to be made. On the other hand, if he judges that the size distribution for some future year of projection will change, he may weight the input structures for different sizes of establishment in accord with their projected relative importance.[1]

Whatever his decision, the investigator should state explicitly the considerations governing it and also the extent to which the decision was effected in subsequent work on the data.

7.1.2 Adjustments for Specialization and Efficiency
The investigator also may advance other hypotheses as he looks at the data. He may observe

---

[1] Bear in mind that in his survey he already may have adjusted in part for the size factor if, as in the Philadelphia study, large firms are overrepresented in his sample of the establishments of the sector.

that the reporting establishments differ greatly with regard to product mix. The primary product of the sector may account for 100 percent of the output of one establishment and for 75 percent of another. It may also account for less than 50 percent of a third establishment, which engages in producing primary products of three or more sectors. Accordingly, the investigator may be inclined to regard the observed differences in the input structures of these establishments as due to differences in product mix, and only product mix. In effect, he postulates that differences in efficiency, size, and technology (if any of these exist) have negligible impact on input structures.

Under these assumptions he may consider weighting the establishments in new ways. For example, he may weight more heavily those establishments that are more specialized in the production of the primary output. He may justify this practice if his aim is to obtain technical production coefficients that depict the production function for the primary output. On the other hand, if he seeks a good statistical representation of an existing economy with all the heterogeneity of its sectors, and if he also wishes to avoid certain projection errors and inconsistencies similar to those arising from the transfer out of secondary production (as discussed in the previous chapter), then he may not be inclined to use this weighting. In any case, he should state his decision.

In similar fashion the investigator may consider adjustments to reflect the different degrees of efficiency among establishments. He may judge that size, product mix, and technology are roughly the same among establishments or, if not, that the effects of differences in these factors are negligible. He then may attribute any observed differences in input structures primarily to differences in efficiency. He therefore may adjust the establishment weights so as to allow for increase in efficiency of production operations among the establishments over time.

7.1.3 Adjustments for Technology and Capital Vintage The investigator may advance still another hypothesis when he observes differences among the input structures of the reporting establishments of a sector. He may attribute them to differences in technology and capital vintage, that is, the time (date) at which plant and equipment of these establishments were constructed and put in place. In effect, he assumes that differences in size, efficiency, and product mix, if any of these exist, have negligible effect on the input structures. In short, he may attribute observed differences in the input structures to the ongoing process of technological change.

Again, the investigator may proceed to calculate coefficients based on a representative sample of establishments in order fully to describe and understand the interindustry structure of a region for the base year.

On the other hand, he may judge the most relevant coefficients to derive are those that he can use for longer-term projection and impact studies. Hence, he searches for input coefficients that for some future year might characterize the production of establishments in operation in that year. Often he then separates out from the reporting establishments in a sector those that are following best practice in production. Such "best practice" establishments may be identified in terms of profit per unit output, man hours per unit output, or some other measure [Miernyk et al., 1969]. Having isolated the "best practice" establishments, often on the basis of subjective as well as objective judgment, he may make an assumption that the "best practice" establishments will be "average practice" establishments (or "worst practice" or some "other practice" establishments) for his relevant year of projection. He calculates the coefficients for his sector accordingly.

Conceptually, of course, there are many other possibilities in the flexible use of input coefficients at the stage of making projections and calculating impacts. At this stage the investigator may be aware of a technological change on the horizon. He may estimate the coefficients for the new technology and substitute the new technology coefficients for those he has calculated on the basis of his survey. He may be inclined to do this if he anticipates, for example, that nuclear power will completely substitute for power produced from coal. Here he may estimate the new coefficients from experience with nuclear power in other regions.

Or having a good set of responses in front of him, the investigator may calculate both "average practice" coefficients and "best practice" coefficients. He may postulate an annual rate of change in technology from "average practice" to "best practice," perhaps by assuming that the transition takes five years or so. Then, having an annual rate of change in practice, he can project average practice for a given future year.

There are of course many serious objections to the derivation and use of coefficients in the several atypical ways already suggested. This is not the place to discuss them fully. The relevant point is that when an investigator does study his responses, he should keep his eyes open in order to identify the "best practice" establishments as against "average practice" and "worst practice" establishments. He may find it enlightening to make additional calculations to determine additional sets of input coefficients when his subsamples are statistically sufficient. Moreover, there is no reason why the investigator cannot employ a cruder or even finer classification than best, average, and poor practice establishments; for example, he may relax the assumption of equal efficiency and consider average inefficient practice and average efficient practice. Furthermore, there may be interesting characteristics of the establishments in a sector that are revealed once the questionnaires are edited and studied. For example, the frequency distribution of establishments by size may be distinctly bimodal, and the investigator may relax the assumption of no scale economies and diseconomies and be inclined to calculate coefficients for "small inefficient," "small efficient," "large inefficient," and "large efficient" establishments. He may find the resulting sets of coefficients very useful in establishing likely conditions of production of establishments in a sector five years hence.

7.1.4 The Number of Coefficients Aside from reaching a decision on whether and how to weight the responses of establishments and calculate additional sets of coefficients, the investigator at this stage must also decide upon guidelines for determining the number of coefficients to be derived for each sector. Specifically, he must decide on how far to go in deriving *minor* coefficients for each sector, or put otherwise, how to determine the cutoff point for calculating additional coefficients. He should have already recognized when he determined his sectoring plan and his questionnaire that each piece of additional information sought involves an added cost. He should have already learned that at some point short of complete information, the wise investigator brings to a halt his search for primary data.

The investigator is very much reminded of the additional cost of information when he confronts the great variety and generally poor quality of data reported on "minor" expenditures. Although establishments generally keep good records on major expenditures in a somewhat standard manner, they often report minor expenditures in aggregate and irregular ways. Consequently, reliable work in developing minor coefficients may often be more costly than the work on major coefficients. Yet some of this work on minor coefficients cannot be forgone, for to the extent that information on minor coefficients is not obtained, to that extent the residual for a sector becomes larger in value and covers more items. Then, when the residual for a sector must be disaggregated, such disaggregation becomes significantly more costly. It should be borne in mind here that no matter how careful the investigation and no matter how detailed the data sought, there will always be some items that will be included within the residuals for each sector. These items, such as machine shop products or lubricants, may not be important for sectors in general. They may be consumed to a minor extent by all or most industries. Yet, as we shall point out again, it is necessary to specify such consumption for each of these items and to obtain the total for each over all consuming sectors in order to account for the output of the particular sectors producing these items.

Finally, the cost of obtaining additional data to yield additional coefficients does vary significantly from sector to sector. For example, in the electronics sectors, in which detailed data printouts are available from the large firms, the cost of securing additional information on minor inputs is small once rapport with firms has been established and agreement reached on reporting data consistent with the classification system of the study. In contrast, it may be very costly to obtain the same kind of detail for sectors in which establishments are small and the information must be obtained by a manual review of the establishment's detailed accounts.

In short, there is no simple answer to the question posed. All the factors mentioned earlier, plus others, must be considered in determining for each sector the efficient cutoff point for the calculation of additional minor coefficients.

At this point we may also make a few more comments on the data available from the Census of Manufactures. As already indicated, the value of its detailed data on materials consumed, as recorded in its Table 7A, were of limited use for interview purposes. These materials are of still less value for the construction of technical coefficients. In large part, this is a consequence of the fact that the Census data relate to the product mix of the nation's industry, and that the national product mix is much different from that of the Philadelphia region.

Further, the Census definitions of the materials listed as consumed are not necessarily compatible with the definitions required by an input–output study. The Census definitions may at times provide some insight into the way in which appropriate 4-, 5-, and 7-digit sectors and commodities might be listed in a questionnaire. However, in general, the Census categories are far too gross to be helpful. Moreover, for any given sector, they reflect delivered prices and thus include average transportation costs on a material used by establishments in the nation as a whole. These costs may be different from those incurred by Philadelphia's or some other region's establishments, since the latter establishments are at different distances from the sources of their inputs than national establishments on the average, and may use a different mix of transport modes charging different rates.

Nonetheless, at times the Census materials can provide approximate magnitudes and reference ratios that are useful for evaluating the data received in questionnaires.

7.2 Calculation Procedures and Alternatives

In addition to issues concerning the character and number of coefficients to be derived, there are many questions relating to the calculation process itself. A first question relates to the extent to which electronic data processing (EDP) can effectively be used in the construction of coefficients.

While there is no doubt that it is very efficient to use EDP for studies in which there exist a very large number of questionnaires that are well prepared and provide responses that are complete and of excellent quality, in practice there is serious question about its use. Many problems arise. When the investigator seeks information over many sectors, there usually is a tremendous variety in the types of responses to his questionnaire that are obtained. A few respondents may provide data on just two or three questions. Others may answer all questions. The investigator's first reaction is to throw away the former. But often in the Philadelphia study the response to one or two questions turned out to be extremely helpful in verifying the responses by other establishments. Moreover, the quality of the data from each respondent varies greatly. Thus, the investigator must carefully sift through and study the data on all the questionnaires in any one sector, and often compare them with the data in one or more closely related sectors. For these reasons and others, we felt it was not desirable to make use of EDP—even though we were inclined to do so for the purpose of margin adjustments.

Put in another way, given the unhealthy mixture of good and poor data that we confronted, we judged that the best procedure initially was to set down the responses of all the establishments in a sector on a worksheet. A first check on the quality of the response and data from each of the several establishments was provided by visual inspection. For example, in the responses of establishments engaged in printing books, one would expect that both paper and ink would be listed. If these items are indeed listed by most establishments in a sector, but not by one or two, then clearly some adjustment should be made in the data of those one or two.

Beyond the filling in of gaps that were immediately apparent by a visual inspection, it was possible to make other rough but extremely valuable checks with the data in worksheet form. For example, the establishments of a sector might tend to report input data in somewhat different ways, reflecting their specializations. These different ways together with the different patterns of inputs reported often suggested desirable improvements in the commodity classification for that sector. Occasionally, examination of these patterns together with either partial or complete data on outputs would indicate that the classification of an establishment should be changed from the 4-digit sector suggested by the Censuses (federal and state), industrial directories, or other public documents to another 4-digit category. More often, we found that the responses of the several establishments suggested that our initial listing of inputs relevant for the establishments of a particular sector was partly inappropriate and partly inadequate. Frequently, one or more of the commodity items listed were not significant, and one or more additional items had to be added.[2]

Another check that could only partially be done by visual inspection was to compare the relative amounts of the different inputs reported by the establishments of a sector. Frequently, differences in the relative importance of inputs reflected the different degrees of vertical integration or inclusion of secondary services—for example, a repair operation might be included within one establishment but excluded from another. Again, judgments were called for as a result of such visual inspection in developing a best compromise list of inputs and outputs relevant for a sector.

Further, even after the data of the responses were adjusted in accord with the points just made, there were inconsistencies remaining among the several responses. These inconsistencies reflected in part the fact that our staff did not have sufficient knowledge of the sector interviewed, and that in a number of instances, at least initially, we were not able to specify the full set of inputs of interest. They also reflected the fact that we insisted on a relatively high coverage for each sector and had to interview many small and medium-size establishments in which the respondents were willing to provide only approximate answers, often erroneous because of failure to understand the questions fully.

In short, there was a wide variety of responses and peculiarities in the questionnaires that were returned to us. To have organized the handling of the raw data mechanically by means of EDP would only have misled us as to the validity of the unadjusted data reported, and could have led to a number of serious errors.

A second question regarding calculation procedures related to the number of decimal digits carried in the computations. In the Philadelphia study we decided to calculate coefficients to six decimal digits. This decision was in large part a consequence of the earlier decision to use a finely disaggregated sectoring scheme involving close to 500 endogenous sectors. To appreciate this point, consider a given sector that provides small amounts of its output to each of many consuming sectors. Or consider another sector that provides a substantial amount of its output to a small number of very large sectors. In each case, the value of the derived coefficient for each consuming sector is very small because of the relatively large magnitude of sector output compared to input value. Hence, for each of the two given sectors, many of the coefficients relating to the use of its product as inputs to consuming sectors may be rounded

---

[2] The relatively large number of such changes was the main reason why prelisting of input goods and services was eventually at least partially abandoned as a questionnaire technique for the Philadelphia study.

to zero if only three, four, or even five decimal digits were used. We would then not be able to account for the distribution of the output of the given sector. To avoid the rounding to zero as much as possible, we decided on the use of six decimal digits for all calculations.

Another question concerning calculation procedures relates to the specific stage or time at which the coefficients are to be computed. If they are computed as soon as the returns are received, the investigator can learn much about the inadequacies of his questionnaire, such as the new input items to be listed and the questions that need restatement. That is, he can prepare a more effective questionnaire for the next set of interviews—as we were able to do in the Philadelphia study when we followed this procedure. On the other hand, if all coefficients are computed at one time, the investigator can achieve a greater uniformity in the calculation of coefficients and undoubtedly greater efficiency.

This point can be elaborated particularly with respect to margin operations. When should the data reported by respondents be consistently adjusted for margins? Specifically, should the margins be calculated on an establishment-by-establishment basis as soon as each questionnaire is received and edited, or should the margin calculations be performed for all the firms simultaneously after their data have been edited and recorded on worksheets?

In theory, it would seem that the most efficient way to make margin adjustments would be to calculate them simultaneously for all the establishments of a sector. In practice, however, this procedure is perhaps not the best. When the questionnaires come in, they do not come in all at once. Very often there is a major establishment in a given sector for which an investigator can expect good data provided that he is patient and can wait for an official of the establishment to fill out the questionnaire, but only when he has some free time. When there are many sectors for which the investigator awaits a return by an important establishment, or for which the investigator is anticipating better coverage through completion of some of the questionnaires that are still outstanding, then the adoption of a practice of simultaneous margin adjustments means that all margin calculations may be delayed for quite some time. Such a practice may mean that the investigator can not employ the slack resources of research assistants' time, which may exist at unpredictable times. Further, such a practice may mean that it will be necessary to provide a large amount of effort at margin calculation and supervision at the time when the deadline is reached on receipt of questionnaires from large as well as small establishments. But the resources of a research project may not permit such intensive effort at any point of time, nor may the research director be able to reserve for that time a large amount of his own time for supervision of this operation. Thus, in practice it may be wise, as we found in the Philadelphia study, to record the data by establishment as they come in, and to make the margin adjustments at the same time as other adjustments are being made, to ask the innumerable small questions of the research director as they arise, and to seek additional information from the respondent if gaps are found in his response.

Another advantage of the immediate, establishment-by-establishment approach lies in the fact that it is possible to use different margins for the several establishments of a sector when specific knowledge exists of their different geographic sources of inputs, use of transport modes, and so forth. On the other hand, making margin adjustments simultaneously does enable the investigator to consider different types and sizes of *sector* margin adjustments much more easily and economically.[3]

Finally, there is always the question of the imputation of missing data. The amount of imputation obviously is related to the kinds of data sought. The more detailed the data sought, the more the responses may be in terms of aggregates of the specified items, the more the gaps in the data, and in general the more the imputations that must take place. Also, the more detailed the data sought, the greater the differences between an excellent and a poor return, and the more ingenious the investigator must be in using estimates based upon the data of excellent returns for filling in the gaps on poor returns.

Frequently, we applied the percentage breakdown for disaggregated items in the excellent returns to the aggregates of the poor returns when the aggregates of the poor returns were comparable to aggregates that could be built up for the excellent returns. To achieve comparable aggregates we often had to estimate one or more items for the poor returns. Such estimates were of course in addition to the estimation of minor coefficients, such as those pertaining to lubricants and machine shop products, which generally had to be made for both excellent returns and poor returns.

In our Philadelphia study, we found that there was no single best procedure for "grafting" the data of excellent returns upon poor returns. The investigator has to use skill, art, and experience in filling in the gaps and in upgrading the quality of poor returns. At times he even has to employ "fictitious statistical" establishments and at other times one or more of numerous other devices spelled out in the *Working Papers* [Isard, Langford, and Romanoff, 1966–1968]. Yet the extensive use of

---

[3] It may be desirable, of course, to set up two types of transaction matrices, one at producers' prices, the other at purchasers' prices. To do so does involve two sets of margin adjustments and hence a sizable increase in cost. Here the advantage of simultaneous adjustments can be significant.

inspection, balance techniques, and comparison with other sources of data can eliminate most if not all serious errors in the calculation of the coefficients.

References
Isard, Walter, Thomas W. Langford, and Eliahu Romanoff (1966–1968). *Philadelphia Region Input–Output Study, Working Papers*, Volumes 1–4. Philadelphia: Regional Science Research Institute.

Miernyk, William H., et al. (1969). *Simulating Regional Economic Development: An Interindustry Analysis of the West Virginia Economy*, Morgantown: Regional Research Institute, West Virginia University.

Once the sample data have been collected, edited, and used to develop coefficients, estimates of the gross output for the input–output sectors can be made. These output estimates, however, can be made relatively independent of the calculations of the technical production coefficients. In fact, some analysts would contend that at least preliminary estimates of sector output should be determined prior to sample selection, or even prior to the selection of a sectoring scheme.

Major errors in input–output analysis frequently occur because of inconsistency in the definitions employed in the measurement of sector output. Hence, whenever output estimates are to be made, we must keep in mind a number of basic considerations, which we discuss in the following sections.

8.1 Alternative Measures of Output

There are several possible ways by which total gross output can be measured—in physical terms, in economic market terms, and by other related indices. Each measure of output represents an attempt to specify in a consistent manner the outcome of a production process—that is, the output that results from the employment of the goods and services as specified by the technical production coefficients.

The output of a sector may be measured in terms of physical units, that is, as tons of steel, bushels of grain, yards of cloth, and so forth. The chief advantage of this kind of measure is that it measures true output and is not subject to the variations of a market pricing system. That is, price changes do not affect what is designated as the outcome of production. The use of this kind of measure, however, has disadvantages within the American economic system. Few establishments maintain records in terms of physical units. Although for input–output analysis physical output measures tend to permit a more accurate accounting for the sector demands for goods and services (row analysis), they do not provide a way to check consistency of the recorded inputs by sector (column analysis). Further, in the application of the model for the evaluation of policy alternatives, few decision-makers are able to "navigate" in the "real world" of physical units.

The output of a sector may be measured in terms of economic market values—that is, in terms of dollars, lire, yen, and so forth. The chief advantages of this kind of measure include the ease with which output can be stated and the capability to effect checks by both row and column in the input–output framework. A basic disadvantage is that fluctuations in prices lead to fluctuations in recorded output, even though production of such output has remained constant. A second basic disadvantage is that two identical units of output may be counted as different amounts simply because one purchaser pays a different price than another—a common occurrence in the American system.

Whether output is measured in terms of physical units or market prices, it may be viewed from three standpoints, as (1) production, (2) shipments, and (3) sales. Although for many industries these standpoints yield relatively identical measures when extreme business cycle conditions do not occur, in some industries these standpoints may yield differences in the measure of output. Therefore, the use of an output measure based on one standpoint in one part of an input–output study and the use of an output measure based on a second standpoint in another part of the study may lead to significant error.

The primary distinction between production and shipments is inventory. In those industries producing relatively few output units of high value (e.g., shipbuilding and construction), the inventory of work in process may be substantial. At the extreme, some establishments, although they engage in production throughout the year, may not fully complete for shipment a single unit; that is, they may be extensively engaged in the production process yet their output is zero from the standpoint of shipments.

A distinction must also be made between sales and either production or shipments. In those industries engaged in long-term leasing, such as the computer industry, relatively few sales may be made in terms of outright purchases; however, a relatively large number of units may be produced and shipped to customers.

Sector output may also be measured in a number of indirect ways designed to reflect specific applications of the input–output model. Some analysts suggest the use of "value-added" as a measure of sector output. This measure, in some forms, has the advantage of consistency with other social accounting measures. However, most input–output analysts consider it inappropriate since its use would require extensive indirect valuations, with the attendant errors of calculation and estimation.

Other investigators have used employment as a proxy measure of output. The data required for this measure, although available on a relatively comprehensive basis, are too often highly unsatisfactory. The great variety of definitions of employment, sources of data, and adjustments for part-time and overtime work makes employment an extremely poor proxy measure of output. Further, employment, as usually described in terms of man-hours, man-years, or average annual employment, seldom considers occupational-skill mixes, substitutability, and other factors important to the measurement of output.

Finally, it is to be noted that whatever measure is selected to describe total gross output, there will always be special problems in handling specific sectors. That is, there will always be sectors for which a strict application of the general output definition is not meaningful. It then becomes necessary to use some substitute measures.

8.2 The Social Accounts Versus the Direct Approach

Ideally, it is desirable, once the measure of total gross output has been selected, to have accurate estimates of control totals from one or more reliable, independent sources of data. The investigator may use these several estimates to check his estimates of sector output, which could have been obtained from a 100 percent coverage of establishments in a sector or from a sample of establishments adjusted to account for 100 percent of total employment in the sector. In practice, there are serious problems in obtaining a single set of reliable control totals from either primary or secondary data, let alone two or more sets from independent data sources. That is, in practice we rarely have the possibility of choosing from among two or more sets of good control totals. Usually, it is necessary to work diligently and long merely to piece together from all available data one set of reasonable estimates.

If, then, estimates of control totals must be pieced together, it may be argued that these control totals should be oriented to the overall social accounting magnitudes that are employed for evaluating the performance of the regional economy. Therefore, the investigator should have available a carefully constructed and relevant set of social accounts for the development of a set of control totals—a set consistent with national income-product accounts, and a set that might also be supplemented with certain key material balance tables. With these social accounts, it is possible to develop a highly aggregate input–output table, involving perhaps 10 to 15 sectors, covering major divisions of the economy and providing control totals for each of these major divisions that are consistent. Then the control totals for each of these major divisions should be disaggregated to obtain a set of consistent totals by sector.

It is only rarely that we have available such a full set of social accounts. Usually, an incomplete set, if any at all, exists for a region.[1] The investigator should then use the incomplete set together with the existing sector data to develop and maintain consistency for his sector control totals.

There is another point of view on this issue, however. This view main-

---

[1] Even when a full set of social accounts can be constructed, in conjunction with an input–output study, there are many issues to be decided, which in turn are to be at least partly related to the objectives of an input–output study that is to use these accounts. For example, there are several ways of identifying and defining regional income. The investigator can use a concept that is based on value-added. But this concept then raises a host of questions. Should the corporate profits earned by a branch plant in a region be assigned to that region? Should the income of nonresidents be included in the gross product of a region? Now, it is clear that the analyst must account for such profits, and income in one way or another. But the real question is what is the best way for a set of social accounts to be designed to be used in connection with an input–output study. Here the reader may refer to the literature, especially the writings of Leven. See the items cited in Leven, Legler, and Shapiro [1970].

tains that the social accounts themselves, while internally and externally consistent, do after all represent selected secondary data. These data, in general, are gross aggregates and implicitly involve a specific product mix. When the investigator uses social accounts data and allocates their gross magnitudes among sectors by means of an allocator such as employment, he may incur all the errors that are associated with using a constant product mix. Additionally, he incurs all those errors associated with the secondary data and the derivation of the allocating index such as employment or other pseudomeasure, which are by their nature imperfect allocators. Even if each of the many possible errors is minor, together they can lead to substantial error in the estimation of a control total for a single sector. Thus, this point of view maintains that the estimate of total gross output for any sector is best derived from primary data and other secondary data unique to the sector itself. Accordingly, it is argued that it is best to use the direct, piecemeal approach to the derivation of a set of control totals, to incur additional cost if necessary, and to bear the risk that the estimated control totals by sector may involve inconsistency and error when aggregated, which may necessitate some additional effort and cost to achieve reconciliation.

8.3 Some Illustrative Problems

In the Philadelphia study we did not attempt to develop a consistent set of social accounts. Rather, we adopted a piecemeal approach to build up a set of output control totals for 4-digit sectors, although we did use the value-of-shipments data from the 1958 Census of Manufactures as guidelines. The problems of developing these control totals were both numerous and varied. We can discuss here only a few that are of general interest.

Let us focus on the estimation of control totals for the manufacturing sectors. For these sectors the problems are often less difficult than for others. We have the long tradition of collecting data in a Census of Manufactures, and relatively speaking, this Census is considered to be a good if not excellent source of secondary data for control total estimation. Yet even here the problems are major. A first problem arises because of the assignment of establishments by the Census to categories other than those suggested by the primary interview data. In the Philadelphia study as well as our related study of the manufacturing sectors of the Boston region, we had to give careful attention to obtaining data from the large establishments. Inevitably it was necessary to examine their classification either in planning the surveys, in checking the reliability of the data, or in other connections. We found many discrepancies between the federal Census classification of these large establishments and the classification by the Pennsylvania Department of Internal Affairs (DIA) and/or industrial directories. There were also discrepancies between the Census classification and that suggested by the interview data on the sales and purchases of these establishments. We found that the federal Census classification often was in error from the standpoint of input–output work. Hence, these errors on large establishments are embedded in the Census data on employment, value of shipments, and so forth. Although neither the Philadelphia nor the Boston region study was designed to check the validity of the Census work on classification, and therefore did not examine the extent to which the Census may also have misclassified small to medium-size establishments, we suspect that here, too, there are many errors of classification. We recognize, of course, that the Census in its classification of establishments may have a bias toward achieving long-term comparability of data—a bias that the publishers of industrial directories may not have. However, it is a bias that, if uncorrected, leads to many serious errors in input–output work.

A second problem in the use of Census of Manufactures data arises if the base year of study is not a Census year. (In the case of the Philadelphia study, the Census was for year 1958, while the study was for year 1959.) The Census data must be updated if they are to be used. Frequently, however, the data on employment, wages and salaries, power consumption, and other benchmarks that the investigator might employ in the updating process are themselves inadequate. This was certainly the situation in the Philadelphia study. From industrial directories we could derive growth rates by sector in terms of employment and number of establishments for the period 1958 to 1959; but we could do this satisfactorily for only the five counties of Pennsylvania. We could also compare the employment growth rates by industry with those for the Commonwealth of Pennsylvania as a whole, and with those for the nation (through the Annual Survey of Manufactures data). Further, we could compare these data with limited data available for the three New Jersey counties, using the County Business Patterns data as a check for gross consistency. But it was clear that the measures and methods we had to employ to estimate 1959 data from 1958 data, even with the relative wealth of independent sources of secondary data, were not very satisfactory.

A third possible problem in the use of the Census of Manufactures arises because the region of study may cut across the counties and states for which the Census provides data. In the Philadelphia study the region did not cut across county lines. In other cases, such as the Boulder study, the study region does cut across the boundaries of the Census geographic units, and it becomes necessary to employ some measure and method, usually inadequate, to adjust the county and state Census data.

A fourth major problem arises if the procedure for the estimation of control totals involves the estimation of employment as an intermediate step, as was the case for the Philadelphia study. In this procedure output estimates are generated by multiplying the employment estimate for each sector by an estimated value of output per employee. There are numerous problems in determining an appropriate output-per-employee figure, and these are discussed in the *Working Papers*. In the Philadelphia study we relied heavily on the Census of Manufactures data (national, state, and metropolitan), generally the best source of such secondary data. Our experience indicates, however, that we would have obtained better results had we used more extensively our own survey returns and the detailed data of the Pennsylvania Department of Internal Affairs (DIA). The DIA classification conformed more closely with that of our study than did the Census classification. Further, the DIA listed the establishments included in each of its sectors, and the publication format of the DIA materials was significantly better than that of the Census.

It is appropriate to point up again two general matters. One concerns the development of control totals for sectors whose output is not placed on the economic market. Among such sectors are government, education, and religious and other nonprofit institutions. For an establishment in any such sector the investigator usually defines total output as the sum of the expenses incurred in its operations. There are, of course, many objections to this procedure, which are discussed in the literature. However, we have not found an alternative procedure that is more acceptable for input–output purposes. A second matter relates to our inclusion in the output of any sector all revenue from sales of secondary products and miscellaneous sources of revenues. The pros and cons for this procedure have been discussed in Chapter 6. We simply wish to state again that whatever the treatment of secondary products, the problem is compounded when a study does pertain to a non-Census year and a non-Census region.

In closing this chapter, we reiterate that Census data are not nearly as valuable as an input–output investigator might anticipate before he digs in. Further, since they are the product of a federal government institution, which has been in existence for a century and a half, they reflect the cultural lags and conservatism that develop in any bureaucratized system. The concepts that the Census employs—the classification of industry that is used, the types of data that it collects—all tend to be somewhat outdated, increasingly so as the years roll by. For example, because of an outdated classification scheme, the 1958 Census of Manufactures failed to provide usable data for the ordnance, electronics, and research and development sectors. Frequently, the very sectors to be examined in detail in an input–output study are the newly emerging sectors, where there is much change and where, by definition, a data-collecting system such as the Census has little to say.

Finally, as a society we are becoming increasingly concerned with noneconomic commodities. For example, amenities as a commodity is increasingly being considered relevant in economic analysis. However, neither the Census nor any other data source has yet been able to measure this commodity. More important, there are other critical noneconomic commodities that must be considered, such as air and water, pollutants, noise level, and others related to the environment in which people live. These may be outputs of economic activity but as such are not indicated in Census or most other publications. Yet from the standpoint of welfare analysis, these commodities are of key importance. In fact, they are of such importance that the analyst might now insist, for example, that steel production that is associated with much air pollution is not comparable with steel production associated with little air pollution. Therefore, it becomes essential for the Census (and other sources of data) to begin to provide reliable information on such outputs as air and water pollutants, solid wastes, and noise so that from a social welfare standpoint more accurate estimates of output control totals and input costs by sector can be developed. Such information would greatly facilitate the use of the input–output technique for measuring combined ecologic-economic impacts along the lines suggested later in Chapter 15.

Reference
Leven, C. L., J. B. Legler, and P. Shapiro (1970). *An Analytical Framework for Regional Development Policy.* Cambridge, Mass.: The M.I.T. Press.

9.1 General Remarks

Before we examine our work on each of the final demand sectors, it is worthwhile to speculate about the function of these sectors.

Although in national input–output studies these sectors have been viewed as exogenous sectors and comprise primarily households, capital formation, inventory change, government, and foreign exports, in regional input–output studies final demand sectors are viewed much more flexibly. Regional scientists recognize much more than others that government, capital formation, and households may function as internal sectors— vital internal sectors—in the regional economy and society. Therefore, they frequently place these sectors within the structural matrix, in ways specific to the region and objectives of the study. That is, regional scientists, much more than national economists, conceive the economic system as a circle of interdependence. Where the investigator cuts the circle, and which variables he determines to be the independent ones, will very much depend on the purpose of the study, the data and resources available, and his inclinations.

In the Philadelphia study, households and local governments were placed within the structural matrix for the calculation of the inverse. Since one of our objectives was to examine the impact of the Vietnam War on the Philadelphia economy, it was natural for the federal government sectors to be placed among the exogenous sectors. But in other analyses that are contemplated, some of these sectors may well be located within the structural matrix. Also, when we come to examine the impact of the expansion of chemicals, steel, and other air- and water-polluting industry, such expansions themselves become the relevant final demand (exogenous) sectors, much as was the case in the Fairless Steelworks study [Isard and Kuenne, 1953].

Further, the flexibility with which the regional input–output analyst defines sectors as exogenous or endogenous is not unrelated to his decision to use an inverse or a round-by-round iteration in making projections. Clearly, when the iterative procedure is used—and this increasingly may be the case in regional input–output work, as noted in Chapter 13—the investigator can exploit this flexibility much more effectively.

9.2 The Households Sector

In regional input–output discussions there has always been considerable thinking concerning the disaggregation of the households sector. The households sector is after all very large; and when such industrial clusters as textile manufacturing are highly disaggregated while households are not, the critical analyst easily can point to serious imbalance in the sector classification scheme.

Beyond the need to correct imbalance, there are strong grounds for disaggregation. Expenditure patterns are known to vary significantly among different income groups and other groups; and at least some data are available on these patterns from the Bureau of Labor Statistics (BLS) and other surveys of households. Hence, any regional input–output study based on BLS data, as the Philadelphia study is, should derive at least three or four if not more personal consumption expenditures vectors, one for each defined income class. In this way, it may be argued, household expenditures can be projected more accurately. However, such an argument is valid only if in the structural matrix wages and salaries, dividends, rents, and profits can be detailed by income-class recipients or, as a proxy, by occupations associated with each set of income-class recipients.

Put otherwise, it is not too meaningful for impact analysis to disaggregate the households sector unless it is also possible to disaggregate the factor payments row in parallel fashion. This point is neatly illustrated in the case of the Boulder study [Miernyk et al., 1967]. There, students (University of Colorado) and nonstudents were treated separately in terms of constructing income-products accounts. However, when the data were to be employed in an input–output table, the authors found it necessary to consolidate these two households sectors into one—because they did not receive from business establishments data on the distribution of employment between student and nonstudent households.

In addition to disaggregation, there has always been extensive discussion of where the households sector belongs within the input–output framework. Some would place it wholly among the final demand sectors as an exogenous sector, where it has been located traditionally in national input–output work. Others, who are sensitive to the local income multiplier effects and needs of regional authorities and decision-makers, would place it in the structural matrix, as an endogenous sector. In general, the latter procedure is preferred by those conducting regional analysis.

However, a third alternative exists that has been considered valid by many—namely, to divide the expenditures of the households sector into two parts. One part would cover the *average* expenditures, which are by and large associated with the social structure and regional economy of the *base year*. This part might be taken to reflect how a level of income equivalent to base-year income might be spent in some future year. It would be associated with a households column in the final demand submatrix. A second part would cover the expenditures generated by *new regional income*, if there is new regional income. This latter part might be derived from *marginal* coefficients that relate to the use of new or "incremental" income, and would be placed in the households column within the structural matrix. By so disaggregating the households sector, the investigator anticipates obtaining more accurate projections. However, in the Boulder study, such disaggregation was found not to be desirable when tested against the data that were gathered.

There is still another useful way of disaggregating the households sector when a considerable amount of growth is projected for a region. This method recognizes that there may be two patterns of household expenditures generated by new income. One pattern is that generated by the income of the new entries into the population system through immigration. Another is the pattern generated by the increased payments to those already in the system—where increased payments result from increased productivity and/or higher wages paid in order to effect the required shift of the labor force among occupations and industries. Hence, we may think in terms of two sets of coefficients, each associated with a households subset. Note that this suggested refinement simply involves a further disaggregation of the sectoring scheme. That is, migrant households in a projected growth situation are to be distinguished from nonmigrant households.

Despite the strong rationale for the disaggregation of the households sector in one or more ways, the typical regional input–output study has not effected any such disaggregation because of costs and inadequate data. In this respect, the Philadelphia study was no different. We constructed a single households column based on BLS data and a single households row based on primary data on wages and salaries and secondary data on other sources of income. However, we could have, and should have, disaggregated the households sector by income class—a disaggregation that is particularly desirable for large metropolitan regions. The BLS data that were employed could have been disaggregated to provide household expenditures vectors for each of several income classes; and we should have collected some primary data on factor payments by type and on wages and salaries by type occupation, to be associated with size of income class.

Although for large metropolitan regional studies it is desirable to disaggregate the households sector, it may not be desirable to do so for other small regions, metropolitan or nonmetropolitan. For such regions a single households sector may be best after all the benefits and costs of disaggregation are accounted for. Further, when a small, lightly populated, primarily agricultural region is being studied, the investigator might even find it desirable to aggregate the households sector with other sectors. That is, he might aggregate personal consumption expenditures with certain kinds of professional expenditures (such as those of doctors, lawyers, and farm realtors) and perhaps with expenditures for certain kinds of agricultural production for home consumption.

In short, there is nothing sacred about a single households sector. Like any other sector in input–output analysis it should be considered for possible disaggregation or aggregation with other sectors.

9.3 Inventory Change

In the past the collection of data on inventory change has not generally yielded satisfactory results. This experience, gained primarily with national input–output tables, reflects the facts (1) that records on inventories have not been particularly good;[1] (2) that these records have been kept in different ways by different establishments; (3) that there exist different notions of how to count and value inventories; and (4) that questions regarding inventories have seldom been as precisely worded as they might have been.

Moreover, once raw inventory data are obtained, many conceptual difficulties arise concerning their proper treatment and use. For example, some analysts contend that the inventory of a commodity should be recorded in the column for the producing industry in order for the technical production coefficients of the using sector to be accurate.[2] However, it is easily seen that if the inventory of an intermediate commodity that is to be processed further by a sector to yield a more finished product is to be kept in the accounts of the producing industry when the region of the producing industry is different from that of the using industry, it is not possible to obtain an accurate accounting for exports for the base year.

When we began the Philadelphia study, we were aware of this highly unsatisfactory experience with inventory data and the numerous difficulties that beset the user of these data no matter how fine a detailed breakdown of inventory by type commodity is achieved. We were also unable to anticipate how successful we might be in obtaining relevant inventory information for constructing the basic technical coefficients. We therefore played it safe. We decided to avoid collecting and processing inventory information, and to assume (implicitly) that net inventory change was zero for all commodities.

Looking back, we perhaps could have proceeded in a more satisfactory

[1] Although many establishments may have available from annual financial reports estimates of inventory change, such estimates are seldom detailed in terms of commodities to be used as inputs, commodities in process of production, and commodities as finished products.

[2] This point would not be valid if consuming establishments were to keep records on their inventories and report as input expenditures only the cost of that amount of a commodity purchased that actually was consumed in production during the course of a year, plus the value of the previous year's inventory of that commodity that was consumed.

manner. We could have reasoned (1) that small firms do not keep good records on their inventory; (2) that these firms probably would not respond adequately to the kinds of questions that we may have asked them; and (3) that in any case, information from small firms is not of key importance for identifying inventory change. We therefore could have rationalized a decision *not* to seek information from most of the establishments in the region. But we could have sought inventory information from the major firms. Such firms do spend considerable time, money, and effort in controlling inventories and hedging against price changes. We know also that the Penn Jersey Transportation Study did receive somewhat adequate responses from the large firms to gross inventory questions.

On the other hand, our assumption of zero net inventory change is not bad in the light of business cycle conditions in 1959. The only major inventory changes that we would have had to make, and that we did make on the raw data received, were changes in the stock of basic steel products resulting from the prolonged steel strike of 1959.

All in all, having in mind the unsuccessful experiences and the difficulties just noted, the authors still consider the case for collecting data on inventory change for a normal base year as not very strong, given the high priorities on and the usefulness of other kinds of data that can be sought.

9.4 Capital Formation

If we were to repeat the Philadelphia study, we would develop our capital formation sectors quite differently. In our study we did not ask establishments for any information on their investments. Neither a total figure for capital expenditures nor any detail regarding its composition was sought at the time of interview. Again, not having had experience with large and detailed input–output studies, and wishing to play it safe, we limited ourselves to questions on current operations to ensure that at the end of the study we would have a table of technical production coefficients useful in themselves. Now that our study is completed, we see how we could have included some questions on capital expenditures without jeopardizing the goal of a complete technical production coefficients table. At the end of the questionnaire, we could easily have asked establishments for information on their total capital expenditures and on their expenditures on plant construction and major items of equipment.

As documented in Volume 3 of the *Working Papers* [Isard, Langford, and Romanoff, 1966–1968], we derived estimates of the total value of capital expenditures in each manufacturing sector. We did so on the basis of the materials gathered by the Pennsylvania Department of Internal Affairs (DIA) for the five Pennsylvania counties in the Philadelphia SMSA, and with the assumption that for any given sector, the capital expenditures pattern was similar for establishments in both New Jersey and Pennsylvania. This assumption is subject to some question, since in general the establishments in New Jersey are somewhat newer and have different product mixes than the establishments for the five Pennsylvania counties, which in large part are located in Philadelphia city proper.

For manufacturing sectors, we relied heavily on the national data contained in the 1958 Census of Manufactures to break down capital expenditures into plant expenditures on the one hand and equipment expenditures on the other. We then used the data of the National Planning Association [1967] to provide an allocation of the capital expenditures on equipment among the diverse equipment-supplying industries. Thus, the coefficients for the manufacturing sectors in the capital formation sector were built strictly from national-type data and represent, in a sense, national average coefficients. They are not oriented to the age and size structure of Philadelphia enterprise, but are oriented to its product-mix structure.

Although it is without question desirable to obtain information from establishments on at least their total capital expenditures and expenditures on major items, the investigator should also recognize on the one hand the limitations of questionnaire data, however good they may be, and on the other hand the usefulness of average national capital coefficients. This point is clear when it is recognized that unlike production operations, capital formation and investment by an establishment is on an irregular basis. For a single establishment, capital investment does not proceed regularly and evenly over the years.[3] It can very well be, then, that the data the investigator obtains from questions on capital expenditures may have limited validity for projection purposes. The data of course would represent the situation of the base year and therefore would be extremely desirable for description purposes. However, when we wish to make projections, we may find that the capital expenditures data when examined by sector do not provide any reasonable basis for estimating a typical set of capital expenditures by sector in some future year. The investigator may attempt to avoid this problem by asking the establishments for information on capital expenditures and on capacity expansion not only for the base year but also for other years—one or more years preceding the base year and one or more subsequent to the base year. He may then argue that over a three- to five-year period the average data might be valid for projection purposes. Perhaps this procedure is somewhat more reasonable.

[3] For example, electric utility companies in the Philadelphia region do not purchase steam turbine generator units regularly over the years. In 1959, they happened to purchase a relatively large number of units as replacements; in the following two years, they purchased none.

The investigator may choose not to follow this procedure, however. He might wish to avoid the additional costs. More important, he might argue that the capital coefficients data, such as those developed in the Philadelphia study, which are strictly average national coefficients, are perhaps the best to use for projection purposes. First, given the possibilities for technological change, an analyst cannot expect past regional data on capital expenditures to be of much validity for projection into the future. Second, even when a set of capital expenditures is projected for a future year against the background of past capital expenditures data for a three- to five-year period, the investigator must rely heavily on information other than that on total capital expenditures and its breakdown provided by establishments for each sector. For example, he needs advice from experts in each sector on rate of obsolescence of existing production processes and new technology to be expected.[4]

In the Philadelphia study, we had no intention whatsoever of using the derived capital coefficients for any type of dynamic regional model. When the Philadelphia study was initiated, it was clear in our thinking that other, more important research areas had to be probed before a dynamic regional input–output model could be considered seriously. Now that the feasibility of constructing highly detailed regional input–output tables has been established, and now that the prospect for the development of some type of interregional model—whether pure interregional, Moses-type, or balanced regional-type—is good, it is worthwhile to consider the possibilities for dynamic models.

The coefficients listed in the capital formation sectors of the Philadelphia table were developed strictly for comparative statics analysis. They relate only to input requirements if in some recent year a decision had been made to invest in new capacity (involving a full complement of plant and equipment) in any given sector. For such a situation, the coefficients in the given sector's column in the capital formation submatrix are relevant. In contrast, in dynamic regional input–output analysis, such a narrow view of capital formation is invalid. In such analysis, it is necessary to proceed from time period to time period, starting with existing capacity, existing output, and therefore existing excess capacity. But what is existing capacity? In the minds of many respondents it will be related to such uncertain factors as the likely work practices adopted by labor unions, air- and water-pollution regulations, and so forth. Furthermore, existing capacity must be detailed by meaningful item to determine the extent to which there exists an imbalance of existing plant

---

[4] In a real sense, it is less valid to project capital formation on the basis of coefficients derived from current and past data on capital expenditures than to project output on the basis of coefficients derived from current data on production operations.

and equipment such that only piecemeal additions to plant and equipment are required to increase capacity. Additionally, the investigator must project replacement requirements (wear and tear) and obsolescence, both for plant and equipment as a whole and for individual pieces of plant and equipment. All these factors and others must be considered in dynamic analysis.

Moreover, there are the definition and data problems. Consider again the definition of existing capacity. Even within a group of specialists—say, engineers—there may be significant differences as to the strict technical capabilities of existing plant and equipment. Different engineers may have in mind different product mixes, different qualities of product, and different performance standards. When economists are brought into the picture, still other notions of existing capacity become relevant. Economists would not define as usable capacity (for input–output analysis) plant and equipment that might be technically able to produce output but only under conditions in which marginal cost well exceeds marginal revenue. But even among economists, who may agree on the concepts and theoretical definitions of marginal cost and marginal revenue, there may be major differences when it comes to the actual measurement of marginal cost and marginal revenue for an existing operating establishment.

Then, even after an acceptable measure of existing capacity is developed, there is the problem of proper timing of investment in new capacity, whether piecemeal or in terms of whole units of plant and equipment. There may be differences among investigators as to the proper date for investment because of differences among them as to what piecemeal additions are required to correct an imbalance of existing plant and equipment. Again, such differences will depend on the product mix that they judge ought to be produced, and so will the particular set of co-efficients that they consider relevant for whole new units of capacity. Further, among investigators there may be differences in their estimates of the life expectancy (wear and tear and obsolescence) of different capital items, and accordingly in their projected programs for replacement over time. These latter factors, of course, are directly related to one's estimate of technological change generated outside a sector, and inside the sector through advance in practice and experience. Such technological change requires changes in the capital coefficients themselves.

Despite all these difficulties, it is desirable to move in the direction of dynamic, interregional input–output analysis. Certainly, crude models are possible that can enhance the utility of whatever interregional models may be developed in the next years. Already, Miernyk, in his West Virginia study [Miernyk et al., 1969], has made considerable progress in attacking some of the difficulties that arise.

9.5 Government Sectors

9.5.1 General Practices Typically, there are three relevant sets of government units whose operations must be encompassed in a regional input–output study: the federal, state, and local. Occasionally, the operations of special government units, such as a multistate river-system, or port authority, or some other special-purpose-district agency, must also be covered.

There are two basic ways to develop a sectoring scheme for government. One is by administrative unit (establishment). This method facilitates the collection of data since it is easy to identify and locate the existing administrative units and since expenditures are usually controlled by the administrative unit.

The second way is by program (function). This way permits a more effective evaluation of the impact of policy alternatives, since it provides for each program the cost (input) data per unit service (output) provided. However, this way also requires extensive imputation (or allocation) of costs of common inputs and services of facilities and administrative personnel among the several programs operated by an administrative unit. Moreover, it requires certain data on programs often operated by agencies not within the region; such data usually are not available except in Washington, D.C. Finally, agencies are rather reluctant to provide information that would permit a benefit-cost evaluation of their programs by persons outside the agency.

Regardless of the sectoring scheme that is adopted, the following practices appear desirable. First, there should be an identification and full listing of all the government units and programs within a region being studied. (In the case of the Philadelphia study, a single comprehensive listing of agencies did not exist; such a listing had to be developed. Further, it is to be noted that the listing of programs recently made available through the U.S. Office of Economic Opportunity is not complete.)

Second, the full set of transfers among the agencies, whether in payments (funds) or real goods and services, should be made explicit. In particular, the set of transfer payments should indicate the flow of funds from funding agency (or funding agencies when interagency programs are involved) through all intermediate agencies to the final spending agency. Associated with any such flow of funds should be the set of purchases of goods and services by the ultimate spending agency and the level of the program supported by these funds.

Third, a system should be devised to reconcile the inconsistencies found in the several sources of secondary data on government expenditures. For example, data in the Census of Governments on total expenditures and its composition for local and state governments do not appear to be consistent with the expenditures recorded by either local or state government authorities for supposedly the same period. The different definitions and practices used by the different sources of secondary data make it necessary for the investigator to develop a set of procedures whereby to arrive at some consistent set of estimates.

Fourth, certain procedures should be established for determining whether certain government purchases are to be regarded as local purchases or imports or exports, and whether certain government sales are local sales or exports or imports. At the one extreme are the local purchases by agencies within the region for purposes of furnishing local services. All these purchases and services are inputs and outputs, respectively, and are to be recorded within the structural matrix as local endogenous transactions. At the other extreme are purchases of nonlocal goods by agencies located outside the region in order to provide local services. The latter are generally identified as imports into the region. Then there are purchases from local producers by agencies within the region to provide services for behaving units in other regions. These services are clearly exports. Further, there are purchases from local producers by agencies not located in the region for the purpose of providing services to the behaving units within the region. Here there may be differences on how to treat such inputs and outputs. If agencies located *outside* the region can be viewed as fictitious units *within* the region, these inputs and outputs may be viewed, respectively, as local purchases and local production for meeting local demands. Otherwise, the inputs may be viewed as exports by the region and the outputs as imports into the region. Still another interesting case is that in which a government agency located in the region purchases goods from other regions and then after simple processing (which may cover just simple accounting operations) exports the goods and services to users in other regions. When such an agency can be viewed as located completely outside the region, then all these transactions can be ignored. However, when the agency does purchase some inputs such as labor services, transportation, and power from households and establishments within the region, then its transactions must be made explicit. Its inputs from other regions then should be viewed as imports into the region, and its services provided to users outside the region as exports.

Fifth, tax receipts (revenues) should be disaggregated and there should be a separate row for each major type of tax and source of revenue. Thus, there should be rows pertaining to revenues from sales taxes (perhaps disaggregated, by type of programs—e.g., education—to which they are assigned), revenues from property taxes (again disaggregated by type of program to which they are assigned), revenues from income tax, and so forth. In this way, the implications of alternative government policies can be more easily and accurately pinpointed, especially at the state and local levels.

9.5.2 The Federal Government As already indicated, one of the strong points of the Philadelphia study is its comprehensive and extensive coverage of expenditures by federal establishments in the region. No other input–output study has collected as much primary information on the federal establishments of a region and at such great detail. However, not every federal establishment was covered intensively. Those that were not covered played rather minor roles in the economy; and over time, as data on their operations are obtained, these data may be incorporated in the study through adjustments to sector 9114, *Civilian Federal Government Agencies, n.e.c.*

However, in line with the preceding general discussion, we suggest that in future studies of a large metropolitan area attempts be made to procure information on a program basis rather than on an agency or establishment basis. Some programs of obvious interest are education, housing, highway construction, welfare, urban renewal, economic development, research and development, and general administration. To the extent that a program orientation can be achieved, the study can provide more basic information on implications of alternative federal legislation.

To sector the federal government activities by program would involve some new problems, but not necessarily difficult ones. There would be the problem, as in any sector analysis, of differentiating between expenditures made under various special program grants and those based on the normal operations of an agency. Another problem, as already suggested, would be to make explicit the transfer of funds among government agencies.

To be specific on the last point, the Philadelphia input–output table indicates expenditures of the ultimate receiving agencies, that is, of the agencies that actually purchase the goods and contract for specific services from the private sectors. This is as it should be. A transfer of funds, say, for highway construction, from federal to state and then to local government, should be associated with expenditures in the local government highway construction sector. However, we should also like to have recorded in the Philadelphia table all moneys allocated by the Bureau of Public Roads (which in 1959 represented many millions of dollars for the Philadelphia region) to the Departments of Highways of the two states. We would also like to have recorded the allocation of these funds by the two states to the several local governments for their highway construction projects.

Another desirable refinement would recognize that some federal government functions should be viewed as endogenous to the system while others should not. The post office function and the general services administration may be considered endogenous and should be placed within the structural matrix, while defense operations such as the Navy Yard are exogenous.

Another improvement that we could have achieved in our Philadelphia study relates to federal government expenditures on account of the military. In the federal government sectors for the Philadelphia region, we included information relating to federal government purchases within the metropolitan region only by federal agencies and establishments within that region. It would have been advisable, especially with regard to military procurement, to have accounted for those purchases from the region's private establishments that were made by federal agencies and units located outside the region. We could have done this at least with respect to prime contracts awarded by the Department of Defense, using the information already compiled by the Regional Science Research Institute for year 1960 [Isard and Ganschow, 1961]. However, we hesitated to do this, partly because of limited resources but also because we anticipated major difficulty in the use of the Regional Science Research Institute data in effecting a distinction between (1) the federal government purchases and contracts awarded to suppliers in the Philadelphia region by federal agencies in that region and (2) those purchases and contracts made by federal agencies outside the region. As we now look back, we see that we could have effected this distinction at small cost and without adding significantly to the problem of data control.

9.5.3 State and Local Government Sectors Although federal government activities are largely outside a region (and thus are largely to be placed in the final demand sectors to the extent that they relate directly to the regional economy being studied), state government activities may not be. When an input–output study is being conducted for a state as a whole or a group of states, obviously most state activities should be covered and many should be viewed as endogenous. Or when a state's set of activities is largely within the region, as might occur when a state capital lies in the region, even though only a portion of a state is physically included in a region, it may still be wise to cover explicitly most of the state's activities. In such a situation, however, parts or even the whole of more of the state's activities may appropriately be excluded from the structural matrix and placed among the final demand sectors.

In the case of the Philadelphia study, too few of the activities of the Commonwealth of Pennsylvania are within the metropolitan region to justify the inclusion of these activities as endogenous sectors. While we included the relevant state government activities as sectors within the *preliminary* structural matrix printed and distributed in December 1966, when the *final* coefficients table was constructed and its inverse derived in 1968, we did exclude such sectors from the structural matrix and place them in the final demand submatrix.

As with the other governments, it is desirable to develop the state sectors in two ways. One way is to disaggregate the state by type of agency and institution, as was done in the Philadelphia study. The second way is to develop the state's sectors by type program. This was not attempted to any major extent in the Philadelphia study.

Practically all local government activities of the region must be covered, and most of them should be placed within the structural matrix. Once again, data should be developed both by agency and institution and by program. A detailed breakdown of local government expenditures for each of the following major functions should be obtained at the minimum: public safety, health and welfare, streets and highways, parks and recreation, utilities, and other government services. However, detailed cost information on these functions are usually not kept systematically by local governments, and hence many purchases may need to be estimated indirectly.

The practice of disaggregating the government receipts row for each major type of tax and source of revenue is particularly important for local governments, since local taxes are tied to specific local programs. At the same time, the rows relating to the local government should be structured so that there can be explicitly recorded receipts of federal and state funds as grants for diverse programs.

9.5.4 Other Governmental Authorities While for some regional input–output studies, it may be of critical importance to cover government agencies other than federal, state, and local, in the Philadelphia study this was not the case. The levels of the operations of these agencies were considered too small to justify an attempt to identify them and collect their expenditures data.

References

Isard, Walter, and J. Ganschow (1961). *Awards of Prime Military Contracts by County, State and Metropolitan Area of the United States, Fiscal Year 1960*. Philadelphia: Regional Science Research Institute.

———, Thomas W. Langford, and Eliahu Romanoff (1966–1968). *Philadelphia Region Input–Output Study, Working Papers*, Volumes 1–4. Philadelphia: Regional Science Research Institute.

———, and R. E. Kuenne (1953). "The Impact of Steel Upon the Greater New York-Philadelphia Industrial Region: A Study in Agglomeration Projection," *Review of Economics and Statistics*, 35: 289–301.

Miernyk, William H., et al. (1967). *Impact of the Space Program on a Local Economy: An Input–Output Analysis*. Morgantown, W. Va.: West Virginia Library.

———, et al. (1969). *Simulating Regional Economic Development: An Interindustry Analysis of the West Virginia Economy*. Morgantown, W. Va.: Regional Research Institute, West Virginia University.

National Planning Association (1967). *Capacity Planning Factors: Manufacturing Industries*, Part II. Washington, D.C.

10.1 General Remarks

In regional input–output analysis the strategic role of imports and exports has almost always been appreciated, and the importance of obtaining data on total imports and total exports and their spatial patterns has rarely been underplayed. In contrast, in national input–output analysis, the need to analyze and project imports and exports is and has been recognized to be much less important. This difference in the relative importance assigned to imports and exports sectors is explainable when we consider certain pertinent data. For example, we find that in 1959, exports of the United States as a nation accounted for 4.7 percent of gross national product, whereas those of the Philadelphia region were $11.4 billion and accounted for 50.2 percent of Philadelphia's gross private production of $22.7 billion. Imports of the United States accounted for 4.8 percent of gross national product, whereas those of the Philadelphia region were $9.7 billion and accounted for 46.2 percent of Philadelphia's gross regional consumption of $21.0 billion.

While import–export analysis is in general much more important in regional input–output analysis than in national, it is also to be appreciated that this importance varies among regions—in accordance with their size, the structure and nature of their industry, their degree of specialization, and their spatial position in a multiregional system. For example, for a large region that is largely self-contained and whose imports and exports may be primarily determined by political considerations, analysis of import–export data may not be of overriding significance. The investigator may seek only to anticipate the levels of exports that may be fixed by political authorities as the extraregional exogenous demand to be met for the year of projection and the amount of foreign exchange available for foreign imports. In contrast, for a small open region that supplies highly competitive markets and largely depends on export trade, it is very important to have detailed data concerning the regional distribution of the sales of its establishment. Yet a hypothesis that states that the smaller the area and the greater its reliance on export trade, the more important it is to detail its exports and imports is perhaps too general. For example, for small areas growing rapidly and experiencing significant structural change within their industrial sectors, the investigator may well question whether an analysis of their trade patterns for a base year can be meaningful for projection purposes. In contrast, for small areas that are growing slowly and have a historically stable pattern of industry whose mix is changing only gradually, import–export analysis with a base year input–output flow table may be very useful.

The points just made do suggest that the data on exports and imports collected in an input–output study should be viewed flexibly in terms of the region being studied. At times in national input–output studies, exports and imports have been recorded, respectively, in a single column in the final demand sector and one corresponding row (occasionally disaggregated) below the structural matrix; at other times, no row has been introduced when the single final demand column has been defined as net foreign trade (exports minus imports). Such treatment, however, is highly inadequate for most regional input–output studies, and accordingly, various methods have been devised in these studies to collect and estimate data on a more disaggregated basis by one or more means to be discussed later.

10.2 The Collection and Processing of Primary Data

The most obvious way to identify the exports and imports of a region is to collect data directly from establishments by interview. Each establishment may be asked to provide data on (1) its sales disaggregated by type of commodity and by region of destination, and (2) its purchases (for production purposes) disaggregated by type of commodity and source (region). As we indicated in Section 5.5, we did seek such data from establishments. Our experience in this regard was mixed. For some moderate and large establishments that had advanced purchasing and sales data systems, we were able to procure good data. For the large majority of smaller firms, we were not successful.

Because the survey materials procured were so inadequate—which consequence in part reflected the fact that some of our questions were not clearly stated—we did not attempt in the Philadelphia study to estimate imports with the use of the primary data only. Rather, as will be reported later, we used a residual-type method and location and other types of analysis in conjunction with our inadequate data. First, however, let us note certain issues that arise when heavy reliance is made upon primary data.

A first issue concerns whether the investigator should seek primary information on both imports and exports, or on only one of these sets of data. This question is partly related to the question raised in Chapter 5 as to whether the investigator should seek data on (1) sales by commodity and region of destination *and* (2) purchases by commodity and source (region), or on only one of these sets of data. Our view, as stated in Chapter 5, is that one set of good data is always better than two sets of poor data. We would hold to this principle even if an investigator were conducting a regional input–output study in connection with other regional input–output studies in such a way that a disjoint and exhaustive set of regions of the United States is covered. We suggest that it is best to focus on the collection of only one set of data, and that the set be on purchases by type of commodity and source (region). We prefer data on purchases by type of commodity and source (region) even though experience on the several regional input–output studies suggests that it is less costly and more accurate to obtain data on the distribution of sales by region. Usually there are more major inputs than major products associated with an establishment, and therefore it is easier for the establishment to provide a single percentage allocation of sales by region for each commodity produced than a single percentage allocation of purchases by region for each input used. For example, a major establishment such as a Westinghouse Electric plant that produces steam turbines probably can make available the data on sales distribution by region of its one or relatively few types of output more easily and at less cost than the data on purchases by region of each of its many inputs.

However, it should be borne in mind that data on sources of inputs by region tend to lead to the more accurate identification of interindustry flows across regions. This point follows since if an establishment does not specify the producing industry (by 4-digit code) of the several regions that serve as sources of an input, the investigator can usually assume with reasonable accuracy that the industry was the one that produces the input in question as primary product. In contrast, when the establishment provides data on distribution of sales by region, specifying only the region of use and not the consuming sectors (by 4-digit code), frequently the investigator cannot make reasonable assumptions as to which sectors were the major consumers. Therefore, when he wishes to link his regional input–output study with one or more other regional input–output studies (hopefully conducted with similar industry sectoring and the same set of regions, or with sectoring and regions that can be adjusted to allow comparison of the data), then clearly he finds data on sources of inputs much more useful than sales distribution data. And clearly, for interregional input–output studies, the investigator will find the greater disaggregation possible with the use of data on sources of inputs to be of critical significance.[1]

A second issue is closely related to this first one. It concerns the identification of the set of regions by which export sales and import purchases are disaggregated. Clearly, the set of regions ought to be exhaustive if it

[1] We may perhaps state the case for "data on sources by input" too strongly. It is to be recognized that usually a series of regional input–output studies, one for each of an exhaustive set of regions, is not being conducted. At best, one or two other studies may be under way while the investigator is pursuing his own study; and these other studies may be oriented to sectoring schemes and survey procedures that do not permit easy coordination and collaboration. Therefore, the investigator may not be able to rely upon other studies to furnish the data on the distribution of the export sales of other regions, by sector, to his region, or the purchases of inputs from each of the sectors of his own region. Consequently, he cannot count on obtaining information on the linkages between the economy of his region and that of others. Therefore,

refers to a nation such as the United States; and it should be disjoint in the sense that there is no overlap among the regions. Otherwise, however, what constitutes a desirable set of regions when regional input–output studies are to be coordinated to achieve the major external economies that can be realized? When confronted with this question, the informal Ad Hoc Committee on Regional Input–Output Analysis of the Regional Science Research Institute urged from a practical standpoint that when possible, the state be used as a standard geographic unit. That is, when possible, all data on nonlocal shipments and nonlocal inputs should be disaggregated by individual states or, if this is not feasible, by composites of states. If composites of states are to be employed, they should conform, where possible, to the following set of five regions (which is consistent with the broadest set of regions used by the U.S. Bureau of the Census):

1. Northeast
2. South
3. Far West
4. Midwest
5. Rest of the World.

The committee suggested that businessmen do in fact think in terms of such broad regions and that information on this basis would not be difficult to obtain.[2] It considered the possibility of using such techniques as the gravity model to allocate regional totals among the state units of a region when primary data are not obtainable. The Committee stated that in some cases it would be easier to obtain information on sales by region than on inputs by source (region), and that in other cases the opposite would be true. It urged that the maximum feasible detail be sought, including exports to and imports from (1) foreign countries and (2) the "rest of the state" (or the "rest of the set of states" if the region of study covers part of more than one state).

Consistent with these recommendations, the current multiregional input–output program of the Harvard Economic Research Project

---

he must reach his own decisions as to which set of data is more useful. When he does consider a decision, he also recognizes (1) that data on distribution of export sales by region can provide valuable information on his region's sensitivity, via the demand channel, to changes in conditions of other regions; and (2) that data on purchases of inputs by sources (region) can yield basic materials for comparative cost and other studies focusing on industrial development and new employment opportunities in his region.

[2] Bear in mind, however, the point made in Section 5.5, namely, that the investigator cannot expect that a respondent will be enthusiastic about reorganizing his establishment's data on marketing areas to conform to the investigator's set of regions.

[Polenske, 1968] is accumulating data for states. These data will serve as building blocks for an exhaustive and disjoint set of regions for the United States, to be demarcated at a later time. Such data development allows considerable flexibility in the implementation of a multiregion model. It allows reshuffling of states so that for each problem or for each set of problems requiring the same regional set, it will be possible to work with the appropriate regions. In this way, the investigator is able to avoid an initial choice of regions, such as the nine Census regions or the eight regions of the Regional Economics Division, Office of Business Economics, U.S. Department of Commerce. Such an initial choice would condition and impose elements of rigidity on the study framework.

It should be noted that while the recommendations of the Ad Hoc Committee and the work of the Harvard Economic Research Project aim to achieve flexibility by taking states as the building blocks, certain inflexibilities are still introduced into the study framework. Counties could have been chosen as the basic units for which to develop data, and such a decision would make possible still greater flexibility regarding the final choice of regions for any problem to be studied, and would permit the study of a greater range of problems with an *appropriate set* of regions. Further, the use of counties would permit investigators to avoid the inappropriate use of states when studies of Eastern and Great Lakes regions are to be conducted and when metropolitan regions involving only parts of several states are the meaningful areas for research. However, collection and processing of data by counties would greatly increase the cost of any multiregion input–output study.

There are other relevant considerations. As we have already asked, why should an investigator expect input–output studies to be completed for even a majority of a set of regions suggested by a group of experts such as the Ad Hoc Committee? Why should he expect this when at the time his study is undertaken, he observes only one or two other regional input–output studies being conducted and few others planned for the near future? In such a situation the investigator may sharply discount the possibility that he will be able to profit from the data of other regional input–output studies that "may" be initiated, let alone completed; or that his data, if appropriately disaggregated by some set of regions judged optimal, would be useful to such other "potential" studies. He therefore may reach the conclusion that it would be best for him to ignore the possibility of several regional studies being pursued concomitantly and to proceed to define a set of regions most useful for the immediate purposes and objectives at hand. Hence, if he were to conduct a study for a region such as the Philadelphia SMSA, he might consider as his second region the rest of the Middle Atlantic states (including, perhaps, southern New England and Maryland); as his third region, the rest of the states east of the Mississippi and north of the Ohio river; and as his fourth, the rest of the United States.

A third issue relates to the difficulty in obtaining directly from establishments primary data on their sales by region and purchases of inputs by region. This difficulty stems from the fact that many manufacturers purchase and sell their goods through merchant wholesalers. Such manufacturers usually are not aware of the distribution of their output by region or of the supply pattern of their inputs by region. Such information must be obtained directly from the wholesalers who handle the establishment's products and inputs. However, it is very difficult, if not impossible, to obtain such information from wholesalers. First, the wholesaler's records on sales and purchase patterns by region are frequently poor. Second, since they handle the outputs and inputs of a large number of establishments, the wholesaler has no effective way of differentiating among these establishments, particularly when these establishments are not all located in the region of study.

The problem, however, is still more complicated. Many establishments of a region may market their outputs and/or purchase their inputs from wholesalers outside the region. Then the investigator may be required to interview and obtain records from merchant wholesalers who may be at some distance from the region and who, not being residents of the region, may have very little incentive to provide information when requested, especially when cost is involved.

Although theoretically it is desirable to identify the sales patterns and input purchase patterns of each local establishment that markets and buys through a wholesaler, local or nonlocal, in practice the investigator's limited resources compels him to be content with obtaining data from a merchant wholesaler on his sales pattern for each commodity marketed and his purchase pattern for each commodity bought, and not to seek differentiation among establishments working through this wholesaler.

A fourth issue relates to the identification of the purchases within the region by nonresident households in their roles as commuters and tourists. Frequently, the information that retail sales establishments in a region provide on their sales to households does not allow the investigator to break these sales down by sales to residents of the region and sales (of an export character) to nonresidents of a region. Yet for an impact study, such a breakdown may be of critical importance.

Also, as indicated, the investigator should estimate purchases by a region's households from sources outside the region (that is, direct imports by households). Frequently, this is done by taking the difference between total household purchases and the reported sales of local establishments (reduced by some percentage figure to eliminate estimated sales to nonresidents). However, these devices for obtaining, first, the exports of retail establishments to households in other regions and, second, the estimate of imports from other regions by the household sector are not really adequate. It would be much more desirable to survey a random sample of households in the region and to ask households how they spend their income for each type of commodity and how the expenditures on each type are distributed among regions.[3] This kind of survey was undertaken in the Boulder study. The added time and expense required was judged to be more than justified in terms of the improved impact analysis that was made possible. Such a survey obviates the need to resort to such indirect estimating procedures as those just mentioned and allows the projection of changes in imports and exports through multiplying per capita estimates of imports and exports by change in population.

Another main issue in import–export analysis deals with financial flows. There currently exists very little information concerning these flows. Perhaps the United States government may be able to provide data on the amount of revenues collected by regions to pay for interest charges on debt, and also may provide information on such debt payments made by regions, so that an investigator can determine interest payment flows on account of the federal government. However, comparable sources of information on interest payments by private enterprise and on rent, dividend, and similar payments that flow across the regions do not exist.

Also, taxes in general give rise to important financial flows among regions. Here again, there does not appear to be any systematic way to determine the outflows of funds from a region because of the payment of federal and state taxes. Hence, these flows must be imputed, even though procedures for imputation are not satisfactory.

Finally, there are flows associated with the provision of educational services. Such services furnished to nonresident students are often conveniently viewed as export services. Other goods and services directly purchased by nonresident students may also be viewed as exports. Payments for the labor services of nonresident students are then to be viewed as imports.

10.3 Estimation Methods of the Philadelphia Study

Having stated some of the issues involved in estimating imports and exports, we now turn to the Philadelphia study and report upon the

---

[3] Such a survey also permits the investigator to go beyond retail sales in order partially to account for exports and imports of the service sectors—such as those associated with hotels, lawyers, doctors, rentals, and recreation.

specific methods employed. As noted, although the data collected on distribution of sales by region were satisfactory for direct use in estimating exports by commodities or sectors, the data collected on input purchases by region were wholly inadequate for estimating imports of goods and services. Imports had to be determined indirectly, at least in large part.

Our procedure for estimating exports was as follows. If a sector was clearly an exporter of its output, we estimated its exports using not only the pieces of data that its establishments reported but also our knowledge of the unique regional organizational structure of the sector, the nature of the products produced, and basic location and marketing theory. We then subtracted the estimated exports of the sector from its total production and compared the resulting magnitude of local sales with the sum of intermediate demand and final demand (excluding exports) for the products of that sector. If total regional production less exports exceeded the total of these two demands, we usually assumed that we had underestimated intermediate demand. We then effected reasonable adjustments of such intermediate demand where possible. If consistency could not be achieved by such adjustment, we then made "reasonable" adjustments to estimated exports and other final demand. In these situations in which we had to adjust intermediate demand, typically we assumed implicitly that the products of an exporting sector were either not imported or imported to a negligible extent only, in order to keep the adjustment as small as possible. This last assumption was, of course, a poor one. If we were to do our study over again, we would seriously consider requesting information from establishments on exports and imports of commodities classified at a 5- to 7-digit level. Thereby, we would be able to obtain more valid data on exports and imports without precluding aggregation to the desired 4-digit sector level.

The usefulness of data on a 5- or 7-digit basis is suggested by Karaska [1966] in his study of the paper and paper products industrial complex in the Philadelphia region. As is widely recognized, United States industry is characterized by a high degree of specialization and product differentiation. A great variety of kinds and grades of manufactured items exist, are demanded, and are able to be supplied cheaply by specialized firms because of scale and other economies. Accordingly, in the paper and paper products industrial complex we find, both within and outside the Philadelphia region, numerous establishments representing various stages in production and making all kinds of specialized products. And we find, for example, that despite the fact that the Philadelphia establishments in sector SIC 2621 *Paper Mills (except building paper mills)* produced roughly twice as much output as was required as inputs by the paper and paper products industrial complex within the Philadelphia region, less than 20 percent of these inputs were purchased from the Philadelphia establishments in sector 2621.

Similar situations exist for other industrial complexes in the Philadelphia region. At first glance, the patterns of sales and purchases associated with these situations suggest extensive crosshauling. On deeper examination they reflect a high degree of specialization—which would be much more apparent if a 5- to 7-digit commodity classification were used. Thus, the estimates of exports in the Philadelphia study could have been greatly improved had data been requested and reported by commodities for such a fine classification.

Imports were estimated almost entirely indirectly. We relied on a "demand equals supply" relationship. We estimated intermediate demand for the output of a sector by multiplying the vector of coefficients along its row by the column vector of sector outputs of the region. To this demand we added deliveries to the final demand sectors, including exports. Thus we obtained our estimates of total demand for the output of each sector. Subtracting actual output produced by any sector from the total demand for its products yielded a residual, which we used as the estimate of imports for those products.

On a number of occasions we found that this procedure yielded a negative value for imports, primarily because we had underestimated intermediate demand. That is, for a number of sectors we found that total production less export sales and less other final demands would exceed the estimated intermediate demand. This inconsistency was adjusted by increasing, uniformly or selectively, the technical coefficients along the row of the table associated with a given sector in order to increase our initially estimated intermediate demand so as to yield zero imports for a sector. Usually in such cases we did not attempt to estimate a positive level of imports for the sector, even though positive imports might have been expected.

For certain other sectors in which the first crude estimates of imports were not negative, intermediate demand was still considered much too low. For these sectors intermediate demand was increased by changing selected coefficients along a row so that our initial estimate of imports was increased, particularly when respondents had provided us with relevant information on their imports of different goods, and when a larger amount of imports was consistent with theoretical and other considerations. Nonetheless, despite the adjustments to our coefficients, in general we have understated these coefficients; and generally speaking we have tended to underestimate both intermediate demand and imports.

Finally, whenever it was necessary to eliminate negative imports and when we could not justify further increases in the technical coefficients along a row, then as a last resort we placed our best estimate of unassigned intermediate demand into the appropriate cell of the "undistributed" column.

In retrospect, we cannot suggest any better procedure to improve estimation of imports and reduce unallocated magnitudes other than to collect directly more information on imports themselves—that is, on the sources of inputs by region. While undoubtedly our estimates of imports for the Philadelphia region are understated, nevertheless we still find them exceedingly useful and relatively good benchmarks for impact analysis and for projection purposes.

10.4 Possible Future Developments

Having reviewed our procedures for estimating imports and exports, we may now look somewhat into the future. First, there exists a possibility that the Census of Transportation and studies supported by the Department of Transportation will develop new data that are more relevant for interregional and regional input–output studies. It is to be hoped that transportation data will be coded by county and state of origin and destination; and that consistent with these data other pertinent regional data will be provided that in part will be required to measure more effectively the efficiency of transportation systems. In particular, sampling on a more extensive basis of goods in transit, for all transportation modes, is to be encouraged. Further, more selective surveys of senders and receivers of goods and materials would be useful. Recall that regional and interregional input–output analysis does not require origin and destination information on all commodities, but merely on those commodities on which transport costs are significant, and which move extensively among regions. Primary data on national-type commodities (with low transport costs) or on local market-oriented commodities (with extremely high transport costs) are not so essential.

Second, it is possible that, in addition to counties (approximately 3,000 in number) and states (50 in number), there will be other areas, intermediate in size, for which important data are collected and processed. If so, the investigator will be in a position to deal with much less than 3,000 areal units, and yet with a set of finer and frequently more meaningful units than states. The collection and processing of data by these new areal units, which are likely to be multicounty units, may be realized if proposals are adopted for the development of a national system of regional accounts, wherein compatibility is achieved among the accounting frameworks of all individual regions and between these frameworks and the corresponding United States aggregative accounts. For example, Leven, Legler, and Shapiro [1970] recommend that a national system of regional accounts be developed for an exhaustive, disjoint set of regions. He urges

that these regions be the *functional economic areas* that have been proposed by the Committee on Areas for Social and Economic Statistics of
the Social Science Research Council. These areas of the United States,
approximately 350 in number, are delineated on the basis of "integration"
criteria, which give primary emphasis to commuting fields and labor
markets of the economic system. The proposal that these functional
economic areas comprise clusters of whole counties would preserve the
extremely valuable character of the historical data on counties.

Yet from the standpoint of future regional input–output studies, we
must observe that while the recommendations of the committee for the
establishment of functional economic areas for the collection and processing of official United States data have many strong underpinnings,
such recommendations do perpetuate an existing set of areas as building
blocks—namely, counties. Consequently, it will be still more difficult in
the future to effect any change in this primary set of building blocks or
to employ in any study a more desirable set of building blocks. It makes
even more difficult a redefinition of a set of regions that would be more
appropriate than counties for a deeper understanding of the emerging
social structures and consequently more appropriate for effective attacks
on social problems. Thus, the recommendations of the committee are in a
sense a compromise between an ideal and political feasibility. The cost of
this compromise can be appreciated fully only when we recognize explicitly that our perception of the world and its problems and the way we
proceed to attack them are very much conditioned by the data we have
collected and processed.

A third development, which we may expect in the future, is that those
conducting regional input–output studies will more and more achieve
external economies through the use of common methodology and classifications (for commodities, sectors, and regions). Equally important,
they will have accumulated experience and will know better what they
are talking about; and their clients are likely to be more easily persuaded
and/or convinced of the value of regional and interregional input–output
studies. Thus, it will be possible to consider the implementation of the
more sophisticated interregional and multiregional input–output models,
whose requirements of export and import data are more extensive.

There is first the *pure interregional* input–output model of the senior
author, initially presented in 1951 [Isard, 1951]. This model has been
questioned on many accounts. A first question concerns the stability of
interareal interindustry coefficients. Are they more or less valid than other
types of crude coefficients that might be utilized to project import–export
magnitudes? A second question concerns the economic feasibility of
obtaining the data for developing the necessary coefficients. Obtaining the

data requires that each respondent be asked to specify (1) the distribution of his sales by sector, where each consuming sector is disaggregated by region;[4] and (2) sources, by region, of each of his inputs. As already indicated, ideally both sets of information are sought so that effective double checks can be realized; in practice, cost considerations are likely to restrict the investigator's collection effort to only one of these two sets of data.

The Philadelphia study was not very successful in obtaining satisfactory answers to these kinds of questions. Looking back, we can attribute the lack of satisfactory answers partly to our failure to pose the relevant questions sharply enough. At times our questions may have been quite confusing. Further, as already indicated, there are many merchant wholesalers both within and outside a region such as Philadelphia through whom establishments sell their output and through whom they buy their inputs. The investigator is not able to ask an establishment dealing through a wholesaler to specify the final geographic distribution of its output or the geographic distribution of sources of its inputs. Therefore, he must obtain such information from merchant wholesalers, both within and outside the region. Now, looking into the future against the background of our study, we see no reason why clear and pointed questions cannot be asked of local establishments that sell directly to industries in the different regions and buy their inputs directly from several producers in different regions. Moreover, having had the experience of interviewing wholesalers and attempting to obtain answers to all kinds of questions, we now judge that it would not be an impossible task to interview wholesalers systematically to derive, by commodity, the sources by region of their purchases and distribution by region of their sales. Then since merchant wholesalers can be viewed as a pool, à la Moses, Chenery, and Stevens type models [Moses, 1955; Chenery, 1953; Stevens, 1958], the

[4] Within this conceptual framework foreign countries together are to be viewed as an additional region. However, it is not necessary at this stage in the development of interregional input–output analysis to break down this additional region into its component sectors. It suffices to record all sales to this "additional region" in a "foreign exports" column within the final demand submatrix and all purchases from it in a "foreign imports" row (placed with the primary factors rows below the structural matrix). At times, depending on the purpose of the study, when imports of a commodity are competitive, they may be subtracted from exports to yield a single net export figure for that commodity (positive or negative) to be placed in the corresponding cell of the foreign exports column. At other times, when imports of a particular product into a given region are noncompetitive, i.e., when the product is not produced at all in the given region (such as certain food products), then the foreign imports row should be used explicitly to record imports of this commodity by consuming sector.

For procedures for developing a foreign exports column for states and regions, see Buechner [1968].

investigator can assign to each establishment that sells and buys through wholesalers a geographic pattern of sales similar to that of the wholesaler through whom it markets its output and a geographic distribution of sources of each of its inputs similar to that of the wholesaler through whom it purchases the input. As has been mentioned several times, we were able to complete successfully the Philadelphia study for 500 endogenous sectors when many scholars had said that this could not be done. We would now judge that there has been sufficient experience in input–output survey work to conclude that the time is ripe for effecting a pure interregional table.

Not all investigators may be inclined to be so bold at this time, however. Some may prefer the cruder approach of a Moses-Chenery-type model, especially if they feel that the trade coefficients thereby derived are stable and perhaps even more valid for projection purposes than interareal interindustry coefficients. Recall that a Moses-Chenery-type model posits the existence of a pool of every commodity in each region. To any commodity pool in a given region all producers of that commodity contribute, including local producers. The set of contributions then yields a geographic pattern of sources of inputs into that pool. Further, any establishment in the region that buys a commodity is postulated to obtain this commodity from its pool and thus to buy this commodity from producers in the several regions in the same proportion that these producers contribute to this pool. Such a postulate then establishes a single import pattern for each commodity applicable to all users of that commodity in that region.

The export pattern also may be established in a similar manner. Each region in a base year sells output to all other regions. We may imagine that the pattern of regional distribution of nonlocal sales of a commodity for a base year for a region is determined by conceiving that another pool of that commodity—a pool for export— comes to exist to which all producers in that region contribute. Since this pool has a geographic pattern of disposition, which is determined by the region's pattern of contributions to the pools of the commodity existing in the other regions, then this pattern of disposition can be conceived of as the geographic pattern of nonlocal sales for any producer producing that output.

Some investigators may wish to eschew entirely the pure interregional and the Moses-Chenery-type models and adopt the still cruder approach of the Leontief balanced regional input–output model [Leontief et al., 1953; Isard, 1960, pp. 345–349]. This model is currently being implemented by Leontief and Polenske[5] with certain adjustments for flows of com-

[5] See current mimeographed papers, Harvard Economic Research Project.

modity in accord with a gravity-type model. Here, national input–output coefficients are employed to derive regional input–output tables; and the geographical allocation of the exports of regions is effected a la the gravity model, whose parameters are adjusted to yield interregional flows consistent with observed data on flows and system totals. The pursuit of this approach, however, raises problems. One problem centers around the use of national coefficients, as are required to estimate for each region intermediate demand and thus total consumption of each commodity (unless data on intermediate demand are available through surveys or other sources). The difference between reported production and total consumption then represents exports or imports. Further, it usually must be assumed that for any given sector of a region there can exist either exports or imports, but not both. The crosshauling that does exist in actuality because of differences in the specialized commodities of the product mix of a sector of a region and of the product mix of the corresponding sector for the rest of the world must be precluded by assumption.

The assumption that national coefficients approximately characterize conditions of production in each of the several regions of a system is particularly strong when one does not use at least a 4-digit sector classification. Also, the assumption that no crosshauling characterizes a multiregional system is very questionable, especially when one does not use a 5- or 7-digit commodity classification. Still more, the abstracting from or the neglect of institutional ties in interregional trade represents another important unreality.

These and other strong assumptions considerably reduce the appeal of a balanced regional national-coefficients gravity-type input–output model. The strong attraction of its relatively simple data requirement gives way to its strong assumptions. It can be stated definitely that when the investigator is considering the study of a single region, and the interrelations of this region with its neighboring regions, the net advantage of such a model is indeed small and certainly does not equal that of the pure interregional model or the Moses-Chenery-type multiregional model. On the other hand, it must be stated, as the senior author has done on so many occasions, that the balanced regional input–output framework is admirably suited for an examination of the impact of alternative national policies when it is desired to consider regional implications *and* when it is not possible to consider each region in and of itself together with its interrelations with the rest of the world.

In sum, not only is it desirable but also we possess the capability to implement the several types of models just discussed. We look forward to their further development in the near future.

References

Buechner, William R. (1968). *State Estimates of Exports from the United States, 1947, 1958, 1963* (Report 9). Cambridge, Mass.: Harvard Economic Research Project.

Chenery, H. B. (1953). "Regional Analysis," in *The Structure and Growth of the Italian Economy*. Rome: U.S. Mutual Security Agency.

Isard, Walter (1951). "Interregional and Regional Input–Output Analysis: A Model of a Space-Economy," *Review of Economics and Statistics*, 33: 318–328.

———, et al. (1960). *Methods of Regional Analysis: An Introduction to Regional Science*. Cambridge, Mass.: The M.I.T. Press.

Karaska, Gerald (1966). "Interindustry Relations in the Philadelphia Economy, *The East Lakes Geographer*, 2 (August): 80–96.

Leontief, W., et al. (1953). *Studies in the Structure of the American Economy*. New York: Oxford University Press.

Leven, C. L., J. B. Legler, and P. Shapiro (1970). *An Analytical Framework for Regional Development Policy*. Cambridge, Mass.: The M.I.T. Press.

Moses, L. N. (1955). "The Stability of Interregional Trading Patterns and Input–Output Analysis," *American Economic Review*, 45: 803–832.

Polenske, Karen R. (1968). *Interim Report on the Multiregional Input–Output Research Program* (Report No. 6). Cambridge, Mass.: Harvard Economic Research Project.

Stevens, B. H. (1958). "An Interregional Linear Programming Model," *Journal of Regional Science*, 1: 60–98.

11.1 General Remarks

In the construction of an input–output table, there always comes that day of reckoning when the various magnitudes recorded must be examined for consistency. In any row the sum of the purchases listed by sectors, including the final demand sectors and estimated exports, must equal the sum of local production, estimated imports, and change in inventories; the coefficients in any column must add to unity; and so forth. Invariably, there are many inconsistencies in the recorded magnitudes of the first rough table constructed. Effort must then be given to (1) analyzing the data to account for these inconsistencies, (2) checking the validity of the data collected and the accuracy of the calculations, (3) developing estimates for at least some empty cells in the table in which the investigator has failed to obtain a complete set of information for each establishment, and (4) adjusting and juggling the processed data since the various estimates the investigator may have made do not balance. These activities must be continued until consistency of the magnitudes is established. Such dirty and gritty activities constitute what is usually called the reconciliation process.

In the Philadelphia study, we faced a full range of inconsistencies, and much effort had to be given to reconciliation. It is appropriate, therefore, to ask: What procedures were used to effect reconciliation? What lessons did we learn? How could we have been more efficient? In answering these questions we recognize, of course, that if in the first place we had done a better job of posing relevant questions, collecting information, and constructing coefficients, the task of reconciliation would have been lightened considerably. However, we must also recognize that no matter how good the work the investigator does in the first stages of an input–output study, there will always be some need for adjustment and reconciliation in the final stages.

11.2 Dummy Sectors

It is often necessary and appropriate to construct dummy (fictitious) sectors in order to adjust for certain unavoidable gaps in the responses to questionnaires. Frequently, the data that are required to account fully for the sales of the output of a sector cannot be obtained realistically by interview. At best the data may be reported irregularly and/or in a manner not suitable for direct incorporation into the table. A classic example of this is the case of office supplies. The investigator cannot expect each establishment to maintain, let alone report, a detailed breakdown of items —paper, paper clips, carbon ribbons, pencils, pens, folders, and so on— purchased in the general office supplies category. There are so many items that fall in this category and are consumed in relatively small quantities by most establishments that these establishments do not keep systematic records on the purchases of these items. Therefore, it becomes necessary to construct a dummy sector to handle in a systematic way both the production of these items for local needs and the local purchases of them. Into the column of this dummy sector in the flows table all sectors producing office supplies deliver some fraction of their outputs in order to meet local needs. The total output of this dummy (fictitious) sector is then distributed among the cells of its row; that is, it is assigned to all sectors purchasing such supplies in accord with the estimates of inputs per dollar output by sector. Frequently, the investigator may use the same common estimate of such inputs per dollar output for all sectors that fall within a category such as light manufacturing, or professional services, or agriculture.

A slightly more sophisticated treatment of a dummy sector—e.g., office supplies—may involve the construction of different modules. One module pertaining to the use of office supply items in a certain fixed-proportions pattern might apply to one category of consuming sectors (such as heavy manufacturing); and another module pertaining to the use of office supply items in a different fixed-proportions pattern might apply to another category of consuming sectors (such as professional services). Although the adoption of this approach represents an improvement, it does raise problems of data collection for the proper determination of applicable modules.

The preceding illustrates a procedure regarding dummy sectors with a category, office supplies, for which the use of the items covered by it may be regarded to be in fixed proportions. However, it may be necessary to develop other dummy sectors whose component items cannot be said to be consumed in relatively fixed proportions. Such is the case with respect to maintenance and repair construction and transportation services.

In the case of the former, most establishments cannot be expected to know the breakdown of expenditures by construction trades (electrical, mechanical, masonry, carpentry, etc.) that might have been involved in the various maintenance and repair jobs performed for them. Realistically, these establishments can be expected to report only the total dollar cost of these jobs. But here, unlike the case of office supplies, the breakdown of items in the diverse repair jobs done for the establishments of a sector can be expected to vary considerably among sectors. In the case of transportation services, most establishments that pay for inputs at purchasers' prices cannot be expected to know the breakdown of the total transportation cost by mode of transportation for each input purchased. They possibly may know the transport costs in aggregate for those items on which they paid transportation charges directly. However, neither they nor the investigator have any realistic notion of how the total transport bill over all purchased inputs breaks down by mode of transportation. Moreover, again unlike the office supplies case, the breakdown of transport costs by mode of transportation over all purchased inputs for the establishments of a sector can be expected to vary greatly among sectors.

Despite the variation in the proportion of purchases of the several dummy sector items by different establishments and sectors, it still is necessary to account for the use of those outputs of producing sectors delivered to the dummy sector. That is, in the case of maintenance and repair construction it is still necessary to assign the outputs of such building trades as the electrical contractors and the plumbing contractors; and in the case of transportation services, we still need to assign fractions of the output of such sectors as the railroad industry, water transportation, and trucking to local consumers. A feasible procedure, then, is to allocate the output among consuming sectors using the investigator's best estimates of inputs of dummy-sector product per dollar output by consuming sector, or by category of consuming sectors. It is to be recognized, of course, that errors in the use of the data for projection will arise because such estimates assume fixed proportions in the use of the component products of the dummy sector. The errors, of course, relate to the composition of the total output of the dummy sectors, that is, to the amounts delivered from producing sectors to the dummy sectors, and to the magnitudes of inputs directly and indirectly required to produce these amounts. Again, the use of modules, if they can be developed, may somewhat reduce the size of these projection errors.[1]

It should be noted that the use of a dummy sector also is appropriate in situations where establishments purchase small quantities of many diverse items that can be aggregated into a single category, such as is the case for office supplies. Here the investigator wishes to avoid the problem of having coefficients being rounded to zero (even when he calculates coefficients to six decimal places), because at a 4-digit SIC level the purchases of any single item—say, a single office supply item—might be negligible in terms of the consuming industry. By using a dummy sector, this problem is encountered less frequently, since for any consuming sector the coefficient for the dummy is the sum of the coefficients for the constituent items.[2]

---

[1] Another source of error arises from the use of a dummy sector, or modules for a dummy sector, when an iterative approach is employed. Such use results in the setting back by one round of the demand for the items of that sector. In general, however, when the number of iterations is five or more, the error generated becomes negligible in size.

[2] Another kind of dummy sector, which was not used in the Philadelphia study, may be employed when, for example, secondary products are to be reallocated. Along the row corresponding to the dummy sector the amount of the commodity to be reallocated appears as a negative magnitude in the cell corresponding to any sector out of which the commodity is to be transferred, and as a positive magnitude in the cell for any sector into which the commodity is to be transferred. Along the row, both negative and positive entries must balance to zero.

11.3 Row Reconciliation and the Undistributed Column

Once the relevant allocations have been made through the use of dummy sectors, it becomes necessary to examine systematically each row and then each column for consistency. Consistency for each row is simply defined as "supply equals demand" for the output of the associated sector. That is, regional production *plus* imports *equals* intermediate demand *plus* final demand (by households, investors, and government) *plus* exports. In the Philadelphia study all these items except imports were estimated from primary sources. It was thus possible to derive imports as a residual item. As previously indicated, errors were most obvious when the magnitude of imports as a residual was negative. We have already indicated a number of adjustments that were made when such was the case.

Before adjustments, there existed imbalances in many rows for several reasons. One was that there were several commodities that were consumed in relatively small amounts by numerous sectors. The case of lubricating oils has already been cited. Clearly, if in a study the investigator has available enough resources and can ask questions and insist upon answers to questions on the consumption of such items, he can avoid some of this imbalance. But surely there will always be some items whose consumption is so minor that the investigator judges that it is not worthwhile to spend the necessary time and effort to collect and process information on them. Accordingly, at the end of the study, he must adjust upward the reported purchases of the output of this sector by consuming sectors so that the "supply equals demand" relationship can be achieved. When it is not possible to account fully for regional production after adjustments of intermediate demand, and even after reasonable adjustments of the other magnitudes (final demand and exports) in the "supply equals demand" relationship, then the discrepancy must be entered into the appropriate cell of the undistributed column, as had to be done in the Philadelphia study.

A second reason for imbalance lies in improper accounting practice on the part of the reporting establishments. For example, consider accounting practices with respect to newspaper advertising, which can be considered the primary product of the newspaper sector since most of the revenue of major newspapers originates from sales of advertising services. Too frequently, the direct purchases of advertising from newspapers are reported by an establishment not as newspaper advertising but rather as expenditures under such general categories as advertising, public relations, or communications. Consequently, the recorded inputs of newspaper advertising by consuming sector are greatly underestimated.

It therefore becomes necessary to adjust the technical coefficients along the newspaper sector row so as to account fully for newspaper advertising. When cost and other factors make it impossible to allocate entirely all newspaper advertising, after the export and other final demands have been fully accounted for, then the remainder of local output must be assigned to the undistributed demand column.

A third reason for row imbalance is closely related to the second— namely, improper accounting for secondary product production. Because of practices we adopted (see Chapter 6), regional production of most sectors includes the value of output of secondary products. However, when establishments report their inputs, they report their inputs by commodity and so by industry producing a commodity as primary product. Hence, the technical coefficients derived for each sector are in terms of the inputs of the primary products of sectors. Thus, the total demand for the output of a sector tends to be the demand for its primary product only, which may be much less or greater than its value of total production (inclusive of value of secondary products). When the total demand is less, as will be the case when the commodity regarded as the sector's primary product is produced only by that sector (that is, when its primary product is not produced as a secondary product by other sectors), and when that sector does produce secondary products, then the total value of the sector's secondary products may be placed in the relevant cell of the undistributed demand column. Sometimes, however, when we had to estimate imports for the primary product of that sector (in situations in which we knew there were imports), we tended to underestimate imports (derived as a residual item) in order to avoid placing too large a magnitude in the undistributed demand column. (Or perhaps sometimes we tended to overstate exports and other final demands.)

In the cases in which the total demand for the output of a sector is greater than its value of total production, the given sector may not be producing much secondary product, whereas other sectors may be producing as secondary product a considerable amount of the commodity regarded as primary product of the given sector. Not being able to recognize the existence of such a situation, the investigator tends to overstate imports for that sector and perhaps to understate exports and other final demands. In none of these cases is there occasion to make entries in the undistributed demand column.

There are a host of other reasons why imbalances crop up. For example, differential pricing systems and discriminatory pricing practices, as occurred in the dairy sectors in the Philadelphia study, can raise havoc for the investigator when some allocations are tied to physical units of output while inputs or deliveries are reported by using sectors in dollar terms. The reader is referred to our *Working Papers* [Isard, Langford, and Romanoff, 1966–1968] for details on some of these questions.

Theoretically, it can be argued that a number of these problems should not occur. Some of the items in the undistributed demand column would not crop up if we were to do the study again, simply because we now know better what kinds of questions to ask. Over half the total dollar value of the undistributed items is accounted for by the outputs from non-manufacturing sectors. Since we learned that we should have given more attention to obtaining primary data on the purchases by the manufacturing sectors of these service outputs and would seek such data more vigorously in a new study, a large number of the entries in the undistributed demand column would not appear. Also, we know that at least one way partially to overcome this problem is to introduce at the early stages of a study design the ability to specify an unallocated category for groups (cluster or aggregates) of commodities or materials. Such a practice would allow the undistributed sector to be disaggregated into component sectors such that there could be an undistributed sector for extractive materials, one for manufactured products, one for services, and so forth. If this could be done effectively, then at a later stage in the reconciliation process appropriate adjustments could be made more easily and perhaps more satisfactorily.

The preceding comments are rather general. We may now ask what specific procedures were used in the Philadelphia study in adjusting technical production coefficients and effecting row reconciliation. Typically, we used proportional assignment and adjustment. For example, the OBE national data on flows and technical coefficients were used to allocate business services across the board to all using sectors. Next, Internal Revenue Service data at a detailed level were used to estimate advertising expenditures for each sector, and these expenditures were separated from business services. Then, for each sector a certain percentage was taken from the advertising expenditures to represent newspaper advertising. The corresponding dollar amount was subtracted from advertising expenditures for each sector and assigned to expenditures on inputs from the newspaper sector.

A second, more satisfactory procedure was to review carefully the allocation of certain basic inputs, especially when the reported data did not conform to an expected or meaningful pattern. For example, we found it necessary to review the allocation of textile inputs into the apparel industry, and paper and selected printing services inputs into the printing industries. Our experience indicates that we should have conducted many more such reviews in our Philadelphia study.

After all feasible adjustments of technical production coefficients and demand magnitudes were made and reviews conducted, we then assigned the residuals to the undistributed demand sector. These residuals and their total were then to be compared for consistency with the residuals of the undistributed inputs row to be discussed later.

Observe that the undistributed demand column was used primarily to achieve balance. In particular, it was used to avoid estimates of negative imports that we know were errors, or in some cases to insure a level of positive imports of which we were fairly certain. Accordingly, the undistributed demand column must be viewed as a set of inputs for local production and should be included within the structural matrix. However, we do not consider it wise to view the undistributed demand column as a *not elsewhere classified* (n.e.c.) sector. The coefficients of an n.e.c. sector, e.g., SIC 3999, relate to production of a specific set of goods or services and imply some stability. Such a statement cannot be made for any coefficients derived for the undistributed demand column, which does not represent production.

It is to be noted that there are certain consistency checks and guidelines that can be applied to the entries in the undistributed demand column. First, in general, the size of the coefficient that results for any cell in the undistributed demand column of the coefficients table does not have significance, for if there is only one entry in the undistributed demand column, and if this entry itself is fairly small or even insignificant in dollar magnitude, the value of the coefficient in that cell still will be unity.

The significant magnitudes are the dollar values in the cells of the undistributed column in the flow table and the percentage that the dollar value in any cell is of the total output of its corresponding sector. Even here, however, it is difficult to provide any guidelines, at least on the basis of our experience. We cannot specify any maximum dollar magnitude or percentage figure below which an entry in a cell should fall. Clearly, for the commodities that are consumed in small quantities by many industries, the percentage figure can be relatively large without introducing serious error into projections and impact analyses; and since the investigator may wish to avoid the large expense involved in collecting the data directly on these items from establishments (or even in attempting to work out refined methods for the allocation of the undistributed sales), a relatively high percentage of output in undistributed outputs can be tolerated and need not indicate low-quality work. Of course, these percentages may be reduced by a simple across-the-board allocation, for example, an allocation in terms of percent of the grand total of the output of all sectors. However, such an allocation would be misleading and might not help significantly to reduce error.

Also, it is possible that there may exist a single large absolute dollar figure in the undistributed demand column that at the same time corresponds to a relatively small percentage of the output of the corresponding sector. This situation need not be cause for concern, especially if one is aware that errors may exist concomitantly because of the inability of a study to identify imports.

A real concern should exist when there is an entry in a cell of the undistributed demand column that is large in both absolute and percentage terms. Then some additional work should be undertaken, including perhaps some reinterviewing, depending upon the resources and time remaining for the study.

11.4 Column Reconciliation and the Undistributed Row

Once row balance is achieved for each sector, it is then necessary to examine systematically the columns and to achieve column balance by sector. Such balance is achieved for a sector when its set of full coefficients adds to unity.

In proceeding with this check in the Philadelphia study, it was also highly desirable to disaggregate the nonwage portion of the value-added residual. For the most part, primary and regional data were not available for the major component items: nonwage employee benefits, dividends and retained earnings, and capital allowance (amortization, depreciation, and depletion). As indicated in our *Working Papers*, these items were estimated on the basis of the Internal Revenue Service data for different size-classes of firms by industry.

After the major component items were estimated, the remaining residual for each of the columns was disaggregated into two parts. One part yielded a dollar value figure from which we derived a coefficient for an undistributed inputs row to be included in the structural matrix. The coefficients of this row corresponded to a total value of undistributed inputs equal to the total value of the demands in the undistributed demand column. A second part yielded a set of residuals to be viewed as an "unspecified import" row, which was not balanced in dollar magnitude with the imports in the import column. This unspecified import row was not included in the structural matrix. For full discussion of procedures used, see our *Working Papers*.

Reference

Isard, Walter, Thomas W. Langford, and Eliahu Romanoff (1966–1968). *Philadelphia Region Input–Output Study, Working Papers*, Volumes 1–4. Philadelphia: Regional Science Research Institute.

12.1 General Remarks

There is one part of the Philadelphia study, as originally conceived, that remains relatively untouched as we write this book—the part that was to develop an intraregional flow matrix and explore intraregional analysis with the use of a regional input–output table. This part of the study remains incomplete because the request for renewal of one of our research grants occurred during the spring and fall of 1968—a time of cutbacks in federal research grants. When the renewal request was finally approved in mid-1969, the key personnel associated with the Philadelphia study were engaged in other basic research projects and it was not possible to find substitute personnel with similar experience and expertise. Also, it should be indicated that from a psychological standpoint, there was little motivation on the part of the senior personnel to reinitiate input–output studies. At that time, a steady six-years' dose of regional input–output was enough. However, although this part of the study remains incomplete, we learned some valuable lessons.

Early in the Philadelphia study, we decided that it would be desirable to explore intraregional analysis within a regional input–output framework. We decided to consider a single county and its relations with the rest of the metropolitan region. Bucks County was chosen.

The mixed structure of this county was of interest for study. The northern portion of Bucks county was and still remains predominantly in agricultural production. The southern portion of the county has experienced extremely rapid growth both in population (Levittown) and in economic activity (U.S. Steel, Benjamin Fairless Works). The county was experiencing growth from the suburbanization of the existing municipalities within the county and of the greater Philadelphia region in general. Of interest, too, was the fact that Bucks County was oriented to different degrees to three urbanized areas: the Allentown-Bethlehem-Easton SMSA, the greater New York metropolitan region, and the greater Philadelphia metropolitan region. We recognized, however, that this situation would make analysis much more difficult.

Another factor that was important in the choice of Bucks County as a county to be studied was the fact that it had an excellent and progressive planning agency in 1963 that was responsible for the development of a high-quality set of data for the county. We therefore judged that an effective survey could be achieved easily.

It should be noted that there were other though less-important reasons why we wanted to focus upon a county such as Bucks County. We wished to study a small region as an entity, since such a region, when it is an open economy, poses many issues in a different light than does a large metropolitan region. One issue is the strategic importance of exports and imports. Another is the question of the differences in technology that may be associated with size and spatial position, after adjustment for differences in technology and capital vintage.

12.2 Lessons Learned

We were successful in interviewing most of the manufacturing establishments in Bucks County. We were able to obtain the relatively high coverage in terms of employment of 74.2 percent.[1] We also gathered excellent data for mining and wholesale and retail trade. However, our questionnaires for other sectors were not adequately structured to provide appropriate data that might depict for each of these sectors the technological differences between Bucks County and the rest of the region.

Once this rather good set of primary data was obtained, we unfortunately were not in a position to exploit it. Preliminary exercises were done on the data by students who were seeking research training with us. One exercise explored the construction of a Bucks County flow table, within the framework of a pure interregional model. In this model, there were three regions: Bucks County, the rest of the Philadelphia region, and the rest of the world. Because of lack of time and resources, this exploration concentrated on the Bucks County manufacturing sectors only and crudely aggregated the 4-digit SIC manufacturing sectors to a 3-digit level. Further, there was time to consider only the input side of these sectors. In particular, for each 3-digit sector there were identified the inputs that came from Bucks County itself, those from the rest of Philadelphia, and those from the rest of the world. Figure 12.1 sketches the three-region pure interregional table; the shaded area indicates the parts for which data were processed.

There were some lessons learned from this and other exercises. Perhaps the most important one is that when data are available on a 4-digit basis, as they were for Bucks County, they should not be aggregated to form 3-digit or other sectors when coefficients are to be constructed, except for unusual situations. It is difficult to define appropriate weights for the various 4-digit sectors so that an aggregate sector emerges with the proper product mix. The technical production coefficients that result from the weighted averaging of data usually are not too relevant, and the implied product mix generally is inaccurate for most of the situations in which the investigator desires to pursue projections and impact analysis.

Further, a rather intractable problem arises when the investigator tries to develop trade coefficients for the aggregate sectors, that is, to associate with these sectors sales by region and input purchases by region. Part of

---

[1] We were not able to conduct interviews with the two largest establishments within the region, both being plants of large national corporations. Excluding these two establishments, the sample coverage represented 92.2 percent of the remaining manufacturing employment.

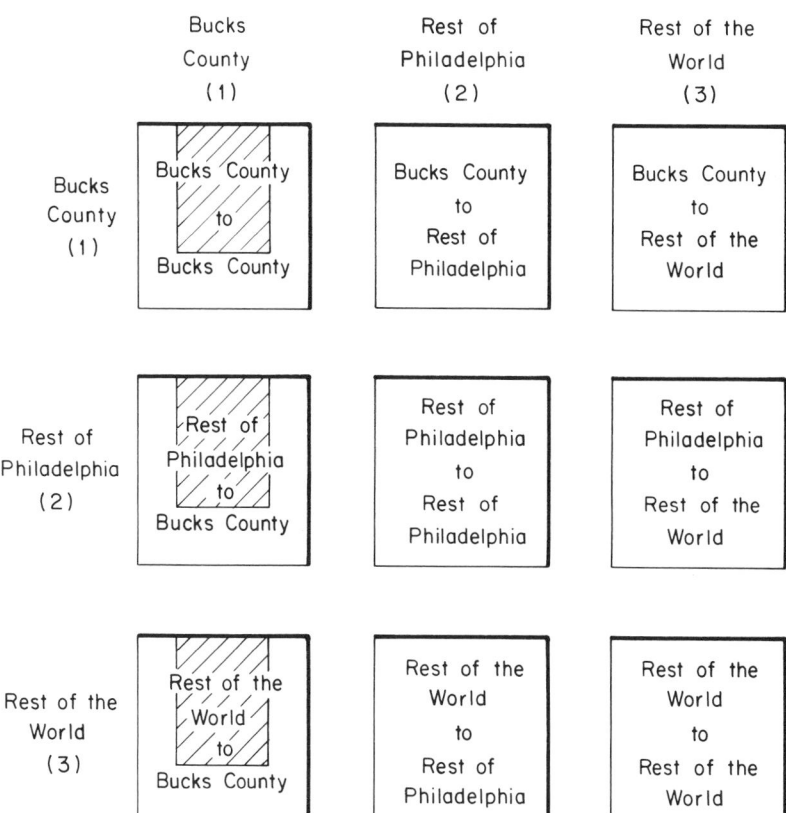

Figure 12.1. Bucks County Interregional Input–Output Table.

this problem arises because the parameters that are used to distribute a given region's exports among other regions, or to determine the region's imports from other regions, are sensitive to the type of commodity being traded. When several commodities are lumped together and associated with a single aggregate sector, the new parameters that are estimated to apply to the product mix of the aggregate sector are not really applicable when each of the other regions does not ship to the given region amounts of these commodities in the same proportion as the product mix, or import from the given region amounts of these commodities in the same proportion as the product mix. This point may be particularly significant in the treatment of smaller regions, which are often more highly specialized with respect to both exports and imports than larger regions.

In short, the investigator should preserve the detailed sectoring for all operations, and should aggregate only after the results are in and when it is desirable to do so for presentation purposes. In fact, as already suggested several times, if there is to be deviation from the 4-digit scheme of primary data, it should be in the direction of further disaggregation by 5- or 7-digit commodities, so as to reflect better the unique features of a subarea or county being studied.

Other points that were apparent at the beginning of our Bucks County work were reinforced by the experience. An input–output study of any suburban area that is to be interconnected with an input–output study for the larger region of which it is a part must involve a careful survey of households of the suburban area. At the minimum, two sets of data must be obtained. One set should relate to a breakdown of the expenditures for households, or each household subsector, in terms of goods purchased in the suburban area and goods purchased in the rest of the region. A second set should relate to the extent to which the workers of the suburban area find employment in the rest of the metropolitan region. Such data are desirably disaggregated by occupation or other characteristic to permit association with specific industries. At the minimum, the data should be obtained and processed so that for each economic sector of the "rest of the region," the investigator can identify the fraction of the labor force that comes from the area under study.

We appreciated the vital importance of these points when we tried to conduct impact analysis in terms of the Bucks County area. Such was not possible with the primary data on just mining, manufacturing, whole-saling, and retail trade.

12.3 Some Other General Issues

There are a number of interesting issues to consider for a study with input–output methodology of a suburban area within a large metro-politan region. A first issue is *how* to obtain a full understanding of the basic linkages of the economic sectors within a suburban area and their basic interconnections with the rest of the metropolitan region. Can this be achieved more efficiently and accurately if we (1) collect primary data comprehensively and process them systematically or (2) impute relation-ships for the suburban area on the basis of a good set of primary data for the larger region, in conjunction with theory, secondary data for the suburban area, and responses from households, government agencies, and establishments to a few key questions on expenditures, sources of pur-chases, and distribution of sales? This issue is particularly relevant if the suburban county being studied has a relatively high growth rate and if, as a consequence, its technical production coefficients derived for a base year become outdated very rapidly. The issue may be even more acute when the economy of the suburban area is dominated by the house-holds, government, and export (import) sectors—that is, when the mag-nitude of both the household and government expenditures plus exports (and imports) far outweighs the value of transactions among the other diverse economic sectors within the area.

There is no single best answer to this question. The answer must depend, of course, upon how detailed an understanding the investigator seeks, how similar the suburban economic structure is to that of the rest of the region, how good the primary data that already exist for the total region are, how good the primary data that can be collected for the suburban area with the resources on hand can be, how good the secondary data for the suburban area are, and finally, how much validity the investigator wishes to assign to the theory at hand. Thus, the investigator may well conclude in certain situations that it is not relevant to conduct a study with input–output methodology for a suburban area like Bucks County. On the other hand, the investigator may easily reach the opposite conclusion, as we did.

Although there were shortcomings in the preliminary analysis for Bucks County, although it would have been desirable to have developed and presented data for all the sectors for Bucks County, and although the Bucks County data should have been made consistent with the Philadelphia data as finally reconciled, certain statements based on the experience can be made. One is that a pure interregional model, such as a model that involves a county, the rest of a metropolitan region, and the rest of the United States, is clearly an operational model. It merely takes time and effort to develop it. Furthermore, in the development of such a model the efficient use of available resources may well suggest that the investigator deviate significantly from following the same sectoring scheme for each region. While it would be ideal to maintain 4-digit detail for all three of the regions, an analyst can easily see that for the rest of the nation much aggregation can occur among those manufacturing sectors that do not have direct linkages to the county of study and the rest of the metropolitan region without appreciably affecting the validity of projections for the county. Moreover, as already indicated, the investigator can seek 5- to 7-digit detail for both the county and the rest of the metropolitan region and for different commodity classifications. Nor need the same kinds of questions be asked of a given sector's establishments within the county as of those in the rest of the metropolitan region. More attention might be paid, for example, to certain details of intracounty sales and expenditures.

Finally, it would seem that sometime in the future a bold investigator may pursue a metropolitan region study with a pure interregional framework wherein each major metropolitan subarea, as a region in itself, is thoroughly studied in terms of internal structure, exports to and imports from the sectors of each other subarea, and exports to and imports from sectors of the rest of the nation. Certainly such a table would lead to great improvement in intrametropolitan analysis and greater understanding of internal interdependencies.

In a regional input–output study, the process of obtaining an inverse and using it is not as simple as most analysts conceive it to be. Moreover, the decisions regarding the form and type of an inverse are critical, especially as the size of the coefficient matrix increases. Like the choice of a region or the choice of a sector classification scheme, these decisions are highly dependent on the problems to be studied. Some of the more relevant questions that arise relate to (1) whether a table of "full" technical coefficients or "reduced" coefficients should be inverted if an inverse is to be used; (2) whether or not a triangularization procedure for computation of indirect effects is justified; and (3) whether or not a round-by-round iterative computation of indirect effects is superior to the use of an inverse. We shall consider these issues in turn.

13.1 The Inversion of a Table of "Full" or "Reduced" Coefficients

At the time the technical production coefficient table for the Philadelphia region was completed and we were prepared for an application, we judged that the most relevant problem at hand was the possible impact of cutback in Vietnam War involvement upon the Philadelphia region economy. Shortly after we focused attention on this problem, we became aware of a conflict in the use of input–output for regional policy formulation and for national (or multiregional) policy formulation. This conflict arose in connection with the issue of the kind of inverse that we should apply; for confronted with the problem of inverting a 500 order matrix with coefficients of six decimal digits—we had no knowledge of any previous inversion of such a large table, and it was necessary to develop our own computer program—and faced with depleted resources, we had no thoughts whatsoever of deriving two or more different types of inverses. We could conceive of developing only one type of inverse.

Two types of inverses came to mind. One would be based on full technical production coefficients, regardless of whether an input of some commodity was furnished 100 percent by local producers or only in part.[1] A second type of inverse would be based on reduced technical production coefficients—that is, coefficients derived from the reduction of the technical production coefficients by the percent by which the input was provided through imports. More specifically, if only 40 percent of the steel used in a steel fabrication operation is furnished by local

---

[1] When a commodity is wholly imported, so that the local production of the sector producing that commodity as primary output is zero, then a table of full technical production coefficients does not contain any coefficients corresponding to the use of a commodity that is wholly imported. This practice can give rise to errors in many situations and represents one of the shortcomings of traditional input–output practice when the imports are not properly specified in an import row below the structural matrix and appropriately projected by a side computation.

producers, then the reduced coefficient pertaining to the steel input would be 40 percent of the technical production coefficient.[2]

On first thought, we were inclined to employ the second type of inverse —the inverse based on reduced coefficients. We reasoned, as in the Fairless Steel study, that our projection of the indirect impact of the Vietnam War on the Philadelphia region should exclude the impact upon the producers in other regions who were exporting commodities to Philadelphia. Our concern was after all with the problem of the Philadelphia region, although we did recognize that by excluding the indirect impact upon regions exporting to Philadelphia we were also excluding impacts upon Philadelphia exports via changes in the demand for Philadelphia's products by consumers in these regions. But our inability to catch such interregional feedback effects by a regional input–output model has always been considered one of the legitimate costs of failing to implement an interregional input–output model.

On deeper thought, however, this line of reasoning proved unacceptable. We soon came to appreciate the fact that changes in Vietnam War expenditures were national changes. They lead to direct as well as indirect effects in all regions in a nation. If we were to have for each region an input–output table like the Philadelphia one and to construct an inverse for each region based on reduced technical coefficients and not the actual, then we would be ignoring all changes in import–export magnitudes of all regions. In the case of Philadelphia we would be ignoring the major impact upon its exports by the aggregate of all other regions in the nation, each of which is directly impacted by Vietnam War expenditures. More important, we would greatly underestimate the national impacts that might logically be derived by summing the impacts upon the several regions; for obviously, the national impacts derived from the use of regional inverses based on many coefficients that are significantly smaller than the actual technical production coefficients are bound to be different from national impacts derived from the use of the full technical production coefficients in the inverse of a national table.[3] Further, we would not be in a position to coordinate effectively regional and national (multiregional) planning.

[2] For cases in which reduced coefficients have been used, although in a round-by-round iteration, see Isard and Kuenne, 1953; Coughlin and Langford, 1969; Coughlin, Douglas, Langford and Stevens, 1970.

[3] To provide some notion of the size of the discrepancy that can be involved, we note that in a study of the direct and indirect total dollar impact of the Frankford Arsenal on the Philadelphia economy, the use of the inverse based on unreduced coefficients gave an estimate of $400 million, whereas the use of reduced technical coefficients for 12 rounds of iteration yielded an estimate of $360 million [Langford, 1969].

Hence, we chose to invert the table of Philadelphia technical production coefficients unreduced by the extent of imports. Thereby the inverse is perhaps not too useful for examining strictly local impacts—say, of a Fairless Steel Works—but it is generally useful in examining the impacts of diverse federal programs (such as poverty and other social welfare programs) in which each program is of a multiregional character. That is, in our situation the conflict regarding which inverse to derive was resolved in favor of the needs for national (multiregional) planning rather than regional planning, primarily because of the nature of the problem being examined.

Note, however, that the particular choice of the inverse that was made leads to two specific types of error in projection. One type arises because we were not able to project those changes in the components of the Philadelphia export vector stemming from the changes in the import demands of other regions for Philadelphia products because of the direct impacts of the Vietnam War expenditures on these other regions.

A second type of error arises from the fact that the use of full technical production coefficients leads to overestimation of the change in local industries that produce a given primary product that is both produced locally and imported. This point follows since all the inputs of this primary product required (released) directly and indirectly by growth (contraction) in all the sectors of the Philadelphia region are provided by increase (decrease) of local production and *not* of local production *and* imports.

These two types of errors constitute major shortcomings of the approach we have taken. It can be argued, of course, that we must adjust the results (from the use of unadjusted coefficients) at least crudely to account for the changed levels and composition of both Philadelphia imports and exports to be anticipated. While it is questionable whether we can do so, it is also clear that if we were able to, we would have a generally useful tool. For we would be able to make projections of other economies on the basis of an application of the inverse of unadjusted Philadelphia coefficients—where the magnitudes yielded by this inverse would need to be adjusted to take into account the particular import–export pattern and competitive cost positions of these other economies.

Another alternative exists, of course, when one has sufficient resources to construct and use consistently both types of inverses—one based on the full technical production coefficients, the other based on the reduced technical production coefficients. We know that the errors in the latter are errors of underestimation, though not by the same percent for all sectors. We know that the errors in the former are errors resulting from the fact that the Philadelphia export vector cannot be developed properly without detailed knowledge of interrelations of the Philadelphia sectors to sectors in each of the other regions of the United States—that is, without the knowledge that would be incorporated in an interregional input–output table. Therefore, having both inverses on hand and in use, the investigator may obtain certain insights from a comparison of the different magnitudes resulting from their use. He might also acquire insight into ways and means by which a region's particular import–export patterns and competitive cost positions may be used to modify the projections for it based on unadjusted coefficients and unadjusted export vectors.

Others might find it valuable to know the range of estimates for any variable that the two inverses would provide. As already mentioned, the inverse based on reduced technical production coefficients clearly provides minimum estimates of projected magnitudes. The second inverse, based on full technical production coefficients, does provide estimates that are not minimum estimates; however, they are not maximum estimates either, since the impact upon certain sectors may still be underestimated because the export demand for their output may be underestimated.

There are other points to be made. Suppose that the investigator does decide that a reduced technical production coefficients matrix should be employed. He still confronts the problem of how to determine what portion of any technical production coefficient is furnished from imports. For example, although for 1959 we estimated the percentages of aggregate intermediate regional demand for every commodity and service that was furnished by local suppliers and by importers, it is questionable whether all the coefficients along any row should be reduced by the same import percentage factor. It seems unreasonable to assume that all purchasing sectors buy a particular input from local suppliers and importers in the same ratio. Yet no other simple criterion is available for immediate use.

Moreover, it is questionable whether the "average" percentage of a commodity that was supplied locally, as estimated for the base year 1959 and as reflecting the total operation of an economy, should be applied to *changes* in intermediate demand generated by changes in final demand. It is clear that if we were to assume greater elasticity in the supply of a commodity from importers than in that from local suppliers, the use of average percentages would overstate the impact on the local economy. Yet again, there is no simple criterion that we can employ to adjust our import and local supply percentages upward and downward, respectively.

Also, we must recognize that once technical input–output coefficients are adjusted (based on knowledge of the local economy's import patterns, competitive cost position, etc.) to reflect only the percentage of each input that is supplied locally, and once these adjusted coefficients are inverted, the resulting inverse has little, if any, value for use in studies of other regional economies. For example, if we were to invert a table of adjusted Philadelphia coefficients, the resulting matrix would reflect the unique import and competitive cost position of Philadelphia and would not have much potential for application in the study of other metropolitan regions. On the other hand, as we have already noted, an inverse based on the full technical production coefficients of Philadelphia seems to be applicable to some extent for the study of other metropolitan regions somewhat similar to Philadelphia—such as Baltimore and Boston.

13.2 Triangularization

Another question that arises concerns triangularization. Triangularization consists of ordering the sectors such that the cells with nonzero entries approximate a right triangle. There are several ways to effect the triangularization. One way involves placing at the top rows of the table those sectors that sell exclusively to final demand. The next rows are assigned to a second set of sectors that sell only to one or more sectors of the first set, and perhaps also to final demand. The third subset of rows is assigned to those sectors that sell only to one or more sectors in the second set and perhaps also to final demand and sectors in the first set, and so forth. Finally, at the bottom of the table is placed those sectors that sell goods to one or more sectors in the previous set and perhaps also to final demand and other sectors in the matrix.

There are, of course, other ways to triangularize. The investigator can start at the bottom, or turn the table 90 degrees to the right or to the left. Each way may be said to have its own advantages and disadvantages. No one way is best, and each does achieve the major goal of triangularization. If the structure of an economy is such that it can be represented in triangularized form, then it is no longer necessary to derive an inverse to estimate the impacts of changes in final demand. Direct computation of required output, sector by sector, is possible.

A more important consideration, however, is that whenever triangularization is possible, it permits the investigator to see more clearly certain aspects of the interdependence of an economy. It casts light on how sectors do and do not cluster, it helps isolate industrial complexes, and so forth.

It is to be recognized fully that perhaps only a relatively few economies can be triangularized effectively. Yet while the deviations from strict triangularity may preclude the exploitation of triangularization for direct computation of required outputs, these deviations may not be so numerous or major as to preclude the additional insight into interdependence that the attempt at triangularization exposes.

It is also to be pointed out that the extent to which triangularization is achieved depends on the degree of disaggregation and definition of sectors, the treatment of secondary products, the definition of region, and numerous other factors. One classification scheme or set of definitions might yield an adequate triangular representation for one regional economy; another scheme for the same economy may not.

In the Philadelphia study, it was clear that we wished to derive an inverse, if for no other reason than to demonstrate that a 500 order coefficient table could be inverted. Once an inverse is obtained, then of course the cost of each additional use of the inverse is relatively small. An investigator is therefore no longer particularly motivated to triangularize in order to ease the problem of computing direct and indirect effects of diverse impacts. It may be that in later stages of our Philadelphia study we may attempt triangularization to expose certain structural interdependencies that we have not thus far observed. However, for such a complex economy as the Philadelphia region, we do not anticipate either much success at triangularization, given our highly disaggregated sectoring scheme, or the disclosure of much new basic information. Our chief concern is still with the identification of the level of disaggregation and the classification system that is most meaningful for the numerous impact studies of interest for metropolitan regional planning and development.

13.3 The Inverse Versus Round-by-Round Iteration

We have now discussed some of the issues involved in the determination of what kind of inverse to construct, and also some of the circumstances under which triangularization of the matrix of coefficients can replace the inverse. There remains still another basic question, namely, the relative advantages of the inverse when compared to a round-by-round iteration for the calculation of direct and indirect effects of changes. To this question we now turn.

A first issue concerns the efficient use of time of research personnel and the cost of computation. It is clear that when impacts are to be examined for a very large number of final demand vectors based on a matrix of technical production coefficients, reduced or unreduced—*without* the introduction of changes in technology, changes in the percentage of any technical production coefficient accounted for by imports, or any other adjustments internal to the structural matrix—then the use of the inverse is highly desirable. Such use involves major savings in time and cost. At the other extreme, when the research necessitates making modifications of the coefficients in successive applications, then the round-by-round iterative approach is far superior. The iterative approach has significantly greater flexibility in permitting changes in coefficients, and is by far cheaper when only a relatively few applications of a given coefficient table are to be made.

The basis for the preceding statements in part derives from our Philadelphia experience. The cost of computer time for a sufficient number of round-by-round iterations in a single application of the Philadelphia 496 order coefficients matrix with eight iterations on an IBM 360-75 system is approximately $60 (March 1970). In contrast, the cost of inverting the matrix, including the necessary programming skill, which did not exist within the project, ran to approximately $4,000 to $5,000 (1968). However, the larger part of the cost was for programming services, since acceptable "canned" programs for inverting a matrix of 496 order, with coefficients of six decimal digits, at double precision did not exist. Such cost would not be incurred if an investigator had an acceptable program for the computer system available to him. Nonetheless, the cost of inverting the matrix would be significantly greater than the cost of a round-by-round iteration; we would estimate that the inversion would cost at least twenty times as much as a single iterative solution. This factor suggests that the point at which the investigator considers using an inverse rather than a round-by-round iteration is when he anticipates that the number of applications of a single given matrix is of the order of twenty or more.

A second issue in considering the relative merits of each procedure relates to the way in which an investigator wishes to check computations. It is clear that the use of an inverse has a certain mathematical elegance. Also, the inverse does yield results that, strictly speaking, are more precise than the results of a round-by-round iteration. On the other hand, in view of the errors inherent in the basic data from which coefficients are derived, such an increase in the precision of results is trivial. The real issue is a practical one. Here some analysts would assert that the use of an inverse does not allow for the continuing checks for inconsistencies and unreasonable assumptions that a round-by-round iteration permits. In the round-by-round approach, they contend, the investigator can see the implications of a bill of goods for the first round of input requirements and expansions and at this point can check for inconsistencies and reasonableness. If he is not satisfied, he can go back and modify some of the coefficients or make other internal adjustments that he considers appropriate and then start again. After verification of the first round of input requirements and expansions, he can then proceed to examine the implications of the first-round expansions for a second round of input requirements, and again check results. In this manner, he can proceed from round to round. By so doing he is clearly in a better position to identify inconsistencies, to check reasonableness of assumptions and to improve upon them where necessary, and to expose data inadequacies and various errors that may have occurred in the construction of technical coefficients and the estimation of imports and exports. Perhaps with city and regional planning agencies that have the constant problem of evaluating implications of large programs and big projects, the capability of a round-by-round check has most appeal. It should also have great appeal in the development work in which the analyst must constantly allocate scarce resources among a number of competing programs.

Yet others may argue that the appeal of the round-by-round iterative approach, because it permits checking at a greater number of places a greater number of times, essentially reflects the fact that the matrix of technical production coefficients was not properly developed and reconciled in the first place. Hence, the back-and-forth checking in a round-by-round iterative approach really constitutes a process by which a final set of valid and reconciled coefficients can be derived. Once such a set is derived, it may be argued, the advantages of the round-by-round iterative approach that are asserted to exist diminish.

In sum, it is apparent from the various arguments put forth that no single conclusion is possible on which procedure is optimal in general. For any given study, the choice of procedure hinges on a number of important factors whose significance is likely to be particular to that study. The choice rests ultimately on the best judgment of the investigator.

Before closing, let us finally address ourselves to the question of whether or not the Philadelphia technical production coefficients are sufficiently stable to justify the use of an inverse, as we do in the next chapter, or a round-by-round iteration.

In answering this question we recognize, of course, that when a region's economy is undergoing major and rapid change, the use of an inverse or round-by-round iteration based on technical coefficients for some base year to make projections into the future or past is subject to major question. But in the case of the Philadelphia region we have an economy that possesses a diversified base of industrial activities, many of them quite old in character and changing slowly. Their technical, managerial, and organizational structures are stable and slowly evolving. In fact, in the Philadelphia region one finds perhaps the strongest case for the use of the inverse. We do not wish to suggest that significant changes in production techniques have not occurred over the past ten years in the Philadelphia region. They have, and it is one of the virtues of our highly disaggregated table that we can make the necessary adjustments of those production functions where specific changes are identified, as in the electronic sectors. We shall continue to verify the stability of these coefficients against new data as they become available. Only after considerable experience with and verification of the 1959 data will we be able to evaluate firmly the stability of these coefficients. If we do find considerable stability in these 1959 coefficients and justification for their continued use, subject to changes in selected sectors, then our findings are likely to be relevant also for other metropolitan regions whose nature, size, and distribution as well as managerial structure and production organization approximate that of Philadelphia.

Also, as we continue to use the Philadelphia table, we shall be examining various aggregations schemes. Consequently, we will have opportunities to compare the aggregated flow and coefficients matrices, and inverses of these, with those of other regions at the same degree of aggregation. In this way, we may obtain additional insight into the validity of the sectoring scheme used for the Philadelphia study and the apparent stability of its coefficients under differing schemes.

References

Coughlin, Robert E., Robert C. Douglas, Thomas W. Langford, and Benjamin H. Stevens (1970). *Economic Impact of the Dallas–Fort Worth Regional Airport on the North Central Texas Region in 1975* (Report to the North Central Texas Council of Governments). Philadelphia: Regional Science Research Institute.

————, and Thomas W. Langford (1969). *Relative Economic Effects on Penjerdel of Two Alternative Jetport Proposals in New Jersey* (Report to the Committee on Regional Development and DVRPC). Philadelphia: Regional Science Research Institute.

Isard, Walter, and Robert E. Kuenne (1953). "The Impact of Steel Upon the Greater New York–Philadelphia Industrial Region: A Study in Agglomeration Projection," *Review of Economics and Statistics*, 35: 289–301.

Langford, Thomas W. (1969). *Economic Impact of the Frankford Arsenal on the Philadelphia Region* (Report to the City of Philadelphia). Philadelphia: Regional Science Research Institute.

14.1 Introduction

In this chapter[1] we make an application of the Philadelphia coefficient table and its derived inverse to a problem of major concern. This problem pertains to (1) the impact of Vietnam War expenditures on the Philadelphia economy and (2) possible offset programs that might effectively utilize resources released through contraction of the Vietnam War effort.

In attacking this problem we follow rather standard input–output procedures. That is, we consider interesting changes in the final demand sectors and, with the use of the inverse, examine their implications. However, as has already been noted, there are three basic aspects of our work that are rather unique. One pertains to the size and detail of the coefficient table itself. A second concerns the systematic coverage and disaggregated character of the federal government activities. The third relates to the use of an inverse based on unreduced technical production coefficients, that is, coefficients unadjusted for imports.

We have already discussed the table containing 496 endogenous sectors with more than 26,000 coefficients, and the final demand subtable comprising 86 sectors with approximately 7,000 coefficients. We have also discussed the rationale for the use of an inverse based on unreduced technical production coefficients. However, we have not yet presented relevant material on the federal agency structure of the Philadelphia region. This we shall do in the next section. Then, in Section 14.3, we shall present our findings on the impact on the Philadelphia region of Vietnam War expenditures; and in Section 14.4, we shall consider the possibility of offset programs based on resources released through a cutback in these expenditures.

14.2 The Federal Agency Structure of the Philadelphia Region

Of the 86 sectors of the final demand subtable of the Philadelphia study, 36 sectors are concerned with the activities of federal government agencies.[2]

In order to permit the identification of those agencies that have unique expenditure patterns, while aggregating those agencies that have similar expenditure patterns or missions, we classified agencies as (1) military (Department of Defense) and (2) civilian. We next subdivided military agencies within the region with respect to their primary activity; namely, (1) procurement, (2) manufacturing or research and development, and (3) military base operations. Table 14.1 presents the sectoring scheme as it was devised in the study.

---

[1] This chapter, including the tables and appendix, is drawn largely from Isard and Langford, 1969.
[2] A tentative listing of approximately 102 federal agencies with offices located in the Philadelphia SMSA was developed with the assistance and cooperation of the Philadelphia Federal Executive Board. The Board, created by presidential memorandum, November 10, 1961, is an interagency group comprising the principal executives of each of the major agencies within the region.

Table 14.1. Federal Government Agencies, Philadelphia SMSA

Sector	Title
9101	U.S. Department of Agriculture
	Agricultural Research Service: Eastern Utilization Research and Development
	Forest Service: Northeastern State and Private Forestry
	Forest Service: Northeastern Forest Experimental Station
	Economic Research Service: Natural Resource Economics Division
	Soil Conservation Service
9102	U.S. Post Office Department
	Regional Post Office
	General Post Offices
	Postal Inspection Services
9103	Social Security Administration
	Social Security Administration Payment Center
	Social Security Administration District Offices
9104	Internal Revenue Service
	Regional Office
	District Offices
	Mid-Atlantic Service Center
9105	Veterans Administration: Medical Institutions
	Hospital: Philadelphia
	Hospital: Coatesville
	Outpatient Clinic: Philadelphia
9106	Veterans Administration: Administrative
	Service Center
	Data Processing Center
9107	U.S. Coast Guard: Gloucester City
9108	U.S. Mint: Philadelphia
9109	U.S. Treasury: Bureau of Customs
9110	U.S. Treasury: Bureau of Accounts
9111	U.S. Department of Housing and Urban Development
	Regional Office
	Renewal Assistance
	Metropolitan Development
	Housing Assistance
	Federal Housing Administration
9112	National Park Service
	Regional Service Center
	Independence National Historic Park
	Hopewell Village National Historic Site
	Bureau of Outdoor Recreation: Regional Office
9113	General Services Administration
	Federal Supply Service
	Public Buildings Service
	Transportation and Communications Service
	Utilization and Disposal Service
	Federal Records Center
9114	Civilian Federal Government Agencies, n.e.c.*
	Department of Agriculture
	Agricultural Marketing Service: Marketing Regulatory Program

Table 14.1. (Continued)

Sector	Title
	Agricultural Marketing Service: Dairy and Poultry Market News
	Engineering and Watershed Planning
	Cooperative State Experimental Stations
	Department of Commerce
	Area Redevelopment Administration
	Business and Defense Services Administration
	Bureau of the Census
	Bureau of Public Roads
	Weather Bureau
	Office of Field Services
	Maritime Administration: Construction Representatives
	Department of Health, Education, and Welfare
	Public Health Service
	Bureau of Federal Credit Unions
	Food and Drug Administration
	Department of the Interior: U.S. Geological Survey
	Department of Justice
	Office of the U.S. Attorney
	Office of the U.S. Marshals
	Antitrust Division
	Federal Bureau of Investigation
	Immigration and Naturalization Service
	Department of Labor
	Bureau of Apprenticeship and Training
	Bureau of Labor Standards
	Bureau of Employees' Compensation
	Office of Labor Management and Welfare Pension Reports
	Department of the Treasury
	Comptroller of the Currency
	Bureau of Narcotics: District Office
	U.S. Savings Bonds Division: Regional and District Offices
	U.S. Secret Service: District Office
	Independent Agencies
	Central Intelligence Agency
	Federal Aviation Agency
	Federal Communications Commission
	Federal Home Loan Bank Board
	Federal Mediation and Conciliation Service
	Federal Trade Commission
	Interstate Commerce Commission
	National Labor Relations Board
	Railroad Retirement Board
	Small Business Administration
	U.S. Civil Service Commission
	U.S. General Accounting Office
	Defense Personnel Support Center
9116	Operations
9117	Procurement
	Defense Industrial Supply Center
9118	Operations

Table 14.1. (Continued)

Sector	Title
9119	Procurement
	U.S. Army Electronics Command: Economic Activity
9120	Operations
9121	Procurement
	U.S. Marine Corps Supply Center
9122	Operations
9123	Procurement
	U.S. Naval Aviation Supply Office
9124	Operations
9125	Procurement
9126	Defense Contract Administration Services: Regional Offices
9128	U.S. Naval Supervisor of Shipbuilding
9129	U.S. Naval Facilities Engineering Command: East Central Division
9130	Frankford Arsenal
9131	U.S. Army Corps of Engineers
9132	Naval Air Engineering Center: Philadelphia
9133	Naval Air Development Center: Johnsville
9134	U.S. Naval Publications and Forms Center
	Naval Publications and Forms Center (Naval Supply Depot)
	Naval Publications and Printing Services Office 4ND
	Naval Air Technical Services Facility
	Naval Oceanographic Distribution Center
9135	Military Hospitals
	Naval Hospital: Philadelphia
	Army Hospital: Valley Forge
9136	U.S. Naval Air Station: Willow Grove
9138	U.S. Naval Shipyard: Philadelphia

* Sector 9114 was included in the initial study for 1959 but was deleted from the empirical analysis of this chapter because adequate data were not available at the time of this analysis.

Government agencies are not significantly different from private establishments insofar as input–output analysis is concerned. These agencies produce goods or services for outside consumption, and in producing these outputs they require specific amounts of various resources as inputs.

The fact that governmental agencies are engaged in providing services does not make them unique. However, unlike many sectors that produce services, the government does not sell its output on the open market, and thus its output is not subject to a direct market valuation. Moreover, the government produces many services that are not intended for or cannot be defined as benefiting individual consumers but rather accrue to society as a whole.

The nonexistence of market prices for government services poses some distinct problems in estimating government output. Typically, the investigator sets the value of output of any government agency equal to its resource costs or its dollar expenditures. Such a practice was used in this study. When transfer payments between government agencies were involved, these payments were excluded from the expenditures (and thus not counted as output) of the originating agency and included in those of the recipient agency or government. HUD grants, for example, appear as materials and service expenditures by the local governmental agencies receiving the funds.

To obtain the data on expenditures by federal agency, special questionnaires were developed that conformed to the accounting terminology and classification used by the agencies. These questionnaires were used to obtain data for the fiscal year 1968, for example. However, for fiscal year 1960 only bench-mark data relating to employment, payroll, and total expenditures were usually available by agency; hence, detailed expenditure information had to be extrapolated from a more recent period for which they were available.

It should be noted that the Philadelphia region is a major procurement center for defense needs. Consequently, there are two distinct purchasing patterns that should be borne in mind. One pattern represents the expenditures for the goods and services procured for usage by other units of the military services. The other pattern represents the expenditures for goods and services directly consumed by the agency in the achievement of its mission.

As examples of these two patterns, consider the activities of the Defense Industrial Supply Center (DISC), sectors 9118 and 9119. This agency catalogs and is responsible for the procurement of approximately 690,000 industrial supply items for the armed services. The procurement categories include such items as hardware, abrasives, metal bars, sheets, shapes, blocks, tackles, rigging, fiber rope, cordage, twine, bearings, chain, wire rope, cable fittings, electrical wire, and cable. The procurement level of this agency for the fiscal year 1960 was estimated to be approximately $120,300,000. The bulk of its purchases are made on a nationwide basis, with little, if any, preference given to local or regional suppliers.

Table 14.2 shows for sector RIS (Regional Interindustry Study) 9119 the allocation of the total procurement within the nation to the specific RIS sectors, and of total procurement within the Philadelphia region to the same sectors. Thus, out of the $120.3 million in national procurement by this agency, only $9.1 million, or 7.5 percent of the total, represents purchases within the region, even though the agency was located in the region.

To procure these goods, DISC required the services of 783 employees. To these employees DISC paid $18,678,374 in wages and salaries. DISC expended an additional $2,006,538 for items for its operations. Table

Table 14.2. Procurement Activities, Defense Industrial Supply Center, Fiscal Year 1960

RIS Sector		Total Procurement ($)	Regional Procurement ($)
2298	Cordage and Twine	3,430,956	147,188
2499	Wood Products, n.e.c.	435,366	11,145
2821	Plastic Materials, Resins, etc.	734,311	111,909
2851	Paints, Varnishes, Enamels	2,203,054	212,154
2852	Putty and Calking Compounds	1,468,743	105,456
2891	Glue and Gelatin	710,973	120,297
3079	Miscellaneous Plastic Products	2,263,685	764,889
3291	Abrasive Products	4,349,687	606,781
3293	Steam Packing and Pipe Cover	4,349,687	729,443
3312	Blast Furnace and Steel Mill Products	8,211,558	515,686
3315	Steel Wire, Nails, and Spikes	4,105,719	219,245
3356	Roll, Draw, Extrude: Non-Ferrous	5,800,265	59,163
3357	Draw and Insulate Non-Ferrous Wire	9,660,210	82,112
3429	Hardware, n.e.c.	7,159,775	234,125
3441	Fabricated Structural Steel	7,843,680	458,071
3452	Bolts, Nuts, Screws, Rivets	31,154,332	2,931,623
3481	Miscellaneous Fabricated Wire Products	7,629,546	434,121
3497	Metal Foil and Leaf	2,185,731	33,442
3499	Fabricated Metal Products n.e.c.	3,088,943	246,807
3562	Ball and Roller Bearings	4,579,460	626,470
3566	Mechanical Power Transmission Equipment	3,052,973	292,170
3981	Brooms and Brushes	2,222,422	124,456
9842	Transportation Services	3,658,924	—
	TOTAL	$120,300,000	$9,066,753

14.3 presents these operating expenditures, disaggregated by RIS sector. The DISC personnel have estimated that at least 95 percent of total operating expenditures were for items produced or provided by establishments within the Philadelphia region.

As can be expected, the expenditure patterns of Tables 14.2 and 14.3 are very different. Since DISC procurement increased 221 percent in the period 1960–1966, while its operating expenditures increased by only 21 percent, the need to assign these activities to two separate RIS sectors in order to avoid projection errors is obvious. It has been estimated that each of the two distinct patterns of expenditures by commodity remained essentially the same during the period 1960–1966.

14.3 Impact of Vietnam War Expenditures

Having sketched the basic structure and data on the federal government sectors, we may now proceed to an application of our coefficient table and its inverse. We specifically examine the impact of Vietnam War expenditures on a regional economy. With reference to the Philadelphia economy, there are several ways in which this examination can be undertaken. We chose to begin with the actual employment and expenditures

Table 14.3. Operating Expenditures, Defense Industrial Supply Center,
Fiscal Year 1960

RIS Sector		Operating Expenditures ($)
2522	Metal Office Furniture	25,977
2542	Metal Office and Store Fixtures	15,586
2621	Paper Mills	37,348
2641	Paper Coating and Glazing	20,748
2645	Die Cut Paper and Cardboard	20,748
2649	Converted Paper Products, n.e.c.	20,748
2655	Fiber Cans, Tubes, Drums, etc.	16,599
2841	Soap and Other Detergents	17,064
2911	Petroleum Refining	46,849
3069	Fabricated Rubber Products, n.e.c.	17,196
3315	Steel Wire, Nails, and Spikes	16,948
3421	Cutlery	12,935
3481	Miscellaneous Fabricated Wire Products	17,246
3555	Printing Trades Machinery	17,416
3571	Computing and Accounting Machines	955,047
3572	Typewriters	15,647
3579	Office Machines, n.e.c.	32,094
3641	Electric Lamps	34,526
3651	Radio and TV Receivers	13,037
3861	Photographic Equipment and Supplies	36,073
3951	Pens, Mechanical Pencils and Parts	30,152
3952	Lead Pencils and Art Materials	30,152
3953	Marking Devices	17,230
3955	Carbon Paper and Ink Ribbons	25,845
4811	Telephone Communications	284,886
4890	Communication Services, n.e.c.	113,822
4911	Electric Company and Systems	50,081
4941	Water Supply	25,040
9842	Transportation Services	39,498
9888	Households (Wages and Salaries)	18,678,374
	TOTAL	$20,684,912

for each of the 35 aggregate governmental sectors,[3] as shown for the
fiscal year 1968 in Table 14.4 and then to estimate the extent and nature
of the changes in these expenditures that can be attributed to the Vietnam
War. We took this last step by projecting what the expenditures for each
agency for fiscal year 1968 would have been had there been no war. Such
projections were based upon the trends of agency expenditures for a period
of years, discussions with appropriate government and private officials,
and staff judgment. To illustrate our procedures, we briefly describe the
treatment of four sectors.

[3] Recall that sector 9114, *Civilian Agencies, n.e.c.*, is not included in this analysis
because of lack of data.

Table 14.4. Actual 1968 Federal Government Activity, by Agency

		Employment	Payroll	Output	Local Purchases	Total Impact
9101	U.S. Agriculture Dept.	576	$ 6,500,667	$ 10,007,001	$ 8,934,575	$ 41,716,666
9102	U.S. Post Office	20,478	135,885,336	170,052,953	161,698,002	745,340,533
9103	Social Sec. Admin.	2,480	19,058,659	21,645,659	20,738,171	93,862,663
9104	Int. Rev. Service	4,013	29,658,579	31,762,717	30,850,872	141,315,016
9105	Vet. Admin: Med. Inst.	1,943	16,577,299	21,794,463	19,862,893	87,694,717
9106	Vet. Admin: Admin.	1,690	12,165,129	12,951,073	12,548,995	57,473,204
9107	U.S. Coast Guard	332	749,063	996,978	933,122	3,980,847
9108	U.S. Mint: Philadelphia	537	4,748,499	31,337,276	7,851,611	34,276,721
9109	Customs Bureau	218	2,594,448	2,671,894	2,617,214	11,970,079
9110	Bureau of Accts: Disburs.	142	920,259	1,570,760	1,313,160	5,983,877
9111	U.S. Dept. Hous., Urban Dev.	725	5,250,944	225,614,152	54,863,240	293,636,690
9112	National Park Service	337	3,558,384	4,231,797	4,031,238	18,576,824
9113	General Services Admin.	446	3,476,250	21,490,918	13,945,865	69,035,708
9116	D.P.S.C. Oper.	5,252	41,279,440	48,100,681	44,574,632	203,127,380
9117	D.P.S.C. Proc.			2,051,908,094	103,498,924	509,926,899
9118	D.I.S.C. Oper.	2,608	20,485,300	25,782,778	22,969,766	104,102,531
9119	D.I.S.C. Proc.			283,600,000	23,919,927	118,647,679
9120	Army Electron., Oper.	3,020	30,465,974	47,866,707	45,477,900	217,311,119
9121	Army Electron., Proc.			956,052,222	163,246,299	880,023,238
9122	U.S.M.C. Oper.	2,232	18,167,122	21,561,377	19,975,235	91,541,207
9123	U.S.M.C. Proc.			181,099,090	14,745,616	73,988,354
9124	A.S.O. Oper.	2,320	20,029,425	26,069,436	19,773,489	91,613,208
9125	A.S.O. Proc.			605,013,172	66,077,529	325,063,958
9126	D.C.A.S.R.	1,446	12,835,355	14,660,589	14,198,111	65,157,715
9128	U.S.N. Sup. Shipbldg.	111	1,210,000	13,975,000	12,622,742	62,025,845
9129	U.S.N. Facils. Eng. Comd.	180	1,833,425	23,630,774	13,915,661	77,465,087
9130	Frankford Arsenal	5,809	56,741,000	490,182,000	91,121,098	407,055,193
9131	Corps. Engineers	613	4,980,668	31,274,366	19,213,087	94,020,305
9132	N.A.E.C.	2,423	19,909,063	123,009,063	65,364,648	305,785,848
9133	N.A.D.C.	2,967	30,306,985	92,945,807	45,912,139	213,470,410
9134	Nav. Pub. Form Ctr.	159	13,050,934	65,867,084	56,000,760	260,300,150
9135	Military Hosps.	3,369	23,062,088	45,107,585	37,395,260	162,243,319
9136	Navl Air Stn: WG	1,033	8,636,801	12,295,963	9,568,176	44,167,642
9138	Nav. Shipyard: Phila.	12,194	113,293,000	295,293,000	206,059,055	1,009,058,222
GRAND TOTAL		79,653	$657,430,096	$6,010,981,429	$1,435,819,012	$6,920,958,854

Source: Isard and Langford, 1969, p. 227.

14.3.1 Sector 9103, Social Security Administration The nature of this service agency suggests that its level of operations is not directly related to the level of defense activities. Examination of the annual operating expenditures of the regional and district offices suggests that there was not a significant reduction in the growth rate of the agency during the past years as a result of increasing military expenditures.

14.3.2 Sector 9111, U.S. Department of Housing and Urban Development Although this agency is not directly related to defense activities, the expenditures of the agency and its employment appear to have been significantly restricted during the period of the Vietnam conflict. The exact changes are not readily determined due to changes in the scope of the mission and programs administered by the agency. It is a widely held opinion, however, that had there been no war, significant additional moneys would have been made available through this agency to aid housing, planning, and development. We estimate that there would have been approximately 150 more persons employed, representing a 20 percent increase in employment. We also estimate that the dollar amount of grants and loans processed by the various constituent agencies would have been approximately 100 percent greater.

14.3.3 Sectors 9118 and 9119, Defense Industrial Supply Center As previously noted, this agency provides procurement activity for general industrial products. From a level of 783 employees in 1960, the agency expanded to a level of 2,687 in 1964. It has experienced a relatively slow decline in personnel in recent years because of an increase in productivity of personnel in handling procurement actions.

Review of the annual data suggests that the procurement levels of the agency would have stabilized at approximately $125 million per year in the absence of the war. For its day-to-day operations, expenditures would have been reduced by approximately $1.85 million and employment by 108 persons.

The generalized nature of the items procured by this agency suggests that the cessation of the war would have had little if any effect upon the spatial pattern of its procurement by four-digit SIC.

14.3.4 Sectors 9120 and 9121, U.S. Army Electronics Command: Philadelphia Office This agency would have undergone significant changes had there been no Vietnam War. In April 1965 it was announced publicly that the operations of the agency were to be transferred to Fort Monmouth, New Jersey. This decision was changed within three months, since such a relocation would have drastically reduced the efficiency of the agency at a time when the buildup for the Vietnam military effort was beginning. In fact, 400 additional personnel were authorized for the agency in August 1965.

It is therefore reasonable to assume that had there been no Vietnam War, the agency would have been relocated. This would have resulted in a 100 percent decrease in the operations in Philadelphia. However, it is estimated that the effect of the relocation upon the procurement purchases from the relative concentration of supplier firms in the Philadelphia region would have been negligible. A "no Vietnam War" situation, however, would have decreased the total procurement to the prewar level of approximately $500 million.

Once employment, payroll, total, and local expenditure estimates by agency for a "no Vietnam War" situation were derived for fiscal 1968, these estimates were subtracted from actual 1968 employment, payroll, and total expenditures. The differences were converted to percentages of actual 1968 magnitudes. These percentages are recorded in Table 14.5 as changes by federal sector of the Philadelphia economy from actual 1968 levels had there been a "no Vietnam War" situation in 1968.

To obtain some notion of the magnitudes involved, we may turn to Table 14.4. For fiscal 1968, total employees summed over all federal sectors in the Philadelphia region were 79,653; total payroll was $657.4 million; and total expenditures were $6.010 billion, of which approximately 24 percent, or $1.44 billion, was for goods and services produced locally. Had there been no Vietnam War, we estimate that this employment would have been 71,509, a net reduction of 8,144, or 10.2 percent; the associated total payroll would have been $586.4 million, a net reduction of $71 million, or 10.8 percent; and the total expenditures would have been $3.466 billion, a net reduction of $2.544 billion, or 42.3 percent. However, 33 percent (in absolute amount, $1.16 billion) rather than 24 percent of these expenditures would have been local. Thus, local expenditures would have decreased by $0.28 billion, or 19.71 percent.

Having crudely identified these differences between what is and what would have been with respect to federal government operations, we ask the following question: What would be the differences in total impacts upon the Philadelphia economy? To help answer this question we multiplied the Philadelphia inverse by each of the 35 local expenditure vectors to determine each government sector's impact on each of the 496 endogenous sectors. These impacts were then summed to obtain the total federal government impact. Thus, for fiscal year 1968, we list in column 4 of Table 14.4 the set of local expenditures (total dollars of inputs required) by each government sector from the Philadelphia region, and in the last column the total impact in terms of total dollars of inputs required directly and indirectly of the Philadelphia region. For example, the local expenditures of the Naval Shipyard in Philadelphia (sector 9138) were $206 million, while total impact was $1.009 billion.

Table 14.5. A No Vietnam War Situation, 1968:
Estimated Changes from 1968 Actual

Sector	Employment (Percent)	Local Purchases (Percent)	Total Impact (Dollars)
9101	+ 64.76	+ 64.88	+ 24,690,663
9102	+ 5.00	+ 4.76	+ 32,375,754
9103	0.00	0.00	0
9104	+ 4.98	+ 4.98	+ 6,424,369
9105	+ 14.98	+ 15.00	+ 11,999,002
9106	− 7.34	− 7.34	− 3,849,844
9107	0.00	0.00	0
9108	0.00	0.00	0
9109	0.00	0.00	0
9110	0.00	0.00	0
9111	+ 20.69	+ 92.24	+ 250,264,277
9112	+ 13.35	+ 13.35	+ 2,262,756
9113	+ 28.25	+ 28.27	+ 17,800,343
9116	− 33.36	− 33.30	− 61,699,644
9117	—	− 65.75	− 307,069,950
9118	− 4.14	− 4.14	− 3,932,432
9119	—	− 55.92	− 60,525,423
9120	− 100.00	− 100.00	− 217,311,119
9121	—	− 46.85	− 375,304,650
9122	− 40.64	− 37.56	− 31,369,832
9123	—	− 83.66	− 56,430,039
9124	− 13.79	− 15.75	− 13,151,614
9125	—	− 21.75	− 64,492,068
9126	− 10.10	− 10.10	− 6,001,120
9128	0.00	0.00	0
9129	− 36.67	− 61.58	− 40,658,028
9130	− 5.32	− 23.39	− 85,656,542
9131	0.00	0.00	0
9132	0.00	− 16.50	− 46,788,023
9133	0.00	0.00	0
9134	0.00	0.00	0
9135	− 34.70	− 34.70	− 51,352,610
9136	− 54.02	− 47.22	− 15,988,914
9138	− 13.89	− 19.54	− 182,074,370
GRAND TOTAL	− 10.22	− 19.71	−1,277,839,058

Source: Isard and Langford, 1969, p. 230.

To determine what would have been had there been no Vietnam War, we list in column 1 of Table 14.5 the percentage change of employment, in column 2 the percentage change in local expenditures (dollar value of inputs required from the Philadelphia region), and in the last column the change in the total impact in terms of dollar value of inputs directly and indirectly required of the Philadelphia region by each government sector. Thus, employment in sector 9101 would have increased by 64.76 percent while that in sector 9116 would have decreased by 33.36 percent. Total dollar change in inputs directly and indirectly required would have corresponded to a $24.7 million increase for sector 9101, and a $61.7 million decrease for sector 9116. The grand totals at the bottom of the columns indicate (1) that federal employment would have been 10.22 percent smaller, (2) that local expenditures of federal agencies would have been 19.71 percent smaller, and (3) that direct and indirect expenditures on locally supplied inputs would have been smaller by an amount of $1.278 billion.

Comparing the last columns of Tables 14.4 and 14.5, we observe that the total inputs directly and indirectly required of the Philadelphia region by actual 1968 federal government operations are approximately $6.9 billion, while without the operations associated with the Vietnam War, the same requirements would have been $5.6 billion, or approximately 18.4 percent smaller.

Thus far, the total impacts and change in impact have been presented by each agency, summed over all 496 sectors. It is equally if not more important to examine the impact of all federal programs as a whole upon each of the 496 endogenous sectors of the Philadelphia economy. Accordingly, we present in columns 1, 2, and 3 in Table A1 of the Appendix to this chapter direct, indirect, and total requirements by all federal agencies as a whole for each of these sectors for fiscal year 1968. These data are summarized by major economic sectors in Table 14.6. For example, from columns 1, 2, and 3 of this table we note that the agriculture, forestry, and fisheries sector furnishes $1.4 million of output directly to federal agencies in the region and another $269.9 million indirectly, for a total of $271.3 million. Aside from households, the electrical machinery sector furnishes *directly* the largest dollar amount of product, $118.7 million; but directly and indirectly, the services sector furnishes the most, $789.1 million.

Next we wish to examine on *net* the estimated Vietnam War impact. The relevant data are recorded by each of the 496 sectors for fiscal year 1968 in columns 4, 5, and 6 of Table A1 in the Appendix. They record, respectively, the changes in the amounts of direct federal requirements, of indirectly generated requirements of federal activity, and of the total of these two. Where no sign is indicated, the change represents an increase as a result of Vietnam War operations. Where a negative sign appears, the change represents a decrease as a result of the Vietnam War operations. Again, we present in columns 4, 5, and 6 of Table 14.6 the relevant data by major economic sector.

For example, as a result of the Vietnam War operations, direct expenditures for construction activities are estimated to be $5.4 million greater than if there had been no war. The indirectly generated expendi-

Table 14.6. Direct, Indirect, and Total Impacts of Regional Federal Agency Expenditures by Major Economic Sector

Major Sectors	Actual Federal Impact Fiscal Year 1968			Estimated Vietnam War Impacts (net) (Actual 1968 federal impacts less estimated federal impact in a no Vietnam War situation)		
	Direct (1)	Indirect (2)	Total (3)	Direct (4)	Indirect (5)	Total (6)
Agric., Forest., Fish.	$ 1,389,224	$269,906,578	$271,295,802	$ 922,167	$ 28,735,823	$ 29,657,990
Extractive	221,596	5,187,139	5,408,735	54,279	962,593	1,016,872
Construction	32,658,045	103,201,984	135,860,029	5,414,474	8,498,171	13,912,645
Ordnance	1,374,659	18,778	1,393,437	1,022,862	− 585	1,022,277
Food	36,628,042	411,959,988	448,588,030	19,014,734	80,714,907	99,729,641
Tobacco	12,525	19,259,134	19,271,659	970	3,277,155	3,278,125
Textiles	6,808,304	83,051,591	89,859,895	4,247,500	18,078,680	22,326,180
Apparel	27,820,580	63,167,172	90,987,752	17,417,150	11,517,702	28,934,852
Lumber, Wood	2,583,222	20,623,123	23,206,345	481,564	2,838,970	3,320,534
Furn., Fixtures	2,559,032	17,298,968	19,827,999	311,145	3,407,563	3,718,708
Paper	3,371,538	115,830,215	119,201,753	536,828	24,218,704	24,755,532
Print., Publish.	37,427,648	110,771,256	148,198,904	11,406,933	23,930,044	35,336,977
Chemicals	18,222,983	102,419,377	120,642,360	7,548,664	18,869,772	26,418,436
Petroleum Ref.	11,538,946	96,608,685	108,147,631	1,632,339	17,609,995	19,242,334
Rubber, Plastics	1,171,056	17,167,089	18,338,145	595,661	3,429,218	3,934,879
Leather	887,242	17,192,131	18,079,373	600,575	3,049,526	3,650,101
Stone, Clay, Glass	6,845,638	34,645,751	41,491,389	2,428,343	6,880,848	9,309,191
Primary Metals	23,093,353	93,823,337	116,916,690	9,809,125	22,055,974	31,865,099
Fab. Metal Prods.	17,119,676	43,524,506	60,644,242	7,356,927	8,660,453	16,017,380
Machinery	47,264,981	37,692,922	84,957,903	13,680,061	8,427,665	22,107,726
Elec. Machinery	118,762,675	67,252,257	186,014,932	46,060,622	20,725,461	66,786,083
Transp. Equip.	54,330,738	90,231,603	144,562,341	9,802,189	16,740,157	26,542,346
Inst. Scient. Equip.	11,407,057	17,289,033	28,696,090	3,482,990	4,440,767	7,923,757
Misc. Mfgr.	1,115,469	29,508,851	30,624,320	439,993	5,199,265	5,639,258
Transp. Services	85,454,784	150,225,901	235,680,685	41,765,461	31,271,210	73,036,671
Utilities, Comm.	40,124,148	213,089,307	253,213,455	5,384,987	39,160,998	44,545,985
Wholesale Trade	1,581,382	167,794,207	169,375,589	219,686	31,874,141	32,093,827
Retail Trade	502,161	429,845,479	430,347,640	55,964	73,288,686	73,344,650
Fin., Ins., R. E.	3,076,882	301,437,920	304,514,802	47,733	51,950,831	51,998,564
Services	129,872,973	659,236,755	789,109,728	50,997,000	96,725,569	147,722,569
Local Govmnt.	49,830,320	127,985,145	177,815,465	−49,682,355	24,347,182	−25,335,173
Households	660,792,133	1,567,893,601	2,228,685,734	70,961,818	308,664,578	379,626,396
TOTAL	$1,435,819,012	$5,485,139,842	$6,920,958,854	$283,928,389	$999,552,023	$1,283,480,412

Source: Isard and Langford, 1969, p. 232.

tures are estimated to be $8.5 million and the total impact is therefore approximately $13.9 million. The total of all direct federal expenditures as a result of Vietnam War operations is estimated at $284 million; the indirectly generated expenditures are estimated at $999 million; and the total of direct and indirect at $1,283 million.

Thus far, we have examined in Tables 14.4 and 14.5 the overall impacts of each federal agency on the Philadelphia economy. In Table 14.6 and Table A1 we have examined the impact upon each sector of the Philadelphia economy of overall federal activity. It is now useful to focus on the impact of specific selected federal activities upon each sector of the Philadelphia economy. For this purpose we choose to concentrate on the impacts of the U.S. Army Electronics Command: Philadelphia Office and the U.S. Naval Shipyard in Philadelphia.

We first consider the U.S. Army Electronics Command: Philadelphia Office. Its impact, as already discussed, is via (1) expenditures associated with its staff employed at the Philadelphia office and (2) the procurement orders given to Philadelphia enterprises. In Table 14.7 and Table A2 (Appendix), columns 1, 2, and 3 refer to agency operations, while columns 4, 5, and 6 refer to procurement activity. Table 14.7 indicates impacts by major economic sectors. Table A2 indicates impacts by selected four-digit sectors. From Table 14.7 it is seen that the direct impacts of its operations in fiscal year 1968 are largely in households (wage and salary payments), and the printing and publishing industry. Its indirect impacts (largely reflecting the expenditure associated with employee earnings) are spread over all sectors. The direct impact of its procurement activity is largely on the three major economic sectors: electrical machinery, equipment and supplies (SIC 36); transportation services; and general services (the SIC definitions for the latter two categories may be found in Table A1). From the details of Table A2, we see that the direct impact on services represents entirely the need for procuring business services, excluding advertising.

As already indicated, had there been no Vietnam War, the U.S. Army Electronics Command in all probability would have relocated to Fort Monmouth, New Jersey. Hence, the impact of the Vietnam War on the Philadelphia economy via the U.S. Army Electronics Command: Operations can be roughly measured by the numbers in columns 1, 2, and 3 of Tables 14.7 and A2.[4] Both direct and indirect requirements of output from sectors of the Philadelphia economy would have decreased by the amounts listed in these columns.

[4] Strictly speaking, these numbers should be adjusted for change in exports to the Fort Monmouth, New Jersey, area were the U.S. Army Electronics Command located there; these adjustments would be minor, however.

Table 14.7. Direct, Indirect, and Total Impacts of U.S. Army Electronics Command: Philadelphia Office, Fiscal Year 1968

Major Economic Sector	Operations			Procurement			Total (7)
	Direct (1)	Indirect (2)	Subtotal (3)	Direct (4)	Indirect (5)	Subtotal (6)	
Agriculture, Forestry, and Fisheries	$ —	$ 8,396,514	$ 8,396,514	$ —	$ 11,529,033	$ 11,529,033	$ 19,925,547
Extractive Industries	—	122,095	122,095	—	245,406	245,406	367,501
Construction	—	2,375,422	2,375,422	—	5,598,562	5,598,562	7,973,984
Ordnance	—	511	511	—	740	740	1,251
Food and Kindred	—	13,745,463	13,745,463	—	18,040,123	18,040,123	31,785,586
Tobacco	—	663,754	663,754	1,716	870,000	870,000	1,533,754
Textiles	—	2,304,388	2,304,388	—	3,142,336	3,144,052	5,448,440
Apparel	—	2,088,278	2,088,278	22	2,747,454	2,747,476	4,835,754
Lumber and Wood	12,503	608,914	608,914	22,332	968,113	990,445	1,599,359
Furniture and Fixtures	318,219	511,624	524,127	2,480	1,359,718	1,362,198	1,886,325
Paper and Allied	11,016,320	6,096,634	6,414,853	68,700	5,387,167	5,455,867	11,870,720
Printing and Publishing	—	3,879,778	14,896,098	70,398	5,956,609	6,027,007	20,923,105
Chemicals and Allied	—	3,349,667	3,349,667	2,795	5,491,228	5,494,023	8,843,690
Petroleum Refining	53,764	3,062,305	3,116,069	1,373	4,429,979	4,431,352	7,547,421
Rubber and Plastics	—	555,228	555,228	7,055	939,394	946,449	1,501,677
Leather	—	585,057	585,057	—	766,357	766,357	1,351,414
Stone, Clay and Glass	—	789,393	789,393	4,987	1,781,174	1,786,161	2,575,554
Primary Metals	—	1,934,318	1,934,318	1,819	5,885,989	5,887,808	7,822,126
Fabricated Metal Products	—	1,014,305	1,014,305	1,267,054	2,608,085	3,875,139	4,889,444
Machinery	151,292	809,073	960,365	2,087,825	3,027,907	5,115,732	6,076,097
Electrical Machinery	—	1,055,972	1,055,972	26,785,878	10,768,792	37,554,670	38,610,642
Transportation Equipment	—	3,174,309	3,174,309	74,460	4,239,969	4,314,429	7,488,738
Inst. and Scientific Equipment	49,366	526,689	526,689	342,716	2,330,884	2,673,600	3,200,289
Miscellaneous Manufacturing	328,031	933,914	983,280	18,983	1,313,622	1,332,605	2,315,885
Transportation Services	2,014,753	4,625,227	4,953,258	8,096,752	7,857,275	15,954,027	20,907,285
Utilities and Communication	—	6,967,157	8,981,910	—	10,689,007	10,689,007	19,670,917
Wholesale Trades	—	5,314,866	5,314,866	—	8,595,216	8,595,216	13,910,082
Retail Trades	—	14,784,600	14,784,600	—	19,381,735	19,381,735	34,166,335
Finance, Insurance, and Real Estate	417,792	9,909,474	10,327,266	—	14,416,685	14,416,685	24,743,951
Services	649,886	21,153,598	21,803,484	37,619,247	31,322,418	68,941,665	90,745,149
Local Government	—	4,125,879	4,125,879	—	6,433,757	6,433,757	10,559,636
Households	30,465,974	46,368,813	76,834,787	—	100,703,324	100,703,324	177,538,111
TOTAL	$45,477,900	$171,833,219	$217,311,119	$76,476,592	$298,828,058	$375,304,650	$592,615,769

Had there been no Vietnam War, we estimate, as already noted, that the procurement activities of the U.S. Army Electronics Command would have been at the prewar level of $500 million. Procurement from sources in the Philadelphia region, however, would not have been adversely affected from a relative standpoint by the *relocation*. Thus, total procurement from the Philadelphia region would have been at the estimated prewar level of $86.8 million rather than at the actual fiscal year 1968 level of $163.2 million, a reduction of $76.5 million, or 46.8 percent. Accordingly, the impact of the Vietnam War via the procurement activities of the U.S. Army Electronics Command may be taken to be measured by the values listed in columns 4, 5, and 6 of Table 14.7 and Table A2.[5]

Next consider the impacts of the U.S. Naval Shipyard in Philadelphia. Data on the expenditure pattern of the U.S. Naval Shipyard were available for both fiscal years 1960 and 1968. On the basis of these data and annual summary data for the intervening years, the changes due to the Vietnam War, for example, the intensified shipbuilding, are clearly discernible. We are then able to approximate expenditure patterns had there been no Vietnam War. We estimate that the level of U.S. Naval Shipyard expenditures in the Philadelphia region would have been $40.2 million, or 19.5 percent less; that is, it would have been at a level of $165.8 million instead of the actual fiscal year 1968 level of $206 million. Its employment would have been 13.89 percent less than the actual fiscal year 1968 employment of 12,194. Its direct and indirect impact would have been smaller by $182 million.

The breakdown of these overall magnitudes is given in Table 14.8 for major economic sectors, and in Table A3 (Appendix) for selected four-digit sectors. Among the manufacturing industries, primary metals and machinery would have been most affected. For example, the direct and indirect impacts on the four-digit sector 3312, *Blast furnaces, Steelworks, and Rolling Mills*, are estimated to be $2.68 million and $2.06 million, respectively. Because of the Shipyard's large employment and payroll, its indirect impacts are diffused over many sectors, as is clear from column 2 of Table 14.8.

Since impacts in terms of employment as well as dollar output are also significant, we present in Table 14.9 the employment impacts upon the Philadelphia region of the U.S. Army Electronics Command, in both its operations and procurement activity, and the U.S. Naval Shipyard—as a result of increased activity engendered by the Vietnam War. Among the major economic sectors most affected are printing and publishing;

[5] In the absence of information to the contrary, the agency procurement expenditures for the Vietnam War were assumed to have been similar in *pattern* to the prewar situation.

Table 14.8. Direct and Indirect Impacts of Increased Operations due to the Vietnam War, by Major Economic Sectors, U.S. Naval Shipyard, Philadelphia, Fiscal Year 1968

(Actual 1968 impact less estimated impact in a no Vietnam War situation)

	Direct (1)	Indirect (2)	Total (3)
Agriculture, Forestry, and Fisheries	$ 383	$ 7,350,065	$ 7,350,448
Extractive Industries	1,331	130,187	131,518
Construction	39,238	2,126,689	2,165,927
Ordnance	—	399	399
Food	1,603,373	10,391,568	11,994,941
Tobacco	970	481,369	482,339
Textiles	9,630	1,755,477	1,765,107
Apparel	8,878	1,526,219	1,535,097
Lumber and Wood	27,917	527,386	555,303
Furniture and Fixtures	216,623	382,925	599,548
Paper	75,927	2,797,906	2,873,833
Printing and Publishing	106,770	2,551,548	2,658,318
Chemicals and Allied	580,864	2,880,074	3,460,938
Petroleum Refining	1,243,203	2,646,704	3,889,907
Rubber and Plastics	31,666	414,752	446,418
Leather	380	422,784	423,164
Stone, Clay, and Glass	886,153	921,639	1,807,792
Primary Metals	4,390,437	4,380,667	8,771,104
Fabricated Metal Products	1,088,471	1,369,515	2,457,986
Machinery	6,422,813	933,906	7,356,719
Electrical Machinery	2,440,441	1,528,520	3,968,961
Transportation Equipment	24,834	2,377,691	2,402,525
Inst. and Scientific Equipment	258,610	305,220	563,830
Miscellaneous Manufacturing	32,923	690,156	723,079
Transportation Services	984,310	4,222,764	5,207,074
Utilities and Communication	2,879,729	5,691,543	8,571,272
Wholesale Trades	219,686	4,596,184	4,815,870
Retail Trades	63,127	10,721,447	10,784,574
Finance, Insurance, and Real Estate	5,640	7,884,501	7,890,141
Services	879,671	16,410,995	17,290,666
Local Government	—	3,415,660	3,415,660
Households	15,738,664	39,975,248	55,713,912
TOTAL	$40,262,662	$141,811,708	$182,074,370

electrical machinery, equipment, and supplies; transportation services; retail trades; and general services.

14.4 Offset Programs and Released Resources

It is not necessary to dwell upon the point that had there not been Vietnam War expenditures in the Philadelphia SMSA, there would have been more of other governmental and private enterprise activity within the region. It is now well recognized that the labor and other resources that were channeled into Vietnam War activities could and would have been profitably occupied in other economic pursuits. Hence, when the Vietnam War effort is reduced, hopefully by 100 percent, the amount of

Table 14.9. Employment Impacts (Direct and Indirect) of Vietnam War, U.S. Army Electronics Command and U.S. Naval Shipyard

(Actual 1968 employment impacts less estimated impacts in a "no Vietnam War" situation)

	U.S. Army Electronics Command		U.S. Naval Shipyard
	Operations	Procurement	
Direct	3,020	0	1,694
Indirect	10,749	22,056	9,188
Agriculture, Forestry and Fisheries	1,330	1,847	1,166
Extractive Industries	6	13	7
Construction	133	311	121
Ordnance	0	0	0
Food and Kindred	438	581	400
Tobacco	15	19	11
Textiles	164	223	125
Apparel	223	292	163
Lumber and Wood	53	85	48
Furniture and Fixtures	41	96	44
Paper and Allied	238	222	118
Printing and Publishing	1,022	389	176
Chemicals and Allied	105	168	108
Petroleum Refining	49	69	60
Rubber and Plastics	27	50	22
Leather	43	73	41
Stone, Clay and Glass	46	107	86
Primary Metals	81	261	399
Fabricated Metal Products	54	244	143
Machinery	76	511	427
Electrical Machinery	79	2,161	256
Transportation Equipment	113	156	87
Inst. and Scientific Equipment	43	230	46
Miscellaneous Manufacturing	72	99	54
Transportation Services	463	1,498	488
Utilities and Communication	587	622	456
Wholesale Trades	308	491	342
Retail Trades	1,783	2,332	1,302
Finance, Insurance and Real Estate	258	391	217
Services	2,489	7,876	1,936
Local Government	410	639	339
TOTAL	13,769	22,056	10,882

the inputs of any of the 496 sectors directly and indirectly required by the Vietnam War effort should not be viewed as indicative of the amount by which the output of that sector is likely to be contracted. Rather, that amount should be viewed as resources (and associated productive capacity) released for the support of other government programs and private undertakings, or as output that may be forgone in order for the economy to turn out products of higher priority.

This view can be developed in some detail. For example, one might estimate, or speculate, what levels of educational programs and low-income-housing construction could have been accommodated in the Philadelphia region had there been no Vietnam War. This question can be examined from the standpoint of the moneys that might have been available or critical inputs in short supply that would have been released. In terms of moneys, the difference between actual fiscal year 1968 federal agency expenditures of $1.443 billion and our estimate of federal agency expenditures of $1.159 billion had there been no Vietnam War—$284 million—is a reasonable indication of the moneys that might have gone into social programs in the Philadelphia region, and also of the moneys that might become available when and if the Vietnam War comes to a halt. For that sum of money, $284 million, the analyst can develop many mixes of reasonable programs that could have been or could be developed as an "offset" policy. One mix to meet some of our urban needs, for example, might involve the following total expenditures:

Elementary and Secondary Education	$170,400,000
Institutions of Higher Education	56,800,000
Low-Income-Housing Construction	56,800,000
	$284,000,000

The details of expenditures required by each of these programs at these suggested levels are presented in columns 1, 3, and 5, respectively, of Table 14.10 (by major economic sectors), and Table A4 (for selected four-digit sectors). As can be expected, payments to households dominate the programs in support of elementary and secondary education and institutions of higher learning. In the former, for example, $120 million of the $170 million expenditure level is for such payments. In the case of the program for low-income-housing construction, however, payments to households represent less than 50 percent of total expenditures, while purchases of stone, clay, and glass products and fabricated metals constitute roughly 10 percent and 9 percent, respectively, of total expenditures.

The support of these programs at the specified levels, just as that of the Vietnam War programs, indirectly requires various other inputs, which are to be identified. These indirect input requirements are listed in columns 2, 4, and 6, respectively, of Table 14.10 and Table A4.

The overall totals of the indirect requirements by program are as follows:

Elementary and Secondary Education	$552,760,222
Institutions of Higher Learning	189,478,244
Low-Income-Housing Construction	211,185,017
	$953,423,483

Table 14.10. Direct and Indirect Impacts of Hypothetical Offset Programs, by Major Economic Sectors, Fiscal Year 1968

	Elementary and Secondary Education		Institutions of Higher Education		Low-Income-Housing Construction	
	Direct (1)	Indirect (2)	Direct (3)	Indirect (4)	Direct (5)	Indirect (6)
Agriculture, Forestry, and Fisheries	$ 566,920	$ 30,656,481	$ 137,115	$ 9,827,058	$ 57,015	$ 9,470,829
Extractive Industries		468,320		186,703	277,204	963,651
Construction	624,005	7,935,730	944,527	3,130,718	14,892	3,104,983
Ordnance		1,726		564		645
Food and Kindred	2,235,139	48,200,656	797,870	15,343,760		15,302,863
Tobacco		2,293,130		726,130		733,045
Textiles		7,901,886	18,005	2,582,668	1,914	2,621,226
Apparel		7,211,139	23,402	2,292,275	319	2,317,315
Lumber and Wood	335,347	2,302,078	11,132	774,640	1,596,638	1,420,346
Furniture and Fixtures	433,498	1,794,107	752,430	588,310	536,219	575,449
Paper and Allied	668,018	11,400,502	333,636	4,086,441	166,153	4,766,504
Printing and Publishing	3,411,924	10,521,273	1,356,808	3,901,021	15,849	4,399,568
Chemicals and Allied	407,587	10,419,337	278,650	3,392,485	446,868	4,101,422
Petroleum Refining	413,220	10,395,660	236,345	3,430,526	987,555	4,055,427
Rubber and Plastics	18,418	1,737,405	7,624	572,029	177,003	646,474
Leather		2,018,955		641,552		643,901
Stone, Clay, and Glass	397,601	2,793,899	30,318	1,109,927	5,536,962	2,113,467
Primary Metals	55,472	6,344,321	3,122	2,415,544	1,241,145	4,368,368
Fabricated Metal Products	302,929	3,623,526	59,933	1,359,556	4,860,972	2,021,158
Machinery	661,691	2,495,557	424,696	922,914	103,392	1,157,986
Electrical Machinery	81,110	3,764,314	328,588	1,299,016	717,690	1,382,857
Transportation Equipment	114,168	10,925,494	13,689	3,497,274	1,488	3,630,253
Inst. and Scientific Equipment	548,742	1,353,281	358,364	429,623	78,077	534,860
Miscellaneous Manufacturing	734,515	3,204,571	262,333	1,020,922	23,721	1,088,649
Transportation Services	551,074	15,041,891	302,971	5,311,350	1,858,312	6,421,584
Utilities and Communication	4,610,854	22,794,684	2,271,603	8,071,559	554,834	8,892,467
Wholesale Trades		18,050,941		6,846,110	7,493,774	6,689,623
Retail Trades		51,075,497	147,737	16,174,810		16,328,065
Finance, Insurance, and Real Estate	19,016,299	24,803,187	2,118,357	11,396,141	773,429	11,861,582
Services	8,541,982	71,654,162	584,018	24,325,844	3,014,996	25,215,458
Local Government		13,667,845	53,108	4,532,662	861,397	4,877,639
Households	119,542,925	145,908,667	34,766,764	49,288,112	25,371,334	59,477,293
Other n.e.c.	6,126,562		10,176,855		30,848	
TOTAL	$170,400,000	$552,760,222	$56,800,000	$189,478,244	$56,800,000	$211,185,017

The totals of direct plus indirect impacts, by major economic sectors, for each of these three programs are recorded in columns 2, 3, and 4 of Table 14.11 and their combined totals in column 5. For example, the combined requirements (direct plus indirect) of labor services of households is $434 million. The breakdown of the combined totals for selected four-digit sectors is presented in column 2 of Table A5 (Appendix). For example, their direct plus indirect requirements for the output of sector 3312, *Blast furnaces, Steelworks, and Rolling Mills,* is $7.8 million.

It is appropriate to ask two basic questions at this point. One relates to the question: In what ways would the Philadelphia economy have been different today had there been no Vietnam War and had the three programs listed earlier taken place at the respective levels? A second question is: To what extent could these three programs, at the respective levels listed, have effectively constituted an offset policy in fiscal year 1968 had the Vietnam War come to a halt in that year?

A preliminary answer to both these questions is obtained from the data of Table 14.11 and Table A5. In Table 14.11 we list in column 1 our estimates of the Vietnam War impacts upon the Philadelphia economy by major economic sectors. In column 5, as already indicated, we list the combined total impact of the three programs at the specified level. Subtraction of column 1 from column 5 yields the figures of column 6. These figures list the amounts by which each major economic sector would have been affected favorably when there is no negative sign and affected adversely when there is a negative sign. For example, the first sector, agriculture, forestry, and fishery products, would have been affected favorably (the demand for its output would have increased) to the amount of $21 million. In contrast, the electrical machinery sector would have been affected adversely (demand for the output decreased) by the amount of $59 million. Perusal of this column indicates certain major effects, in particular the adverse effects in the electrical machinery sector and the transportation services sector and the favorable effects in the local government and household sectors. From the standpoint of social welfare, such changes cannot be said to be, in general, undesirable. The availability of more income in the local government and households sectors could be viewed as desirable, particularly since such income is more likely to accrue to the relative benefit of low-income segments of our population. The decline in output in the electrical machinery and transportation services sectors is likely to be a burden, relatively speaking, on the middle- and higher-income groups. But these groups may be judged to be well able to forgo some of the improvement in their income position experienced during the Vietnam War years.

The overall total of column 6 is a negative figure of $40 million. This

Table 14.11. Comparison of Impacts (Direct Plus Indirect) of Vietnam War and Offset Programs, Fiscal Year 1968

| | Vietnam War Impacts (net) (1) | Impacts of Offset Programs | | | | Offset – War (6) |
		Elementary and Secondary Education (2)	Institutions of Higher Education (3)	Low-Income-Housing Construction (4)	Total Impacts of Offset Programs (5)	
Agriculture, Forestry, and Fisheries	$ 29,657,990	$ 31,223,401	$ 9,964,173	$ 9,527,844	$ 50,715,418	$ 21,057,428
Extractive Industries	1,016,872	468,320	186,703	1,240,855	1,895,878	879,006
Construction	13,912,645	8,559,735	4,075,245	3,119,875	15,754,855	1,842,210
Ordnance	1,020,181	1,726	564	645	2,935	− 1,017,246
Food and Kindred	99,729,641	50,435,795	16,141,630	15,302,863	81,880,288	− 17,849,353
Tobacco	3,278,125	2,293,130	726,130	733,045	3,752,305	− 474,180
Textiles	22,326,180	7,901,886	2,600,673	2,623,140	13,125,699	9,200,481
Apparel	28,934,852	7,211,139	2,315,677	2,317,634	11,844,450	− 17,090,402
Lumber and Wood	3,330,534	2,637,425	785,772	3,016,984	6,440,181	3,119,647
Furniture and Fixtures	3,718,708	2,227,605	1,340,740	1,111,668	4,680,013	961,305
Paper and Allied	24,755,532	12,068,520	4,420,077	4,932,717	21,421,314	− 3,334,218
Printing and Publishing	35,336,977	13,933,197	5,257,829	4,415,417	23,606,443	− 11,730,534
Chemicals and Allied	26,418,436	10,826,924	3,671,135	4,548,290	19,046,349	− 7,372,087
Petroleum Refining	19,242,334	10,808,880	3,666,871	5,042,982	19,518,733	276,399
Rubber and Plastics	3,934,879	1,755,823	579,653	823,477	3,158,953	− 775,926
Leather	3,650,101	2,018,955	641,552	643,901	3,304,408	345,693
Stone, Clay, and Glass	9,309,191	3,191,500	1,140,242	7,650,429	11,982,174	2,672,983
Primary Metals	31,865,099	6,399,793	2,418,666	5,609,513	14,427,972	− 17,437,127
Fabricated Metal Products	16,017,380	3,926,455	1,419,489	6,882,130	12,228,074	− 3,789,306
Machinery	22,107,726	3,157,248	1,347,610	1,261,378	5,766,236	− 16,341,490
Electrical Machinery	66,786,083	3,845,424	1,627,604	2,100,547	7,573,575	− 59,212,508
Transportation Equipment	26,542,346	11,039,662	3,510,963	3,631,741	18,182,366	− 8,359,980
Inst. and Scientific Equipment	7,923,757	1,902,023	787,987	612,937	3,302,947	− 4,620,810
Miscellaneous Manufacturing	5,639,258	3,939,086	1,283,255	1,112,370	6,334,711	695,453
Transportation Services	73,036,671	15,592,965	5,614,321	8,279,896	29,487,182	− 43,549,489
Utilities and Communication	44,545,985	27,405,538	10,343,162	9,447,301	47,196,001	2,650,016
Wholesale Trades	32,093,827	18,050,941	6,846,110	14,183,397	39,080,448	6,986,621
Retail Trades	73,344,650	51,075,497	16,322,547	16,328,065	83,726,109	10,381,459
Finance, Insurance, and Real Estate	51,566,965	43,819,486	13,514,498	12,635,011	69,968,995	− 17,970,431
Services	125,566,965	80,196,144	24,909,862	28,230,454	133,336,460	7,769,495
Local Government	− 25,335,173	13,667,845	4,585,770	5,739,036	23,992,651	49,327,824
Households	379,626,396	265,451,592	84,954,876	84,848,627	434,355,095	− 54,728,699
Other, n.e.c.		6,126,562	10,176,855	30,848		
TOTAL	$1,261,322,712	$723,160,222	$246,278,244	$267,985,017	$1,221,089,218	−$40,233,494

constitutes 3.1 percent of the total of column 3, Table 14.5 which represents the total impact of the war. This percentage decline is of minor significance, particularly in light of the various errors that unavoidably exist in the data.

On the question of offset policy, interest goes well beyond the magnitudes that relate to the highly aggregated major economic sectors. An investigator should have the data in as fine detail as possible so as to be able to pinpoint any critical areas of contraction. Accordingly, we present such detail for selected four-digit sectors in Table A5. Note that the major contractions are $48 million in sector 7400, *Research and Development*; $10 million in sector 3312, *Blast Furnaces, Steelworks, and Rolling Mills*; and $9 million in sector 2311, *Men's, Youths', and Boys' Suits, Coats, and Overcoats*. Of these three contractions, only that in sector 2311 could be of real concern, since both the research and development and the steel industry need not have expanded as much as they did during the Vietnam War. (Our economy would have been just as well off, and possibly much better off, if some of the $10 million of basic steel that was produced in the Philadelphia steelworks had not been lost to productive use by society as bulkheads, and so forth, in aircraft carriers but had instead been embodied as structural steel in new schools and hospitals.)

14.5. Some Closing Remarks

Before closing this chapter we wish to make some general remarks. First, we wish to reiterate that the research findings must be viewed as preliminary only; for while the work on the technical input–output coefficients for the Philadelphia region is complete and while our materials on the federal agency structure of the Philadelphia region are also in satisfactory shape, we still must engage in further explorations on appropriate methodology. As discussed in the previous chapter, we must develop at least some crude methodology for adjusting the results (from the use of full, unreduced coefficients) to account for the changed levels and composition of both Philadelphia imports and exports to be anticipated. We then will be in a better position to examine the implications of different policies regarding economic and social problems, whether they relate to the closing down of wartime operations and conversion programs or to diverse national welfare and development programs.

Second, we wish to repeat a point of general significance. This point has been brought into bold relief by the recent discussions concerning the Vietnam War and its relationships to social programs that might be undertaken by the federal government. Of necessity, any given government program must always be viewed in terms of the revenues required to support it. It cannot be contracted or expanded without changing the revenue available for some other government program, whether it be housing, schools, health care, or anything else. There exists, of course, the parallel to this two-sided relationship for every behaving unit we may consider. An individual cannot increase any of his programs—for example, his investments—without changing the revenues available for some other programs—for example, his consumption. The same is true for an organization. In input–output analysis, we frequently have been able to consider only one side of the coin when we have treated individuals or production organizations—for somehow or other we generally have been able to assume that money they do not spend is saved, perhaps stored away, without having any further major repercussions. This assumption is questionable, but nonetheless, for short-run analysis, it has been found acceptable in the sense that the errors and inconsistencies in the resulting analysis have been judged implicitly to be minor. However, in the case of a government unit, there is no mattress or other storage place in which the government can hide its surplus funds. Even when the United States accumulates gold in Fort Knox, this accumulation is generally known to the world and affects interest rates, prices, credit availability, and so forth. In short, we have learned that when analyzing impacts of government programs, we cannot treat any one in isolation. We cannot consider, for example, the impact of change in military expenditures in isolation— as many analysts have tended to do in the past. Such an impact is pure fiction. We unavoidably must consider simultaneously the impact of such change and the corresponding change in one or more other government programs, such as low-income housing, education, and health care.

Finally, the problem attacked in this chapter may be more broadly conceived. It is more than a problem of national dimensions that has regional repercussions—repercussions that on any one region are direct and also indirect via other regions. It is a problem of international dimensions also. It has international dimensions in the sense that the level of United States imports from foreign countries and the composition of these imports is highly dependent upon the national policy with respect to Vietnam War expenditures. Likewise, the level of foreign exports from the United States and its composition are much affected by this policy. Thus, the economies of many nations of the world are directly affected, and almost all are indirectly affected. Further, a number of these economies are strongly oriented to specialized export trade, and any change in foreign trade by major nations such as the United States can result in highly disruptive effects on them. We therefore need to examine the international dimensions of U.S. Vietnam policy and accordingly could employ effectively a multinational input–output table. Such a table would disaggregate for each nation its foreign exports column by receiving nation and its foreign imports row by sending nation.

It may be argued (1) that after all we are studying the Philadelphia region and various direct and indirect impacts upon it, (2) that both the United States and the Philadelphia economies are oriented only to a minor extent to international trade, and (3) that for their study, therefore, a multinational input–output framework is not required. However, if we were to conduct a regional input–output study for a region such as the Calcutta metropolitan region, we could not ignore changes in international trade; the multinational framework would be as important as either the multiregional framework or the strictly regional framework.

Hence, to study the regional impact of any major national policy such as contraction of the Vietnam War effort, we may need to relate such policy to the regional economy in three ways: directly via final demand and a regional input–output matrix; indirectly via a multiregional frame work; and indirectly, via a multinational framework.

Reference

Isard, Walter, and Thomas W. Langford (1969). "Impact of Vietnam War Expenditures on the Philadelphia Economy: Some Initial Experiments with the Inverse of the Philadelphia Input–Output Table," *Papers and Proceedings of the Regional Science Association*, 23: 217–265.

Table 14A.1. Direct, Indirect, and Total Impacts of Regional Federal Agency Expenditures by 4-Digit SIC Sector

Sector		Actual Federal Impact Fiscal Year 1968			Estimated Vietnam War Impacts (net) (Actual 1968 federal impacts less estimated federal impact in a no Vietnam War situation)		
		Direct (1)	Indirect (2)	Total (3)	Direct (4)	Indirect (5)	Total (6)
Agriculture, Forestry, Fisheries							
Fruit, Veg. Prod.	0120	$ 1,273,230	$ 52,549,534	$ 53,822,764	$ 889,401	$ 9,631,859	$ 10,521,260
Dairy Prod.	0132	—	28,012,914	28,012,914	—	5,686,076	5,686,076
Poultry Prod.	0133	76,493	23,636,215	23,712,708	41,072	4,204,970	4,246,042
Other Ag. Prod.	0190	11,313	151,925,992	151,937,305	7,844	6,403,589	6,411,433
Agric., Forest, Fish. Serv.	0708	28,188	8,854,802	8,882,990	-16,150	1,801,708	1,785,558
Forest, Fish. Prod.	0809	—	4,927,121	4,927,121	—	1,007,621	1,007,621
Extractive							
Dimension Stone	1411	10,120	153,766	163,886	2,545	30,296	32,841
Crushed, Broken Stone	1421	89,879	2,370,239	2,460,118	22,604	427,589	450,193
Sand, Gravel	1441	121,597	1,685,217	1,806,814	29,310	309,371	338,681
Mining, n.e.c.	1490	—	977,917	977,917	—	195,157	195,157
Construction							
Maint., Repair Const.	1509	14,032,829	—	14,032,829	3,414,404	—	—
General Contr.	1511	5,116,568	—	5,116,658	76,496	—	76,496
Hgwy., Street Const.	1611	72,220	—	72,220	-9,644	—	-9,644
Heavy Const.	1621	11,802,411	2,528,518	14,330,929	1,299,965	547,514	1,847,479
Special Trade Contr., n.e.c.	1701	38,582	82,696,054	82,734,636	-10,910	7,777,291	7,766,381
Plmb., Heat, Air Cond. Contr.	1711	261,046	10,237,002	10,498,048	-73,797	2,057,907	1,984,110
Elec. Contr.	1731	38,471	7,740,320	7,778,791	-10,873	1,510,575	1,499,702
Resid. Const.	6560	1,295,918	—	1,295,918	728,833	—	728,833
Ord., Access.	1900	1,374,659	18,778	1,393,437	1,022,862	-585	1,022,277

Food						
Meat Packing	2011	4,448,503	101,996,785	106,445,288	3,027,605	18,627,843	21,655,448
Sausage, Prep. Meats	2013	1,918,436	24,046,920	25,965,356	1,310,718	4,640,732	5,951,450
Poultry Dress., Packing	2015	199,986	14,576,196	14,776,182	133,563	2,584,408	2,716,971
Butter, Cheese	2020	128,899	24,145,334	24,274,233	83,832	4,193,872	4,277,704
Ice Cream, Froz. Dess.	2024	2,181,548	5,827,364	8,008,912	903,350	980,478	1,883,828
Fluid Milk	2026	11,404,214	42,472,214	53,876,455	3,422,506	7,513,163	10,935,669
Canned, Cured Seafood	2031	36,561	2,002,584	2,039,145	21,605	336,902	358,507
Canned Specialties	2032	3,157,284	6,311,212	9,468,496	2,241,374	1,114,845	3,356,219
Can. Fruits, Veg., Jams, etc.	2033	746,803	14,548,305	15,295,108	486,304	2,468,900	2,955,204
Pickled Fruit, Veg.	2035	186,446	4,033,332	4,219,778	114,536	696,051	810,587
Fresh, Froz. Pckgd. Fish	2036	268,563	2,558,190	2,826,753	152,095	451,201	603,296
Froz. Fruit, Juice, Veg., Spec.	2037	57,784	6,195,268	6,253,052	25,871	1,053,756	1,079,627
Flour, Grain 'Prod.	2041	6,776	8,865,409	8,872,185	4,499	1,748,180	1,752,679
Prepared Feeds	2042	—	15,760,641	15,760,641	—	2,939,478	2,939,478
Cereal Preparations	2043	92,097	2,734,749	2,826,846	47,958	460,140	508,098
Blend., Prep. Flours	2045	10,409	772,198	782,607	4,575	129,904	134,479
Wet Corn Milling	2046	2,157	1,218,161	1,220,318	902	260,785	261,687
Bread, Bakery Prod.	2051	5,559,173	30,879,600	36,438,773	2,768,611	5,348,247	8,116,858
Biscuits, Crackers, Pretzels	2052	1,270,755	6,018,983	7,289,738	885,714	759,194	1,644,908
Cane Sugar Refining	2062	1,358,891	11,379,351	12,738,242	955,244	4,180,216	5,135,460
Candy, Confections	2071	1,150,197	8,153,549	9,303,746	796,359	1,377,999	2,174,358
Chocolate, Cocoa Prod.	2072	168,932	1,743,708	1,912,640	117,565	324,294	441,859
Chewing Gum	2073	371,218	1,084,752	1,455,970	259,471	182,504	441,975
Malt Liquors	2082	—	8,982,263	8,982,263	—	1,530,610	1,530,610
Wine, Brandy, Brandy Spirits	2084	—	2,242,480	2,242,480	—	394,278	394,278
Distld., Rectfd., Blend Liquor	2085	—	4,949,319	4,949,319	—	844,446	844,446
Soft Drinks, Carbon. Water	2086	740,119	9,314,093	10,054,212	519,000	1,567,020	2,086,020
Flavoring Extracts, Sirups	2087	50,669	4,577,440	4,628,109	33,800	995,335	1,029,135
Food Prep., n.e.c.	2090	937,077	32,022,859	32,959,936	630,010	4,315,354	4,945,364
Grease, Tallow	2094	—	3,465,750	3,465,750	—	6,950,211	6,950,211
Animal, Marine Fats, Oils	2095	65,599	1,577,139	1,642,738	—	340,390	340,390
Shorten., Oils, Marg.	2096	—	6,879,407	6,879,407	41,527	1,283,386	1,324,913
Manufactured Ice	2097	108,919	624,433	733,352	26,140	121,785	147,925

Table 14A.1. (Continued)

Sector		Actual Federal Impact Fiscal Year 1968			Estimated Vietnam War Impacts (net) (Actual 1968 federal impacts less estimated federal impact in a no Vietnam War situation)		
		Direct (1)	Indirect (2)	Total (3)	Direct (4)	Indirect (5)	Total (6)
Tobacco							
Cigarettes	2111	$ 6,157	$ 16,205,123	$ 16,211,280	$ 86	$ 2,757,169	$ 2,757,255
Cigars	2121	6,214	2,086,762	2,092,976	863	355,228	356,091
Tobacco, Snuff	2131	154	967,249	967,403	21	164,758	164,779
Textiles							
Broadwoven Fab., Cotton	2211	347,561	12,994,462	13,342,023	208,505	299,850	508,355
Broadwoven, Manmade, Silk	2221	363,069	8,551,445	8,914,514	221,996	2,302,738	2,524,734
Broadwoven Fab., Wool	2231	1,743,700	8,945,819	10,689,519	1,135,558	2,962,366	4,097,924
Narrow Fab., Smallware	2241	2,175,884	1,222,427	3,398,311	1,402,626	292,791	1,695,417
Fullfashion Hose. Mills	2251	—	1,618,026	1,618,026	—	275,609	275,609
Seamless Hose. Mills	2252	—	3,032,284	3,032,284	—	516,507	516,507
Knit Outerwear Mills	2253	289,355	5,120,145	5,409,500	187,980	882,206	1,070,186
Knit Underwear Mills	2254	—	1,408,529	1,408,529	—	239,925	239,925
Knit Fab. Mills	2256	1,003,986	2,336,444	3,340,430	654,053	587,124	1,241,177
Knitting Mills, n.e.c.	2259	—	557,171	557,171	—	94,907	94,907
Finish., Broadwoven Cotton	2261	6,909	917,788	924,697	960	231,515	232,475
Finish., Manmade, Silk	2262	2,135	499,328	501,463	297	141,418	141,715
Dying, Finish., n.e.c.	2269	148,967	1,098,335	1,247,302	27,556	248,859	276,415
Woven Carpets, Rugs	2271	—	1,950,017	1,950,017	—	333,180	333,180
Tufted Carpets, Rugs	2272	783	1,668,957	1,669,740	109	240,361	240,470
Carpets, Rugs, Mats, n.e.c.	2279	—	1,319,275	1,319,275	—	2,424,880	224,880
Yarn Spinning Mills	2281	—	13,023,768	13,023,768	—	3,347,769	3,347,769
Yarn Throw, Twist, Wind Mills	2282	—	4,824,428	4,824,428	—	1,218,103	1,218,103
Yarn Mills, Wool	2283	—	2,245,306	2,245,306	—	652,235	652,235
Thread Mills	2284	2,549	1,135,280	1,137,829	354	331,567	331,921

	Code						
Felt Goods	2291	12,548	664,396	656,944	1,845	268,943	270,788
Lace Goods	2292		368,231	368,231	—	66,567	66,567
Padding, Uphol. Filling	2293	44,810	554,832	599,642	1,716	165,137	166,853
Proc. Waste Fibers	2294	—	1,486,974	1,486,974	—	441,592	441,592
Artif. Leather, etc.	2295	6,862	240,998	247,860	953	41,533	42,486
Wool Scour., Comb. Mills	2297	—	2,225,367	2,225,367	—	851,169	851,169
Cordage, Twine	2298	582,618	1,317,667	1,900,285	336,659	363,675	700,334
Textile Goods, n.e.c.	2299	76,568	1,743,892	1,820,460	66,333	456,154	522,487
Apparel							
Men-Boys Suits, Coats	2311	15,448,743	11,680,427	27,129,170	9,502,300	1,894,290	11,396,590
Men-Boys Shirts, Nightwr.	2321	697,513	3,868,015	4,565,528	452,331	658,474	1,110,805
Men-Boys Underwear	2322	—	707,738	707,738	—	120,163	120,163
Men-Boys Neckwear	2323	—	140,407	140,407	—	23,917	23,917
Men-Boys Sep. Trous.	2327	2,490,748	2,722,825	5,213,573	1,622,613	463,295	2,085,908
Work Clothing	2328	740,562	1,985,398	2,725,960	302,743	346,036	648,779
Men-Boys Clothing, n.e.c.	2329	1,492,378	1,583,678	3,076,056	928,627	276,462	1,205,089
Womens Blouses	2331	977,015	965,637	1,942,652	636,843	163,594	800,437
Womens Dresses	2335	456,807	6,994,091	7,450,898	297,590	1,191,500	1,489,090
Womens Suits, Skirts, Coats	2337	51,066	6,069,095	6,120,161	137,675	1,006,768	1,144,443
Women-Misses Outerwr.	2339	—	1,701,983	1,701,983	17,720	281,190	298,910
Women-Infants Underwr.	2341	—	2,715,785	2,715,785	—	462,207	462,207
Girdles, Allied Garments	2342	—	1,631,160	1,631,160	—	277,847	277,847
Millinery	2351	824,814	824,814	824,814	—	140,463	140,463
Men-Boys Hats, Caps	2352	2,063,966	986,261	3,050,227	1,344,583	214,743	1,559,326
Girls-Infants Dresses	2361	—	1,836,437	1,836,437	—	312,811	312,811
Girls-Infants Coats, Suits	2363	—	862,584	862,584	—	146,206	146,206
Girls-Infants Outerwr, n.e.c.	2369	—	2,121,709	2,121,709	—	361,406	361,406
Fur Goods	2371	53,368	1,772,345	1,825,713	34,767	304,044	338,811
Dress, Work Gloves	2381	36,290	342,547	378,837	23,641	58,510	82,151
Robes, Dressing Gowns	2384	—	216,183	216,183	—	36,824	36,824
Raincoats	2385	207,191	785,684	992,875	134,976	127,588	262,564
Leather, Lined Clothing	2386	717	60,175	60,892	100	10,252	10,352
Apparel, Belts	2387	—	372,190	372,190	—	63,399	63,399

Table 14.A.1. (Continued)

Sector		Actual Federal Impact Fiscal Year 1968			Estimated Vietnam War Impacts (net) (Actual 1968 federal impacts less estimated federal impact in a no Vietnam War situation)		
		Direct (1)	Indirect (2)	Total (3)	Direct (4)	Indirect (5)	Total (6)
Apparel, n.e.c.	2389	$ 104,192	$ 244,052	$ 348,244	$ 26,204	$ 41,598	$ 67,802
Curtains, Draperies	2391	—	2,124,437	2,124,437	—	363,570	363,570
Housefurnishings	2392	70,782	1,728,422	1,799,204	23,160	293,158	316,318
Textile Bags	2393	257,514	631,897	889,411	165,093	122,115	287,208
Canvas Products	2394	923,599	304,030	1,227,629	601,684	53,877	655,561
Pleating etc. for the Trade	2395	—	155,549	155,549	—	32,193	32,193
Apparel Findings, Related	2396	607,672	3,926,726	4,534,398	387,035	1,460,652	1,847,687
Schiffli Mach. Embroid.	2397	—	385,496	385,496	—	94,640	94,640
Fab. Textile Products, n.e.c.	2399	1,140,457	719,395	1,859,852	777,465	113,910	891,375
Lumber, Wood							
Sawmills, Planing Mills	2421	110,201	10,289,871	10,400,072	23,100	1,813,522	1,836,622
Millwork Plants	2431	56,898	4,902,334	4,959,232	10,401	856,823	867,224
Prefab. Wood Buildings	2433	1,572,529	91,342	1,663,871	27,128	17,391	44,519
Nailed Wood Boxes, Shook	2441	81,242	590,460	671,702	20,433	143,081	163,514
Veneer, Plywood Containers	2443	—	930,772	903,772	—	178,324	178,324
Cooperage	2445	—	130,171	130,171	—	27,954	27,954
Wood Products, n.e.c.	2490	762,352	3,715,173	4,477,525	400,502	733,226	1,133,728
Furniture, Fixtures							
Wood Hsld. Furn.	2511	40,974	5,541,390	5,582,364	8,171	976,454	984,625
Wood Hsld. Furn., Uphol.	2512	—	4,141,256	4,141,256	—	761,551	761,551
Metal Hsld. Furn.	2514	383,695	1,250,297	1,633,992	53,303	324,347	377,650
Mattresses, Bedsprings	2515	4,633	2,289,131	2,293,764	644	388,819	389,463
Hsld. Furn., n.e.c.	2519	—	93,478	93,478	—	15,931	15,931

SIC	Industry				
2521	Wood Office Furn.	93,421	233,688	4,188	41,423	45,611
2522	Metal Office Furn.	746,639	1,295,430	42,589	519,609	562,198
2531	Public Bldg., Rel. Furn.	136,407	1,452,844	73,889	194,751	268,640
2541	Wood Office Store Fixt.	352,936	184,326	40,629	28,912	69,541
2542	Metal Office, Store Fixt.	658,771	132,470	72,207	36,775	108,982
2591	Venetian Blinds, Shades	6,650	607,243	924	101,452	102,376
2599	Furn., Fixt., n.e.c.	105,106	77,214	14,601	17,539	32,140
	Paper					
2621	Paper Mills	812,356	42,821,415	44,401	9,356,694	9,401,095
2631	Paperboard Mills	117,944	15,342,285	—	3,150,836	3,150,836
2640	Converted Paper Prods., n.e.c.	156,273	7,025,656	28,733	1,228,212	1,256,945
2641	Paper Coating, Glazing	389,304	5,384,356	190,793	1,118,446	1,309,239
2642	Envelopes	1,333,408	1,652,713	37,137	358,551	395,688
2643	Bags, Exc. Textile	6,398	7,722,262	914	1,481,122	1,482,036
2645	Die Cut Paper, Cdbrd.	270,556	3,714,708	181,223	596,852	778,075
2651	Folding Paperboard Boxes	1,188	10,177,691	—	2,185,584	2,185,584
2652	Set-Up Paperboard Boxes	28,577	3,028,728	3,970	614,702	618,672
2653	Corrug., Solid Fiber Boxes	1,781	10,447,129	850	2,292,715	2,293,565
2654	Sanitary Food Containers	—	7,179,818	—	1,514,537	1,514,537
2655	Fiber Cans, Tubes, Drums, etc.	109,948	895,729	25,563	216,829	242,392
2661	Building Paper, Board	143,805	437,725	23,244	103,624	126,868
	Printing, Publishing					
2711	Newspapers	109,907	29,517,847	14,159	8,881,412	8,895,571
2721	Periodicals	273,690	3,189,645	98,621	541,644	640,265
2731	Books, Publ., Print.	4,633,437	10,169,771	35,763	2,108,270	2,144,033
2732	Books, Printing	6,233,539	2,753,892	-1,672	476,830	475,158
2741	Misc. Publishing	28,479	2,455,110	3,966	411,132	415,098
2751	Comm. Print., Exc. Litho	5,535,195	15,376,434	192,944	2,776,675	2,969,619
2752	Comm. Print., Litho	19,217,528	8,461,880	10,950,738	1,663,455	12,614,193
2753	Engraving, Plate Print.	—	1,343,612	—	242,101	242,101
2761	Manifold Business Forms	465,317	20,655,443	111,880	3,670,813	3,782,693
2771	Greeting Cards	1,729,271	1,729,271	—	294,560	294,560

Table 14A.1. (Continued)

Sector		Actual Federal Impact Fiscal Year 1968			Estimated Vietnam War Impacts (net) (Actual 1968 federal impacts less estimated federal impact in a no Vietnam War situation)		
		Direct (1)	Indirect (2)	Total (3)	Direct (4)	Indirect (5)	Total (6)
Blankbooks, Binders, etc.	2782	$ 280,350	$ 3,647,300	$ 3,927,650	$ 534	$ 613,895	$ 614,429
Bookbinding, Rel. Work	2789	395,389	5,165,548	5,560,937	—	877,951	877,951
Typesetting	2791	—	2,640,924	2,640,924	—	589,784	589,784
Photoengraving	2793	16,952	2,462,740	2,479,692	—	497,416	497,416
Electro, Stereotyping	2794	—	944,505	944,505	—	201,807	201,807
Print. Trade Services, n.e.c.	2799	237,865	257,334	495,199	—	82,299	82,299
Chemicals							
Industrial Gases	2813	949,195	909,690	1,858,885	215,660	240,451	456,111
Cyclic Crudes	2814	325,506	310,745	636,251	168,927	94,901	263,828
Dyes, Intermed., Pigments	2815	—	4,347,711	4,347,711	—	1,105,651	1,105,651
Inorganic Pigments	2816	23,686	679,345	703,031	3,290	158,354	161,644
Ind. Organic Chem., n.e.c.	2818	131,438	13,347,460	13,478,898	45,391	2,963,067	3,008,458
Ind. Inorganic Chem., n.e.c.	2819	377,230	14,753,449	15,130,679	182,864	3,304,921	3,487,785
Plastic Mtls., Resins, etc.	2821	481,371	6,094,377	6,575,748	173,321	1,522,052	1,695,373
Pharma. Preparations	2830	12,521,168	10,439,662	22,960,830	5,785,228	1,639,237	7,424,465
Soap, Other Detergents	2841	338,340	16,077,773	16,416,113	73,782	2,737,604	2,811,386
Special Clean. Polish Preps.	2842	179,971	5,447,319	5,627,290	37,026	932,245	969,271
Surface Agents, Oils, etc.	2843	69,048	778,391	847,439	12,011	160,755	172,766
Perfumes, Cosmetics, Others	2844	—	6,910,811	6,910,811	—	1,199,001	1,199,001
Paints, Varnishes, Enamels	2851	1,637,135	5,243,689	6,880,824	592,981	1,048,357	1,641,338
Putty, Calking Compounds	2852	187,099	700,550	887,649	84,169	126,668	210,837
Gum, Wood Chemicals	2861	1,326	1,158,911	1,160,237	180	220,223	220,403
Agricultural Chemicals	2870	1,419	2,174,522	2,175,941	197	360,284	360,481
Fertilizers	2871	—	2,537,623	2,537,623	—	499,003	499,003
Glue, Gelatin	2891	107,203	1,483,602	1,590,805	55,739	448,043	503,782

Industry	Code						
Explosives	2892	270,240	2,065,457	2,335,697	153,860	401,842	555,702
Printing Ink	2893	338,019	2,903,699	3,241,718	—	629,503	629,503
Fatty Acids	2894	—	2,241,399	2,241,399	—	494,151	494,151
Carbon Black	2895	—	85,209	85,209	—	16,514	16,514
Chemical Products, n.e.c.	2899	283,589	1,727,983	2,011,572	107,038	294,706	401,744
Petroleum Refineries							
Petroleum Refining	2911	11,277,580	91,750,039	103,027,619	1,568,855	16,844,136	18,412,991
Paving Mixtures, Blocks	2951	198,579	661,799	860,378	49,942	-5,935	44,007
Asphalt Felts, Coatings	2952	24,860	67,221	92,081	4,006	13,531	17,537
Lub. Oils, Greases	2999	37,927	4,129,626	4,167,553	9,536	758,263	767,799
Rubber, Plastic							
Tires, Inner Tubes	3011	91,982	7,942,406	8,034,388	8,924	1,545,757	1,554,681
Rubber Footwear	3021	405,042	686,435	1,091,477	263,867	116,926	380,793
Reclaimed Rubber	3031	—	121,290	121,290	—	25,121	25,121
Fab. Rubber Prods., n.e.c.	3069	360,360	3,892,599	4,252,959	102,148	797,577	899,725
Misc. Plastic Products	3079	313,672	4,524,359	4,838,031	130,722	943,837	1,074,559
Leather							
Leather Tanning, Finish	3111	1,404	3,915,333	3,916,737	195	763,550	763,745
Ind. Leather Belting	3121	—	44,363	44,363	—	9,078	9,078
Boot, Shoe Stock, Findings	3131	—	339,883	339,883	—	69,359	69,359
Footwear	3141	529,274	11,182,644	11,711,918	368,095	1,903,701	2,271,796
House Slippers	3142	—	75,774	75,774	—	12,907	12,907
Luggage	3161	—	603,974	603,974	—	102,876	102,876
Womens Handbags, Purses	3171	—	913,760	913,760	—	155,648	155,648
Personal Leather Goods	3172	197,893	24,212	222,105	128,918	11,164	140,082
Leather Goods, n.e.c.	3199	158,671	92,188	250,859	103,367	21,243	124,610
Stone, Clay, Glass							
Flat Glass	3211	29,712	3,770,296	3,800,008	7,201	757,211	764,412
Glass Containers	3221	1,390	3,696,527	3,697,917	293	788,680	788,973
Pressed, Blown Glassware	3229	34,010	1,930,854	1,964,864	11,353	498,078	509,431

Table 14A.1. (Continued)

Sector		Actual Federal Impact Fiscal Year 1968			Estimated Vietnam War Impacts (net) (Actual 1968 federal impacts less estimated federal impact in a no Vietnam War situation)		
		Direct (1)	Indirect (2)	Total (3)	Direct (4)	Indirect (5)	Total (6)
Prods. from Purchased Glass	3231	$ 1,373,163	$ 1,294,738	$ 2,667,901	$ 200,100	$ 341,385	$ 541,485
Cement, Hydraulic	3241	115,202	4,107,950	4,223,152	28,741	716,119	744,860
Brick, Structural Tile	3251	111,334	3,075,477	3,186,811	27,798	547,548	575,346
Ceramic Wall, Floor Tile	3253	279,896	1,558,353	1,838,249	70,326	288,936	359,262
Clay Refractories	3255	90	1,027,112	1,027,202	—	291,389	291,389
Struct. Clay Prod., n.e.c.	3259	562	132,905	133,467	78	4,626	4,704
Vitreous China Plumb. Fixt.	3261	52,927	50,002	102,929	9,166	7,769	16,935
Pottery Products, n.e.c.	3269	49,850	969,355	1,019,205	6,925	197,989	204,914
Concrete Brick, Block	3271	325,959	2,191,130	2,517,089	82,005	418,236	500,241
Concrete Products, n.e.c.	3272	34,112	830,194	864,306	3,938	136,479	140,417
Ready Mixed Concrete	3273	253,865	1,380,281	1,634,146	32,655	134,897	167,552
Lime	3274	247,993	1,816,432	2,064,425	61,785	344,666	406,451
Gypsum Products	3275	100,958	2,093,489	2,194,447	24,872	335,214	361,086
Cut Stone, Stone Prod.	3281	8,739	142,929	151,668	2,198	23,549	25,747
Abrasive Products	3291	868,812	456,250	1,325,062	330,848	138,922	469,770
Asbestos Products	3292	228,485	1,283,778	1,512,263	107,980	272,399	380,379
Steam Packing, Pipe Cover	3293	1,478,278	284,560	1,762,838	784,728	52,922	837,650
Minerals, Earths, Treated	3295	165,088	1,649,162	1,814,250	23,952	397,960	421,912
Mineral Wool	3296	1,052,325	472,118	1,524,443	608,318	70,218	678,536
Nonclay Refractories	3297	29,194	376,469	405,663	2,570	99,210	101,780
Nonmet. Min. Prods., n.e.c.	3299	3,694	55,390	59,084	513	15,446	15,959
Primary Metals							
Blast Furn., Steel Mill	3312	15,552,205	47,202,032	62,754,237	7,254,818	10,979,988	18,234,806
Steel Wire, Nails, Spikes	3315	1,111,427	4,102,849	5,214,276	393,334	494,586	887,920
Cold Roll Sheet, Strip, Bar	3316	29,057	2,305,916	2,334,973	5,600	561,398	566,998

Steel Pipe, Tube	3317	972,528	2,020,140	2,992,668	548,667	344,886	893,553
Gray Iron Foundries	3321	68,043	2,612,764	2,680,807	12,813	564,618	577,431
Steel Foundries	3323	221,019	3,602,856	3,823,875	75,453	1,064,274	1,139,727
Prim. Smelt, Ref., Nonfe., n.e.c.	3330	1,371,203	4,537,075	5,908,278	84,152	1,295,815	1,379,967
Prim. Smelt, Ref., Zinc	3333	6,063	359,734	365,797	389	84,438	84,827
Prim. Reduction, Alum.	3334	33	4,653,198	4,653,231	3	1,094,521	1,094,524
Secondary Smelt, Ref., Nonfe.	3341	521,179	1,349,223	1,870,393	7,150	377,250	384,400
Roll, Draw, Extrude, Copper	3351	628,672	5,706,701	6,335,373	161,722	1,491,693	1,653,415
Roll, Draw, Extrude, Alum.	3352	685,502	5,241,070	5,926,572	168,723	1,140,648	1,309,371
Roll, Draw, Extrude, Nonfe.	3356	754,871	1,309,685	2,064,556	360,906	417,108	778,014
Draw, Insulate Nonfe. Wire	3357	453,070	4,282,352	4,735,422	274,206	1,009,046	1,283,252
Aluminium Castings	3361	—	877,272	877,272	—	195,038	195,038
Brass, Bronze, Copper Casts	3362	680,949	999,720	1,680,669	460,486	110,045	570,531
Nonfe. Castings, n.e.c.	3369	—	995,991	995,991	—	237,592	237,592
Prim. Metal Indust., n.e.c.	3390	35,842	85,606	121,448	467	26,355	26,822
Iron, Steel Forgings	3391	1,699	1,579,153	1,580,852	236	566,675	566,911
Fabricated Metal Products						
Metal Cans	3411	—	9,363,867	9,363,867	—	2,006,242	2,006,242
Cutlery	3421	23,399	709,353	732,752	4,676	120,418	125,094
Hand, Edge Tools	3423	100,487	341,505	441,992	31,974	41,053	73,027
Hand Saws, Blades	3425	50,323	117,316	167,639	8,311	13,349	21,660
Hardware, n.e.c.	3429	380,610	6,362,438	6,743,048	183,867	1,303,175	1,487,042
Enameled Ironware	3431	125,099	2,323,335	2,448,434	17,594	76,631	94,225
Plumb. Fixt., Fitt.	3432	90,521	630,199	720,720	15,673	111,709	127,382
Heating Equipment	3433	730,829	1,717,605	2,448,434	121,321	306,326	427,647
Fabricated Struct. Steel	3441	1,565,746	1,239,455	2,805,201	940,688	222,193	1,162,881
Met. Doors, Sash, Frame, etc.	3442	77,292	1,304,743	1,382,035	10,737	241,607	252,344
Fabricated Plate Work	3443	99,298	328,694	427,992	19,393	69,560	88,953
Sheet Metal Work	3444	177,015	1,312,178	1,489,193	33,004	239,559	272,563
Arch., Misc. Metal Work	3449	1,290,205	1,113,483	2,403,688	91,468	224,267	315,735
Screw Machine Products	3451	—	1,229,114	1,229,114	—	353,741	353,741
Bolts, Nuts, Screws, Rivets	3452	6,590,838	2,231,783	8,822,621	3,557,029	510,356	4,087,385
Metal Stampings	3461	3,281	4,261,770	4,265,051	456	1,059,736	1,060,192

Table 14A.1. (Continued)

Sector	Actual Federal Impact Fiscal Year 1968			Estimated Vietnam War Impacts (net) (Actual 1968 federal impacts less estimated federal impact in a no Vietnam War situation)		
	Direct (1)	Indirect (2)	Total (3)	Direct (4)	Indirect (5)	Total (6)
3471 Electroplating	$ 73,159	$ 583,197	$ 656,356	$ 10,163	$ 127,145	$ 137,308
3479 Coating Services, n.e.c.	32,795	130,621	163,416	6,473	26,751	33,224
3481 Misc. Fab. Wire Prods.	3,074,503	1,563,466	4,637,969	1,481,358	261,223	1,742,581
3491 Metal Barrels, Drums, Pails		1,472,695	1,472,695		316,381	316,381
3493 Steel Springs	16,551	307,648	324,199	2,299	61,155	63,454
3494 Valves, Pipe Fittings	2,048,572	2,162,094	4,210,666	525,556	339,251	864,807
3496 Collapsible Tubes		77,377	77,377		13,967	13,967
3497 Metal Foil, Leaf	248,877	433,901	682,778	139,181	76,709	215,890
3498 Fab. Pipe, Fittings	96,420	763,520	859,940	22,064	251,814	273,878
3499 Fab. Metal Prods., n.e.c.	223,856	1,443,209	1,667,065	113,642	286,135	399,777
Machinery						
3510 Engines, Turbines, Generator	8,995,969	2,675,019	11,670,988	5,985,389	261,317	6,246,706
3522 Farm Machinery, Equipment	25,830	2,734,385	2,760,215	−16,623	497,935	481,312
3531 Construction Mach. Equip.	2,525,751	777,400	3,303,151	266	89,241	89,507
3534 Elevators, Moving Stairs	112,668	142,168	254,836	17,675	25,640	43,315
3535 Conveyors, Equip.	3,901,390	378,628	4,280,018	−179,920	346,636	166,716
3536 Hoists, Cranes, Monorails	775,793	165,616	941,409	48,197	8,904	57,101
3537 Ind. Mtrl. Hand Equip., n.e.c.	4,330,840	639,164	4,970,004	−79,189	174,723	95,534
3541 Machine Tools, Cutting	6,176,120	333,457	6,509,577	1,908,831	68,421	1,977,252
3542 Machine Tools, Forming	1,229,038	78,995	1,308,033	561,145	21,377	582,522
3544 Dies, Tools, Jigs, Fixt.	1,187,633	1,564,490	2,752,123	841,697	416,645	1,258,342
3545 Mach., Tool Access., Devices	135,434	333,477	468,911	73,158	81,737	154,895
3548 Metalwork Machines, n.e.c.	210,704	1,491,419	1,702,123	29,482	492,841	522,323
3551 Food Products Machinery	272,602	34,608	307,210	37,870	9,218	47,088

Textile Machinery	3552	33,664	67,400	101,064	4,677	23,777	28,454
Woodworking Machinery	3553	33,328	80,178	113,506	4,630	2,033	6,663
Paper Ind. Machinery	3554	—	37,527	37,527	—	10,802	10,802
Print. Trade Machinery	3555	849,717	1,538,084	2,387,801	15,899	266,274	282,173
Spec. Indust. Mach., n.e.c.	3559	21,255	263,073	284,328	7,471	53,686	61,157
Pumps, Compress., Equip.	3561	307,185	700,903	1,008,088	41,573	155,054	196,627
Ball, Roller Bearings	3562	1,421,229	875,538	2,296,767	738,052	192,345	930,397
Blowers, Fans	3564	47,334	239,283	286,617	4,091	23,063	27,154
Industrial Patterns	3565	52,214	209,154	261,368	7,254	45,305	52,559
Mech. Pwr. Transmiss. Equip.	3566	883,220	1,109,421	1,992,641	453,601	155,807	609,408
Industrial Furnace, Oven	3567	455,014	5,064	460,078	45,350	1,309	46,659
Gen. Ind. Mach., Equip., n.e.c.	3569	435,678	858,658	1,294,336	198,995	350,243	549,238
Computing, Acct. Machines	3571	9,108,222	9,108,222	18,402,130	2,467,564	2,180,130	4,647,694
Scales, Balances	3576	11,526	84,622	96,148	1,601	15,894	17,495
Office Machines, n.e.c.	3579	1,830,727	769,315	2,600,042	411,451	196,068	237,519
Automatic Mdse. Mach.	3581	—	55,872	55,872	—	10,348	10,348
Coml. Laund., Dryclng. Equip.	3582	542	73,585	74,127	75	11,794	11,869
Refrigs., Refrig. Mach.	3585	1,223,407	2,902,315	4,125,722	169,313	562,028	731,341
Measure, Dispense Pumps	3586	6,832	62,440	69,272	4,354	11,688	16,042
Service Ind. Machinery, n.e.c.	3589	286,242	557,844	844,086	36,072	79,769	115,841
Machine Shops	3591	259,745	4,802,734	5,062,479	173,917	1,184,328	1,358,245
Machinery, Parts, n.e.c.	3599	118,128	1,757,178	1,875,306	36,143	401,285	437,428
Electrical Machinery							
Elec. Instr., Test Equip.	3611	4,423,606	2,186,871	6,610,477	1,651,675	733,318	2,384,993
Transformers	3612	140,835	4,116,599	4,257,434	14,934	732,745	747,679
Switchgear, Switchboards	3613	2,927,035	2,425,698	5,352,733	1,690,844	526,534	2,217,378
Motors, Generators	3621	612,197	5,055,823	5,668,020	172,739	1,190,823	1,363,562
Industrial Controls	3622	144,202	912,744	1,056,946	42,177	185,345	227,522
Welding Apparatus	3623	1,424,303	253,621	1,667,924	262,844	50,936	313,780
Carbon, Graphite Prod.	3624	29,345	58,394	87,739	4,159	14,801	18,960
Elec. Ind. Apparatus, n.e.c.	3629	275,686	1,834,245	2,109,931	100,580	450,500	551,080
Hsld. Cooking Equip.	3631	—	1,339,027	1,399,027	—	241,453	241,453
Hsld. Laundry Equip.	3633	2	2,853,028	2,853,030	1	486,320	486,321

Table 14A.1. (Continued)

Sector		Actual Federal Impact Fiscal Year 1968			Estimated Vietnam War Impacts (net) (Actual 1968 federal impacts less estimated federal impact in a no Vietnam War situation)		
		Direct (1)	Indirect (2)	Total (3)	Direct (4)	Indirect (5)	Total (6)
Elec. Housewares, Fans	3634	$ 17,484	$ 1,184,633	$ 1,202,117	$ 2,429	$ 255,710	$ 258,139
Hsld. Vacuum Cleaners	3635	—	1,321,439	1,321,439	—	230,768	230,768
Hsld. Appliances, n.e.c.	3639	333	1,290,275	1,290,608	—	220,340	220,340
Lighting Fixtures	3642	1,491,348	4,179,254	5,670,602	560,502	387,899	948,401
Current Carry. Wiring Device	3643	346,816	3,984,675	4,331,491	122,094	1,062,309	1,184,403
Noncurrent Carry, Wiring Devices	3644	339,438	787,000	1,126,438	79,477	163,060	242,537
Radio, TV Receivers	3651	1,646,675	1,598,327	3,245,002	430,591	450,187	880,778
Phonograph Records	3652	1,714	856,105	857,819	238	145,939	146,177
Telephone, Telegraph Equip.	3661	9,979	14,559	24,538	1,980	768	2,748
Radio, TV Transmiss. Equip.	3662	97,525,678	1,595,075	99,120,753	38,890,778	462,782	39,353,560
Radio, TV Electron Tubes	3671	3,818,731	2,017,985	5,836,716	861,798	621,614	1,483,412
Cathode Ray Tubes	3672	260,714	1,437,429	1,698,143	60,696	540,801	601,497
Electronic Components, n.e.c.	3679	2,196,334	28,625,551	30,821,885	478,677	10,458,417	10,937,094
Elec. Mach., Equip., n.e.c.	3690	114,598	583,978	698,576	25,827	370,016	395,843
Storage Batteries	3691	389,780	3,288,489	3,678,269	220,997	298,703	519,700
X-Ray Apparatus, Tubes	3693	500,763	809,043	1,309,806	184,773	347,522	532,295
Elec. Equip., Int. Comb. Eng.	3694	125,079	582,390	707,469	199,812	95,851	295,663
Transportation Equipment							
Motor Vehicles	3711	1,078,133	56,506,662	57,584,795	112,138	9,476,337	9,588,475
Truck, Bus Bodies	3713	51,338	159,960	211,298	604	4,633	5,237
Motor Vehicle Parts, Accs.	3714	2,194,902	34,439,858	36,634,760	1,556,654	5,750,429	7,307,083
Truck Trailers	3715	—	158,214	158,214	—	38,821	38,821
Aircraft	3721	808,899	185,145	994,044	197,088	31,687	228,775
Aircraft Engines, Parts	3722	4,160,782	1,351,837	5,512,619	881,198	245,162	1,126,360
Aircraft Parts, Equip., n.e.c.	3729	32,892,321	4,392,074	37,284,395	7,045,266	905,729	7,950,995
Ship Building, Repairing	3731	13,124,674	170,778	13,295,452	5,372	41,192	46,564
Boat Building, Repairing	3732	7,542	1,256,663	1,264,205	2,182	215,005	217,187
Locomotives, Parts	3741	—	42,095	42,095	—	13,587	13,587

Product	SIC						
Trailer Coaches	3791	—	—	—	—	—	—
Transp. Equip., n.e.c.	3799	12,147	289,849	301,996	1,687	17,575	19,262
Scientific, Control Instruments							
Scientific Instruments	3811	2,297,484	2,454,213	4,751,697	524,744	854,678	1,379,422
Mech. Measure, Cont. Inst.	3821	3,004,474	1,625,995	4,630,469	654,721	420,285	1,075,006
Auto Temperature Controls	3822	126,814	368,890	495,704	15,446	62,749	78,195
Optical Inst., Lenses	3831	583,909	2,057,997	2,641,906	57,582	424,283	481,865
Surgical, Medical Inst.	3841	1,780,648	1,195,223	2,975,871	844,860	259,050	1,103,910
Orthopedic, Prosthetic Accs.	3842	1,166,206	1,574,524	2,740,730	373,679	212,500	586,179
Dental Equip., Supplies	3843	1,820,593	2,066,236	3,886,829	907,045	774,340	1,681,385
Photog. Equip. Supplies	3861	626,929	5,945,955	6,572,884	104,913	1,432,882	1,537,795
Miscellaneous Manufacturing							
Jewelry, Prec. Metal	3911	1,212	1,133,261	1,134,473	168	205,573	205,741
Lapid. Work. Diamonds	3913	—	168,512	168,512	—	28,892	28,892
Silverware, Plated Ware	3914	1,387	272,607	273,994	481	43,842	44,323
Musical Inst., Parts	3931	—	1,612,741	1,612,741	—	276,524	276,524
Games, Toys	3941	103	2,533,523	2,533,626	14	430,932	430,946
Dolls	3942	—	768,244	768,244	—	130,897	130,897
Sport, Athletic Goods, n.e.c.	3949	369	5,013,338	5,013,707	51	828,578	828,629
Pens, Mech. Pencils, Parts	3951	149,304	615,330	764,634	38,139	109,247	147,386
Lead Pencils, Art Mtls.	3952	83,811	1,045,869	1,129,680	17,083	158,776	175,859
Marking Devices	3953	73,971	1,413,982	1,487,953	13,889	234,604	248,493
Carbon Paper, Ink Ribbons	3955	85,197	3,121,038	3,206,235	39,341	537,003	576,344
Costume Jewelry	3961	—	851,743	851,743	—	156,964	156,964
Feathers, Artif. Flowers	3962	—	172,780	172,780	—	33,105	33,105
Needles, Pins, Misc. Notions	3964	8,049	1,049,504	1,057,553	1,118	232,747	233,865
Brooms, Brushes	3981	214,032	1,004,090	1,218,122	85,193	164,680	249,873
Linoleum, Other Floor Cover	3982	35,052	1,326,866	1,361,918	8,503	218,999	227,502
Candles	3984	—	115,891	115,891	—	19,740	19,740
Lamp Shades	3987	—	323,892	323,892	—	57,429	57,429
Morticians' Goods	3988	83,577	2,436,674	2,520,251	11,611	413,381	424,992
Furs, Dressed, Dyed	3992	—	547,139	547,139	—	101,565	101,565
Signs, Adv. Displays	3993	2,204	1,170,050	1,172,254	1,052	194,253	195,305
Umbrellas, Parasols, Canes	3995	—	271,354	271,354	—	46,268	46,268
Misc. Mfg. Indust., n.e.c.	3999	377,201	2,540,423	2,917,624	223,350	575,266	798,616

Table 14A.1. (Continued)

Sector		Actual Federal Impact Fiscal Year 1968			Estimated Vietnam War Impacts (net) (Actual 1968 federal impacts less estimated federal impact in a no Vietnam War situation)		
		Direct (1)	Indirect (2)	Total (3)	Direct (4)	Indirect (5)	Total (6)
Transportation Services							
Railroads	4011	$ 451,736	$ 66,085,168	$ 66,536,904	$ 1,415	$ 21,476,553	$ 21,477,968
Local, Suburban Transit.	4111	207,104	19,586,254	19,793,358	32,511	3,514,645	3,547,156
Taxicabs	4121	61,907	3,143,417	3,205,324	−17,394	611,441	594,047
Transport. Services, n.e.c.	4190	301,709	32,403,838	32,705,547	41,913	11,269,623	11,311,536
Trucking	4210	1,206,745	76,119,976	77,326,721	156,629	26,147,358	26,303,987
Public Warehousing	4220	2,808	841,666	844,474	390	99,266	99,656
Water Transportation	4400	179,055	24,682,259	24,861,314	24,874	7,500,125	7,524,999
Air Transportation	4500	2,740,582	7,666,461	10,407,043	313,518	1,863,804	2,177,322
Transport. Margin Alloc.	9842	80,303,138		—	41,211,605		
Utilities, Communication							
Telephone Comm.	4811	9,748,976	61,819,261	71,568,237	840,749	11,492,919	12,333,668
Radio Broadcasting	4832	—	3,784,002	3,784,002	—	733,795	733,795
Television Broadcasting	4833	—	7,858,985	7,858,985	—	1,524,020	1,524,020
Comm. Services, n.e.c.	4890	828,755	9,888,172	10,716,927	144,608	2,008,639	2,153,247
Elect. Company, Systems	4911	22,588,363	79,642,313	102,230,676	2,529,693	14,761,372	17,291,065
Gas Company, Systems	4920	522,978	37,148,925	37,671,903	−434	6,622,374	6,621,940
Water Supply	4941	6,322,183	9,838,872	16,161,055	1,870,254	1,905,096	3,775,350
Sanitary, Other Systems	4990	112,893	3,108,777	3,221,670	117	112,783	112,900
Wholesale Trade							
Motor Vehicle Whslr.	5012	—	2,895,064	2,895,064	—	493,134	493,134
Auto Equip. Whslr.	5013	50,453	127,035	177,488	7,009	21,640	28,649
Tire, Tube Whslr.	5014	—	4,885,663	4,885,663	—	946,925	946,925
Drug Whslr.	5022	—	2,645,513	2,645,513	—	461,235	461,235
Paint, Varnish Whslr.	5028	1,109	2,126,186	2,127,295	154	448,862	449,016
Chemical Whslr.	5029	8,312	1,075,934	1,084,246	1,155	205,898	207,053
Dry Goods Whslr.	5032	4,138	1,119,307	1,123,445	575	200,876	201,451

Apparel Whslr.	5035	—	8,067,842	8,067,842	—	1,374,248	1,374,248
Footwear Whslr.	5039	1,847	2,554,074	2,555,921	257	435,053	435,310
Grocery Whslr.	5042	7,241	2,208,306	2,215,547	1,006	389,627	390,633
Dairy Product Whslr.	5043	—	1,716,090	1,716,090	—	292,313	292,313
Poultry Product Whslr.	5044	15,442	1,893,881	1,893,881	—	334,826	334,826
Confectionery Whslr.	5045	—	1,869,867	1,885,309	2,145	318,506	320,651
Fish, Seafood Whslr.	5046	—	619,574	619,574	—	105,534	105,534
Meat Whslr.	5047	8,047	3,551,395	3,559,442	1,118	605,087	606,205
Fruit, Veg. Whslr.	5048	2,926	4,080,724	4,083,650	407	695,095	695,502
Grocery Whslr., n.e.c.	5049	5,069	19,615,600	19,620,669	704	3,387,012	3,387,716
Farm Product Whslr.	5051	—	21,813	21,813	—	4,416	4,416
Electrical Mdse. Whslr.	5062	—	4,121,001	4,121,001	—	888,428	888,428
Elect. Apparat., Equip., Whslr.	5063	21,551	251,840	273,391	2,994	42,897	45,891
Elect. Appliance Whslr.	5064	5,172	3,944,144	3,949,316	718	763,027	763,745
Electron. Part, Equip. Whslr.	5065	16,058	1,221,855	1,237,913	2,231	97,344	99,575
Hardware Whslr.	5072	24,876	2,263,881	2,288,757	3,456	456,748	460,204
Plumb., Heat. Equip. Whslr.	5074	45,934	1,968,232	2,014,166	6,381	421,146	427,527
Air Cond., Refrig. Equip. Whslr.	5077	58,716	360,146	418,862	8,157	66,350	74,507
Coml., Ind. Mach., Sup. Whslr.	5082	478,005	4,658,471	5,136,476	66,405	1,002,957	1,069,362
Farm Equip., Mach. Whslr.	5083	—	177,890	177,890	—	32,342	32,342
Professional Equip. Whslr.	5086	3,768	899,295	903,063	523	189,787	190,310
Service Equip. Whslr.	5087	9,606	1,090,913	1,100,519	1,334	204,510	205,844
Mach., Equip., Supply Whslr., n.e.c.	5089	5,616	207,268	212,884	780	35,305	36,085
Metal, Mineral Whslr.	5091	271,834	19,502,299	19,774,133	37,763	4,197,193	4,234,956
Petro. Bulk Stations, Term. Whslr.	5092	—	10,638,017	10,638,017	—	1,974,643	1,974,643
Scrap Waste Whslr.	5093	—	3,665,829	3,665,829	—	989,937	989,937
Misc. Whslr., n.e.c.	5099	535,662	51,749,258	52,284,920	74,414	9,791,240	9,865,654
Retail Trade							
Lumber, Bldg. Mtl. Rtlr.	5210	175,114	12,761,455	12,936,569	24,327	2,173,741	2,198,068
Heat., Plumb. Equip. Rtlr.	5221	—	815,700	815,700	—	138,943	138,943
Paint, Glass, Wallpaper Rtlr.	5231	—	1,733,917	1,733,917	—	295,349	295,349
Electrical Supply Rtlr.	5241	—	274,128	274,128	—	46,695	46,695
Hardware, Farm Equip. Rtlr.	5250	3,694	5,003,399	5,007,093	513	852,261	852,774
Department Stores	5311	9,605	46,597,367	46,606,972	1,334	7,937,231	7,938,565
Variety Stores	5331	—	9,313,679	9,313,679	—	1,586,457	1,586,457
Mail Order, Vend. Machines	5342	13,300	3,113,474	3,126,774	1,848	530,337	532,185

Table 14A.1. (Continued)

Sector		Actual Federal Impact Fiscal Year 1968			Estimated Vietnam War Impacts (net) (Actual 1968 federal impacts less estimated federal impact in a no Vietnam War situation)		
		Direct (1)	Indirect (2)	Total (3)	Direct (4)	Indirect (5)	Total (6)
Direct Selling Orgs.	5351	$ —	$ 18,212,822	$ 18,212,822	$ —	$ 3,102,307	$ 3,102,307
Misc. General Mdse. Rtlr.	5390	—	7,882,862	7,882,862	—	1,342,739	1,342,739
Grocery Rtlr.	5411	—	49,909,192	49,909,193	—	8,501,353	8,501,353
Meat, Fish Rtlr.	5420	—	6,489,935	6,489,935	—	1,105,472	1,105,472
Fruit, Vegetable Rtlr.	5431	—	1,482,077	1,482,077	—	252,452	252,452
Candy, Nut, Confect. Rtlr.	5441	—	904,863	904,863	—	350,886	350,886
Retail Bakeries	5460	—	7,820,459	7,820,459	—	800,633	800,633
Misc. Food Rtlr., n.e.c.	5490	—	1,811,921	1,811,921	—	633,362	633,362
Motor Vehicle Dealers	5511	739	52,240,399	52,241,138	103	8,898,446	8,898,549
Used Motor Vehicle Dealers	5521	—	2,257,033	2,257,033	—	386,691	386,691
Tire, Access. Dealers	5531	—	3,251,653	3,251,653	—	553,874	553,874
Gasoline Service Stations	5541	—	16,380,841	16,380,841	—	2,790,253	2,790,253
Misc. Aircraft, Marine Rtlr.	5599	5,911	1,060,854	1,066,765	821	180,702	181,523
Mens-Boys Clothing Rtlr.	5610	—	8,243,908	8,243,908	—	1,404,237	1,404,237
Womens Ready-to-Wear Rtlr.	5621	—	11,865,523	11,865,523	—	2,021,131	2,021,131
Womens Access., Spec. Rtlr.	5630	—	3,594,871	3,594,871	—	612,339	612,339
Child-Infant Clothing Rtlr.	5641	—	1,613,568	1,613,568	—	274,850	274,850
Family Clothing Stores	5651	—	3,942,546	3,942,546	—	671,559	671,559
Shoe Rtlr.	5660	—	6,001,851	6,001,851	—	1,022,333	1,022,333
Misc. Apparel, Access. Rtlr.	5690	—	2,810,374	2,810,374	—	478,709	478,709
Furniture Home Furn. Rtlr.	5710	739	14,080,838	14,081,577	103	2,398,480	2,398,583
Household Appliance Rtlr.	5722	4,433	4,386,058	4,390,491	616	747,105	747,721
Radio, TV, Music Rtlr.	5730	—	2,676,652	2,676,652	—	455,931	455,931
Eating Places	5812	233,486	46,213,459	46,446,945	32,436	7,874,379	7,906,815
Drinking Places	5813	47,751	21,332,032	21,379,783	7,163	3,648,918	3,641,755
Drug, Proprietary Stores	5912	—	15,129,268	15,129,268	—	2,561,769	2,561,769
Liquor Stores	5921	—	1,201,262	1,201,262	—	204,618	204,618
Book, Stationery Rtlr.	5940	—	1,914,442	1,914,442	—	326,098	326,098

	Code						
Sporting Goods Rtlr.	5950	—	1,045,253	1,045,253	—	253,602	253,602
Jewelry Rtlr.	5971	—	3,057,757	3,057,757	—	520,849	520,849
Fuel, Ice Rtlr.	5980	—	13,403,318	13,403,318	—	2,283,074	2,283,074
Retail Stores, n.e.c.	5990	7,389	18,014,468	18,021,857	1,026	3,068,521	3,069,547
Finance, Insurance, Real Estate							
Federal Reserve Bank	6011	—	312,753	312,753	—	67,723	67,723
Comm., Stock Sav. Banks	6020	203,931	68,286,320	68,490,251	70,761	10,385,628	10,456,389
Mutual Savings Banks	6030	—	22,773,279	22,773,279	—	4,373,518	4,373,518
Savings, Loan Assoc.	6120	—	376,655	376,655	—	64,223	64,223
Misc. Financial Inst., n.e.c.	6190	—	13,254,205	13,254,205	—	2,611,572	2,611,572
Brokers, Dealers, Exchanges	6200	—	6,112,703	6,112,703	—	1,295,720	1,295,720
Nonlife Insurance Carriers	6301	109,305	95,156,640	95,265,945	40,656	16,988,643	17,029,299
Life Insurance Carriers	6310	—	9,887,526	9,887,526	—	1,562,148	1,562,148
R. E., Ins., Other Agents	6590	2,763,646	85,277,839	88,041,485	-63,684	14,601,656	14,537,972
Services							
Hotel, Pers., Repair Serv.	7200	2,027,413	127,199,830	129,227,243	276,365	21,879,239	22,155,604
Bus. Services, Exc. Adv.	7301	19,740,005	106,001,929	125,741,934	2,171,518	21,419,081	23,590,599
Advertising	7310	—	33,296,690	33,296,690	—	6,456,921	6,456,921
Research, Development	7400	98,829,557	1,184,126	100,013,683	48,106,713	183,292	48,290,005
Auto Repair, Service, Garage	7500	3,329,647	38,444,378	41,774,025	20,293	7,845,624	7,865,917
Amusement, Rec. Service	7900	2,162	25,658,059	25,660,221	750	4,482,262	4,483,012
Hospitals	8061	156,577	41,816,932	41,973,509	22,918	6,617,902	6,640,820
Med., Health Service, n.e.c.	8090	4,563,037	58,945,060	63,508,097	867,970	9,538,553	10,406,523
Elem., Second. Education	8211	—	128,117,244	128,117,244	—	1,760,866	1,760,866
Inst. Higher Education	8220	1,201,848	17,433,798	18,635,646	-474,645	3,018,691	2,544,046
Other Educ. Inst., n.e.c.	8290	9,310	3,925,533	3,934,843	1,293	546,400	547,693
Nonprofit orgs., etc.	8486	13,417	48,652,566	48,665,983	3,825	8,112,726	8,116,551
Private Household Services	8800	—	28,560,610	28,560,610	—	4,864,012	4,864,012
Local Government							
Local Government	9300	49,830,320	127,985,145	177,815,465	-49,682,355	24,347,182	-25,335,173
Households							
Households (Wages, Salaries)	9888	660,792,133	1,567,893,601	2,228,685,734	70,961,818	308,664,578	379,626,396

Table 14A.2. Direct and Indirect Impacts of U.S. Army Electronics Command: Philadelphia Office, by Selected 4-Digit Sectors, Fiscal Year 1968

Sectors	SIC	From Operations			From Procurement Activity			Total (7)
		Direct (1)	Indirect (2)	Subtotal (3)	Direct (4)	Indirect (5)	Subtotal (6)	
Chemicals	28	—	$ 3,349,667	$ 3,349,667	$ 2,795	$ 5,491,228	$ 5,494,023	$ 8,843,690
Industrial Gases	2813	—	26,618	26,618	146	103,336	103,482	130,100
Cyclic Crudes	2814	—	5,892	5,892	—	12,471	12,471	18,363
Dyes, Intermed., Pigments	2815	—	133,346	133,346	—	213,132	213,132	346,478
Inorganic Pigments	2816	—	25,986	25,986	—	26,698	26,698	52,684
Ind. Organic Chem., n.e.c.	2818	—	381,868	381,868	227	863,671	863,898	1,245,766
Ind. Inorganic Chem., n.e.c.	2819	—	465,876	465,876	1,196	854,434	855,630	1,321,506
Plastic Mtls., Resins, etc.	2821	—	140,674	140,674	—	455,580	455,580	596,254
Pharma. Preparations	2830	—	342,724	342,724	—	577,330	577,330	920,054
Soap, Other Detergents	2841	—	545,547	545,547	—	728,403	728,403	1,273,950
Special Clean., Polish Preps.	2842	—	182,967	182,967	—	244,434	244,434	427,401
Surface Agents, Oils, etc.	2843	—	24,173	24,173	—	32,352	32,352	56,525
Perfumes, Cosmetics, Others	2844	—	235,712	235,712	—	320,112	320,112	555,824
Paints, Varnishes, Enamels	2851	—	148,325	148,325	196	256,508	256,704	405,029
Putty, Calking Compounds	2852	—	23,760	23,760	155	34,655	34,810	58,570
Gum, Wood Chemicals	2861	—	53,036	53,036	—	47,804	47,804	100,840
Agricultural Chemicals	2870	—	68,578	68,578	—	92,153	92,153	160,731
Fertilizers	2871	—	80,667	80,667	—	110,960	110,960	191,627
Glue, Gelatin	2891	—	50,057	50,057	415	67,971	68,386	118,443
Explosives	2892	—	47,806	47,806	—	106,186	106,186	153,992
Printing Ink	2893	—	242,262	242,262	—	116,458	116,458	358,720
Fatty Acids	2894	—	63,826	63,826	—	140,642	140,642	204,468
Carbon Black	2895	—	2,984	2,984	—	3,920	3,920	6,904
Chemical Products, n.e.c.	2899	—	56,983	56,983	460	82,018	82,478	139,461
Primary Metals	33	—	$ 1,934,318	$ 1,934,318	1,819	$ 5,885,989	$ 5,887,808	$ 7,822,216

Industry	Code							
Blast Furn., Steel Mill	3312	—	993,920	993,920	—	2,485,251	2,485,251	3,479,171
Steel Wire, Nails, Spikes	3315	—	81,071	81,071	1,819	344,164	345,983	427,054
Cold Roll Sheet, Strip, Bar	3316	—	27,821	27,821	—	170,664	170,664	198,485
Steel Pipe, Tube	3317	—	35,035	35,035	—	71,939	71,939	106,974
Gray Iron Foundries	3321	—	57,175	57,175	—	119,000	119,000	176,175
Steel Foundries	3323	—	40,445	40,445	—	137,690	137,690	178,135
Prim. Smelt, Ref., Nonfe., n.e.c.	3330	—	63,388	63,388	—	352,885	352,885	416,273
Prim. Smelt, Ref., Zinc	3333	—	7,044	7,044	—	24,394	24,394	31,438
Prim. Reduction, Alum.	3334	—	87,467	87,467	—	302,678	302,678	390,145
Secondary Smelt, Ref., Nonfe.	3341	—	190,631	190,631	—	58,494	58,494	249,125
Roll, Draw, Extrude, Copper	2251	—	91,917	91,917	—	586,436	586,436	678,353
Roll, Draw, Extrude, Alum.	3352	—	114,883	114,883	—	314,190	314,190	429,073
Roll, Draw, Extrude, Nonfe.	3356	—	15,822	15,822	—	177,091	177,091	192,913
Draw, Insulate Nonfe., Wire	3357	—	66,028	66,028	—	448,958	448,958	514,986
Aluminium Castings	3361	—	17,024	17,024	—	54,377	54,377	71,401
Brass, Bronze, Copper Casts	3362	—	7,996	7,996	—	79,912	79,912	87,908
Nonfe., Castings, n.e.c.	3369	—	19,337	19,337	—	123,808	123,808	143,145
Prim. Metal Industries, n.e.c.	3390	—	1,105	1,105	—	4,434	4,434	5,539
Iron, Steel Forgings	3391	—	16,209	16,209	—	29,624	29,624	45,833
		$ 649,886	$21,153,598	$21,803,484	$37,619,247	$31,322,418	$68,941,665	$90,745,149
Services								
Hotel Pers., Repair Serv.	7200	—	4,365,709	4,365,709	—	5,796,121	5,796,121	10,161,830
Bus. Services, Ex. Adv.	7301	649,886	3,505,064	4,155,950	—	5,797,646	5,797,646	9,953,596
Advertising	7310	—	1,041,419	1,041,419	—	1,700,652	1,700,652	2,742,071
Research, Development	7400	—	27,781	27,781	37,619,247	60,983	37,680,230	37,708,011
Auto Repair, Service, Garage	7500	—	1,171,769	1,171,769	—	1,945,288	1,945,288	3,177,057
Amusement, Rec. Serv.	7900	—	849,326	849,326	—	1,253,420	1,253,420	2,102,746
Hospitals	8061	—	1,417,009	1,417,009	—	1,885,192	1,885,192	3,302,201
Med., Health Services, n.e.c.	8090	—	1,997,639	1,997,639	—	2,645,258	2,645,258	4,642,897
Elem., Second. Education	8211	—	3,421,862	3,421,862	—	5,720,023	5,720,023	9,141,885
Inst. Higher Education	8220	—	594,070	594,070	—	804,915	804,915	1,393,985
Other Educ. Inst., n.e.c.	8290	—	130,929	130,929	—	173,857	173,857	304,786
Nonprofit Orgs., etc.	8486	—	1,645,283	1,645,283	—	2,248,549	2,248,549	3,893,832
Private Household Services	8800	—	984,738	984,738	—	1,290,514	1,290,514	2,275,252

Table 14.A3. Direct and Indirect Impacts of Increased Operations due to Vietnam War, by Selected 4-Digit SIC Sectors, U.S. Naval Shipyard, Philadelphia, Fiscal Year 1968 (actual 1968 expenditures less estimated expenditures of a no Vietnam War situation)

Sector		Direct (1)	Indirect (2)	Total (3)
Chemicals		$ 580,780	$ 2,880,159	$ 3,460,939
Industrial Gases	2813	100,156	31,912	132,068
Cyclic Crudes	2814	84	8,325	8,409
Dyes, Intermed., Pigments	2815	—	188,781	188,781
Inorganic Pigments	2816	3,290	35,130	38,420
Ind. Organic Chem., n.e.c.	2818	9,351	424,388	433,739
Ind. Inorganic Chem., n.e.c.	2819	11,942	465,158	477,100
Plastic Mtls., Resins, etc.	2821	28,139	192,080	220,219
Pharma. Preparations	2830	12,354	250,217	262,571
Soap, Other Detergents	2841	4,467	401,298	405,765
Special Clean., Polish Preps.	2842	5,411	135,338	140,749
Surface Agents, Oils, etc.	2843	4,070	18,578	22,648
Perfumes, Cosmetics, Others	2844	—	171,213	171,213
Paints, Varnishes, Enamels	2851	386,396	147,225	533,621
Putty, Calking Compounds	2852	1,259	14,300	15,559
Gum, Wood Chemicals	2861	175	27,755	27,930
Agricultural Chemicals	2870	197	52,637	52,834
Fertilizers	2871	—	64,933	64,933
Glue, Gelatin	2891	358	34,783	35,141
Explosives	2892	—	42,201	42,201
Printing Ink	2893	—	59,210	59,210
Fatty Acids	2894	—	71,591	71,591
Carbon Black	2895	—	1,978	1,978
Chemical Products, n.e.c.	2899	13,215	41,043	54,258
Primary Metals		$ 4,390,437	$ 4,380,667	$ 8,771,104
Blast Furnace, Steel Mill	3312	2,683,173	2,060,521	4,743,694
Steel Wire, Nails, Spikes	3315	422	110,755	111,177
Cold Roll Sheet, Strip, Bar	3316	2,108	76,206	78,314
Steel Pipe, Tube	3317	519,928	59,152	579,080
Gray Iron Foundries	3321	5,305	102,403	107,708
Steel Foundries	3323	75,453	413,970	489,423
Prim. Smelt, Ref., Nonfe., n.e.c.	3330	84,152	417,909	502,061
Prim. Smelt, Ref., Zinc	3333	389	14,471	14,860
Prim. Reduction, Alum.	3334	—	209,615	209,615
Secondary Smelt, Ref., Nonfe.	3341	195	31,781	31,976
Roll, Draw, Extrude, Copper	3351	155,672	262,191	417,863
Roll, Draw, Extrude, Alum.	3352	162,959	120,514	283,473
Roll, Draw, Extrude, Nonfe.	3356	19,467	21,139	40,606
Draw, Insulate Nonfe., Wire	3357	220,790	124,992	345,782
Aluminium Castings	3361	—	16,138	16,138
Brass, Bronze, Copper Casts	3362	459,721	16,066	475,787
Nonfe. Castings, n.e.c.	3369	—	11,857	11,857
Prim. Metal Industries, n.e.c.	3390	467	1,672	2,139
Iron, Steel Forgings	3391	236	309,315	309,551

Table 14.A3 (Continued)

Sector		Direct (1)	Indirect (2)	Total (3)
Services		$ 879,671	$ 16,410,995	$ 17,290,666
Hotel Pers., Repair Serv.	7200	263,832	3,198,174	3,462,006
Bus. Services, Ex. Adv.	7301	406,014	2,820,022	3,226,036
Advertising	7310	—	832,654	832,654
Research Development	7400	3,644	62,331	65,975
Auto Repair, Service, Garage	7500	171,530	964,339	1,135,869
Amusement, Rec. Serv.	7900	—	643,746	643,746
Hospitals	8061	—	1,038,206	1,038,206
Med., Health Services, n.e.c.	8090	7,938	1,459,162	1,467,100
Elem. Second. Education	8211	—	2,921,615	2,921,615
Inst. Higher Education	8220	24,866	439,524	464,390
Other Educ. Inst., n.e.c.	8290	1,293	95,870	97,163
Nonprofit Orgs., etc.	8486	554	1,221,378	1,221,932
Private Household Services	8800	—	713,974	713,974

Table 14A.4. Direct and Indirect Impacts of Hypothetical Offset Programs, by Selected 4-Digit Sectors, Fiscal Year 1968

Sectors	RIS Code	Elementary, Secondary Education Direct (1)	Indirect (2)	Institutions of Higher Education Direct (3)	Indirect (4)	Low Income Housing Construction Direct (5)	Indirect (6)
Apparel							
Men-Boys Suits, Coats	2311	$ —	$ 1,371,631	$ 682	$ 436,053	$ —	$ 442,319
Men-Boys Shirts Nightwr.	2321	—	460,654	—	145,867	—	147,253
Men-Boys Underwear	2322	—	84,244	—	26,678	—	26,937
Men-Boys Neckwear	2323	—	16,723	—	5,295	—	5,345
Men-Boys Sep. Trous.	2327	—	324,239	—	102,672	—	103,652
Work Clothing	2328	—	227,330	—	72,058	—	73,024
Men-Boys Clothing, n.e.c.	2329	—	186,859	—	59,169	—	59,728
Womens Blouses	2331	—	114,894	—	36,385	—	36,746
Womens Dresses	2335	—	832,106	—	263,732	—	266,215
Womens Suits, Skirts, Coats	2337	—	703,563	—	222,784	—	224,896
Womens-Misses Outerwear	2339	—	196,630	1,079	62,263	—	62,852
Womens-Infants Underwear	2341	—	323,416	—	102,411	—	103,386
Girdles, Allied Garments	2342	—	194,282	—	61,519	—	62,100
Millinery	2351	—	98,217	—	31,100	—	31,394
Men-Boys Hats, Caps	2352	—	105,898	—	33,533	—	33,849
Girls-Infants Dresses	2361	—	218,732	—	69,261	—	69,915
Girls-Infants Coats, Suits	2363	—	102,642	—	32,505	—	32,826
Girls-Infants Outerwr, n.e.c.	2369	—	252,710	—	80,020	—	80,776
Fur Goods	2371	—	210,567	—	66,676	—	67,305
Dress, Work Gloves	2381	—	40,709	—	12,949	—	13,058
Robes, Dressing Gowns	2384	—	25,749	—	8,153	—	8,230
Raincoats	2385	—	92,559	—	29,515	—	29,762
Leather, Lined Clothing	2386	—	7,167	—	2,270	—	2,291
Apparel Belts	2387	—	44,330	—	14,037	—	14,170
Apparel, n.e.c.	2389	—	29,009	—	9,205	—	9,290

Curtains, Draperies	2391	—	249,923	852	80,043	—	81,380
Housefurnishings	2392	—	204,586	20,789	65,169	—	65,916
Textile Bags	2393	—	73,824	—	23,945	213	23,070
Canvas Products	2394	—	34,379	—	11,147	—	11,590
Pleating etc. for the Trade	2395	—	16,649	—	5,273	—	5,325
Apparel Findings, Related	2396	—	254,233	—	81,689	—	81,682
Schiffli Mach. Embroid.	2397	—	36,065	—	13,865	—	13,316
Fab. Textile Products, n.e.c.	2399	—	76,620	—	25,034	106	27,717
SUBTOTAL		$ 0	$ 7,211,139	$ 23,402	$ 2,292,275	$ 319	$ 2,317,315
Primary Metals							
Blast Furnace, Steel Mill	3312	—	3,583,882	2,954	1,346,082	507,286	2,391,009
Steel Wire, Nails, Spikes	3315	55,472	310,387	168	124,889	5,638	117,874
Cold Roll Sheet, Strip, Bar	3316	—	99,193	—	42,072	—	92,118
Steel Pipe, Tube	3317	—	127,286	—	48,680	72,226	100,089
Gray Iron Foundries	3321	—	152,162	—	56,994	171,152	109,815
Steel Foundries	3323	—	156,338	—	56,612	—	135,276
Prim. Smelt, Ref., Nonfe., n.e.c.	3330	—	220,689	—	83,897	—	260,559
Prim. Smelt, Ref., Zinc	3333	—	24,536	—	9,586	—	22,723
Prim. Reduction, Alum.	3334	—	315,400	—	114,972	—	371,025
Secondary Smelt, Ref., Nonfe.	3341	—	108,641	—	43,297	—	42,751
Roll, Draw, Extrude, Copper	3351	—	342,935	—	134,446	353,473	225,865
Roll, Draw, Extrude, Alum.	3352	—	411,985	—	151,710	59,462	217,585
Roll, Draw, Extrude, Nonfe.	3356	—	54,687	—	18,938	23,083	53,416
Draw, Insulate Nonfe., Wire	3357	—	242,235	—	110,807	14,786	114,932
Aluminium Castings	3361	—	56,184	—	21,327	—	22,629
Brass, Bronze, Copper Casts	3362	—	32,363	—	10,497	—	40,625
Nonfe. Castings, n.e.c.	3369	—	41,411	—	20,473	—	19,139
Prim. Metal Industries, n.e.c.	3390	—	3,499	—	1,469	34,039	9,612
Iron, Steel Forgings	3391	—	60,508	—	18,796	—	21,326
SUBTOTAL		$ 55,472	$ 6,344,321	$ 3,122	$ 2,415,544	$ 1,241,145	$ 4,368,368

Table 14A.4. (Continued)

Sectors,	RIS Code	Elementary, Secondary Education		Institutions of Higher Education		Low Income Housing Construction	
		Direct (1)	Indirect (2)	Direct (3)	Indirect (4)	Direct (5)	Indirect (6)
Services							
Hotel Pers., Repair Serv.	7200	$ 1,534	$ 15,021,215	$ 110,930	$ 4,777,054	$ —	$ 4,865,795
Bus. Services, Ex. Adv.	7301	442,188	10,606,128	246,342	4,169,650	2,263,269	4,217,641
Advertising	7310	21,300	3,493,757	35,898	1,160,534	193,171	1,305,610
Research, Development	7400	—	93,850	99,968	30,093	—	38,819
Auto Repair, Services, Garage	7500	—	3,977,283	1,931	1,348,780	435,592	1,556,340
Amusement, Rec. Serv.	7900	625,368	3,140,507	—	970,821	—	1,009,933
Hospitals	8061	—	4,893,732	—	1,563,173	25,316	1,585,189
Med Health Services, n.e.c.	8090	2,639,326	7,158,972	22,834	2,207,964	51,058	2,231,373
Elem., Second. Education	8211	4,809,199	11,635,142	—	4,346,357	—	4,641,932
Inst. Higher Education	8220	3,067	2,050,709	—	667,317	—	668,671
Other Educ. Inst., n.e.c.	8290	—	451,048	—	143,391	12,126	147,184
Nonprofit Orgs., etc.	8486	—	5,730,057	66,115	1,863,547	34,464	1,859,636
Private Household Services	8800	—	3,401,762	—	1,077,163	—	1,087,335
SUBTOTAL		$ 8,541,982	$ 71,654,162	$ 584,018	$ 24,325,844	$ 3,014,996	$ 25,215,458

Table 14A.5. Comparison of Total Impacts: Vietnam War and Offset Programs, Fiscal Year 1968

		Vietnam War	Offset Programs	Offset − War
Apparel				
Men-Boys Suits, Coats	2311	$ 11,396,590	$ 2,250,685	$ − 9,145,905
Men-Boys Shirts, Nightwr.	2321	1,110,805	753,774	− 357,031
Men-Boys Underwear	2322	120,163	137,859	17,696
Men-Boys Neckwear	2323	23,917	27,363	3,446
Men-Boys Sep. Trous.	2327	2,085,908	530,563	− 1,555,345
Work Clothing	2328	648,779	372,412	− 276,367
Men-Boys Clothing, n.e.c.	2329	1,205,089	305,756	− 899,333
Womens Blouses	2331	800,437	188,025	− 612,412
Womens Dresses	2335	1,489,090	1,362,053	− 127,037
Womens Suits, Skirts, Coats	2337	1,144,443	1,151,243	6,800
Womens-Misses Outerwear	2339	298,910	322,824	23,914
Womens-Infants Underwear	2341	462,207	529,213	67,006
Girdles, Allied Garments	2342	277,847	317,901	40,054
Millinery	2351	140,463	160,711	20,248
Men-Boys Hats, Caps	2352	1,559,326	173,280	− 1,386,046
Girls-Infants Dresses	2361	312,811	357,908	45,097
Girls-Infants Coats, Suit	2363	146,206	167,973	21,767
Girls-Infants Outerwr., n.e.c.	2369	361,406	413,506	52,100
Fur Goods	2371	338,811	344,548	5,737
Dress, Work Gloves	2381	82,151	66,716	− 15,435
Robes, Dressing Gowns	2384	36,824	42,132	5,308
Raincoats	2385	262,564	151,836	− 110,728
Leather, Lined Clothing	2386	10,352	11,728	1,376
Apparel, Belts	2387	63,399	72,537	9,138
Apparel, n.e.c.	2389	67,802	47,504	− 20,298
Curtains, Draperies	2391	363,570	412,198	48,628
Housefurnishings	2392	316,318	356,460	40,142
Textile Bags	2393	287,208	121,052	− 166,156
Canvas Products	2394	655,561	57,116	− 598,445
Pleating etc. for the Trade	2395	32,193	27,247	− 4,946
Apparel Findings, Related	2396	1,847,687	417,604	− 1,430,083
Schiffli Mach., Embroid.	2397	94,640	63,246	− 31,394
Fab. Textile Products, n.e.c.	2399	891,375	129,477	− 761,898
Primary Metals				
Blast Furnace, Steel Mill	3312	18,234,806	7,831,213	− 10,403,593
Steel Wire, Nails, Spikes	3315	887,920	614,428	− 273,492
Cold Roll Sheet, Strip, Bar	3316	566,998	233,383	− 333,615
Steel Pipe, Tube	3317	893,553	348,281	− 545,272
Gray Iron Foundries	3321	577,431	490,123	− 87,308
Steel Foundries	3323	1,139,727	348,226	− 791,501
Prim. Smelt, Ref., Nonfe., n.e.c.	3330	1,379,967	565,145	− 814,822
Prim. Smelt, Ref., Zinc	3333	84,827	56,845	− 27,982
Prim. Reduction, Alum.	3334	1,094,524	801,397	− 293,127
Secondary Smelt Ref., Nonfe.	3341	384,400	194,689	− 189,711
Roll, Draw, Extrude, Copper	3351	1,653,415	1,056,719	− 596,696
Roll, Draw, Extrude, Alum.	3352	1,309,371	840,742	− 468,629
Roll, Draw, Extrude, Nonfe.	3356	778,014	150,124	− 627,890

Table 14A.5. (Continued)

		Vietnam War	Offset Programs	Offset— War
Draw, Insulate Nonfe., Wire	3357	1,283,252	482,760	−800,492
Aluminium Castings	3361	195,038	110,140	−84,898
Brass, Bronze, Copper Casts	3362	570,531	83,485	−487,046
Nonfe. Castings, n.e.c.	3369	237,592	81,023	−156,569
Prim. Metal Industries, n.e.c.	3390	26,822	48,619	21,797
Iron, Steel Forgings	3391	566,911	100,630	−466,281
Services				
Hotel Pers., Repair Serv.	7200	22,155,604	24,776,528	2,620,924
Bus. Services, Ex. Adv.	7301	23,590,599	21,945,278	−1,645,321
Advertising	7310	6,456,921	6,210,270	−246,651
Research, Development	7400	48,290,005	262,730	−48,027,275
Auto Repair, Service, Garage	7500	7,865,917	7,319,926	−545,991
Amusement, Rec. Serv.	7900	4,483,012	5,746,629	1,263,617
Hospitals	8061	6,640,820	8,067,410	1,426,590
Med., Health Services, n.e.c.	8090	10,406,523	14,311,527	3,905,004
Elem., Second. Education	8211	1,760,866	25,432,630	23,671,764
Inst. Higher Education	8220	2,544,046	3,389,764	845,718
Other Educ. Inst., n.e.c.	8290	547,693	753,749	206,056
Nonprofit Orgs., etc.	8486	8,116,551	9,553,819	1,437,268
Private Household Services	8800	4,864,012	5,566,260	702,248

We now have completed the Philadelphia region input–output study. In retrospect, we would seek many improvements if we were to do the study over again. A number of these have already been discussed. However, we would also probe some new directions, two of which we shall discuss briefly.

Since the inception of the study, both the variety and relative significance of pressing research problems have changed. There has been a major shift away from the impact of scientific development and military expenditures upon the economy to the problems of developing programs to meet new social demands and reduce the mounting tensions within society. We also confront environmental problems that have increased in severity almost without limit. It is to these environmental problems that we wish first to address ourselves.[1]

15.1 Environmental Quality Analysis

Perhaps in no area more than that relating to environmental quality is the strategic importance of input–output more clear. It appears that an approach involving an input–output framework is almost a sine qua non for meaningful analysis of environmental problems on a *comprehensive* scale. There does not seem to be any other systematic way of projecting conditions of both demand and supply regarding environmental commodities—resources and pollutants.

As demonstrated in our book on ecologic and economic analysis for regional planning [Isard, Choguill, Kissin, et al., 1971], the input–output framework can rather easily be extended to cover the ecologic system—to embrace new ecologic commodities, of which air and water are only two; to embrace diverse ecologic processes, of which photosynthesis and the replenishment of the oxygen supply in water are two; and to pertain to different sets of regions, of which air, marine, and land are three.

Let us elaborate on these statements in some detail. Consider ecologic commodities. We would insist that the technical production coefficients for any economic sector, for example, the steel sector, cover as inputs not only economic commodities such as coal, ore, professional services, and labor but also ecologic commodities such as water (for sanitary, production, cooling, boiler, irrigation, and other purposes), air, and land of diverse types. We would also insist that they cover the several outputs not only of economic commodities such as steel by type, slag, and by-product gas, but also of ecologic commodities such as polluted water (from sanitary, production, cooling, and other uses), biological oxygen demand (BOD, 5-day), ultimate oxygen demand (UOD), chemical oxygen demand (COD), suspended solids, settleable solids, turbidity, alkalinity, acidity, and temperature (BTU). They should also cover the

[1] The first section of this chapter draws heavily on Isard, 1968.

outputs of the ecological commodities hydrogen sulfide (H_2S), sulfur dioxide (SO_2), particulates, and other air pollutants, diverse solid wastes, noise, and all other items of significance in terms of environmental quality and potential disturbance to the environment. In short, for each sector of the economy, we would insist on complete data for ecologic as well as economic commodities, as both inputs and outputs.

To develop such coefficients implies that we extend the number of rows in an input–output table by as many as the number of ecologic commodities to be encompassed. We have already begun this process [Isard, 1968; Isard, et al., 1967; Isard, Choguill, Kissin, et al., 1971].

Once ecologic commodities are introduced into the framework, it also becomes important to encompass those processes that yield these commodities as outputs. Such processes may, of course, use some of these commodities as inputs. For example, we must incorporate the ecologic process that replenishes the oxygen supply of water depleted by biological oxygen demand (BOD) and other demands. We also should include those natural processes that remove particulates from the air, such as rain and wind movement. These processes may be viewed essentially as employing as inputs the diverse pollutants that are generated and yielding as outputs water and air of specified quality. The relevant data on inputs and outputs are to be recorded in appropriately titled columns of an input–output table.

The conceptual framework and the operational model must be extended still further. We know that pollutants that are "exported" to the ecologic system at a given location interfere with processes going on there. For example, an increase in turbidity of the water decreases the depth of penetration of light and thus reduces the phytoplankton output from photosynthesis in the marine area. This in turn affects the supply of plankton, algae production, and so on, and finally fish production (for example, winter flounder production in the context of New England coastal areas). Change in the supply of fish then affects the desirability and profitability of recreational fishing at any location for which that production represents a significant resource. Since these and other feedback effects upon recreation and other sectors of the economy are significant, it becomes essential to examine in detail the interrelationships between pollutants and the outputs of diverse environmental processes to the economy. To conduct such analysis requires that there be a full and systematic collection of data on all the environmental processes involved. Thus, we require specification of the photosynthesis process—to be exact, the several photosynthesis processes—as well as the zooplankton grazing process, the herbivorous invertebrates production process, the carnivorous invertebrates production process, and so forth, and finally recreational or commercial fish production processes.

In short, if we are conducting an impact study of a new facility upon a region—for example, the New England region—and seek a complete study incorporating indirect effects on recreational resources and growth potential of the recreation industry, it becomes necessary to spell out all the stages involved in the relevant food chains—beginning with the incidence of the sun's radiation on the marine surface and ending with the processes that may be characterized as the fish production processes.

As detailed elsewhere, one can easily visualize for empirical analysis a four-part table such as that in Table 15.1. The upper left quadrant corresponds to a table that might be characterized as an input–output table

Table 15.1. Matrix of Economic and Ecologic Processes

		Economic Activities						Ecologic Processes			
		Agriculture	Textile	...	Petroleum Refining	...	Sport Fishing	...	...	Plankton Production	Herring Production	Cod Production
Economic Commodities	Wheat											
	Cloth											
	⋮			Economic System: Intersector Coefficients				Ecologic Processes: Their Input and Output Coefficients re Economic Commodities				
	Crude Oil											
Ecologic Commodities	Water Intake											
	Alkalinity											
	⋮			Economic Sectors: Their Input and Output Coefficients re Ecologic Commodities				Ecologic System: Interprocess Coefficients				
	Detritus											
	Plankton										+	−
	Herring										+	−
	Cod						−					+

Source: Isard, 1968, p. 87.

or an activities analysis table. It refers to the Economic System: Intersector Coefficients. Along the columns are listed the standard economic sectors, such as those in the Philadelphia input–output table, or alternatively, the activities of a programming problem. Along the rows are listed, in corresponding order, commodities (as primary output) of the respective sectors and activities.

However, economic activities may require ecologic commodities as inputs and yield ecologic commodities as outputs. Therefore, to record systematically the data on such commodities, the lower left quadrant of the table is required. It refers to the Economic Sectors: Their Input and Output Coefficients re Ecologic Commodities. Along the rows of this quadrant are listed the relevant ecologic commodities. The columns of this quadrant still refer to the traditional input–output or activity sectors.

Further, we must consider diverse ecologic processes such as replenishment of the oxygen supply of water, photosynthesis, and winter flounder production. These are listed at the head of the columns in the right half of the table. The ecologic commodities that are involved either as inputs or outputs are recorded in the lower right quadrant. It refers to the Ecologic System: Interprocess Coefficients. Finally, the economic commodities that may be involved as inputs or outputs are listed in the upper right quadrant. It refers to Ecologic Processes: Their Input and Output Coefficients re Economic Commodities.

Table 15.1 provides a conceptual framework. However, to be able to attack environmental quality problems, we must also be able to implement the conceptual framework empirically. Therefore, we now illustrate how the conceptual framework of Table 15.1 can be implemented.

Let us begin by considering a classic polluting economic sector, namely, the petroleum refining industry. In the upper part of Table 15.2 are listed its typical inputs and outputs of economic commodities in coefficient form. For example, the first coefficient, —0.555848, is the dollar's worth of input of crude petroleum and natural gas per dollar output of the industry, and the coefficient for sector 9888, —0.089378, is wages and salaries per dollar output of the industry.

But the petroleum refining industry requires inputs of water and yields as outputs pollutants discharged via water to the environment. To consider this set of inputs and outputs, a workable classification of noneconomic commodities is needed. A very preliminary classification with reference to water use and pollution has been developed and is presented in Table 15.3. For example, the fourth item in Table 15.3 is water intake for cooling (in 1,000 gallons per dollar output) and the third from the last item is toxic material. If one lists the set of noneconomic commodities as shown in Table 15.3 along the left-hand stub in the lower half of Table

Table 15.2. Input–Output Coefficients: RIS Sector 2911, Petroleum Refining

Sector			Coefficient
RIS	1311	Crude Petroleum and Natural Gas	−0.555848
	1509	Construction, Maintenance, and Repair	−0.001410
	2652	Set-Up Paperboard Boxes	−0.008054
	2655	Fiber Cans, Tubes, Drums, and Similar Products	−0.001557
	2711	Newspapers	−0.001404
	2812	Alkalies and Chlorine	−0.000935
	2818	Industrial Organic Chemicals, n.e.c.	−0.027180
	2819	Industrial Inorganic Chemicals, n.e.c.	−0.009199
	2911	Petroleum Refining	+0.954950
	2992	Lubricating Oils and Greases	−0.014054
	3411	Metal Cans	−0.005294
	3591	Machine Shop Products	−0.000018
	3599	Machinery and Parts, n.e.c.	−0.000002
	4811	Telephone Communications	−0.001210
	4890	Telegraph and Other Communications	−0.000100
	4911	Electric Utilities	−0.007629
	4920	Gas Companies and Systems	−0.012336
	4941	Water Supply	−0.001082
	4990	Sanitary and Other Systems	−0.000142
	6020	Interest	−0.005088
	6301	Insurance, Nonlife	−0.001242
	6510	Rent	−0.002907
	6590	Real Estate Agents, Managers, etc.	−0.000153
	7301	Business Services, excluding Advertising	−0.017228
	7310	Advertising	−0.002312
	7400	Research and Development	−0.000390
	7500	Automotive Repair	−0.001040
	9100	Federal Government Taxes	−0.022576
	9200	State Government Taxes	−0.004102
	9300	Local Government Taxes	−0.010881
	9826	Office Supplies	−0.000280
	9842	Transportation Costs	−0.040831
	9888	Wages and Salaries	−0.089378
	9891	Net Profits	−0.024331
	9892	Capital Allowance	−0.082876
	9893	Non-Wage Employee Benefits	−0.005597
WPC	1001	Water Intake, Sanitary Use, 1,000 Gal./$ Output	−0.000455
	1002	,, Production ,,	−0.022827
	1003	,, Cooling ,,	−0.114861
	1011	Water Discharged, Sanitary Use ,,	+0.000323
	1012	,, Production ,,	+0.070219
	1013	,, Cooling ,,	+0.050100
	1031	Biochemical Oxygen 1,000 Lb./$ Output Demand BOD, 5-Day,	+0.000065
	1032	Ultimate Oxygen Demand, UOD ,,	+0.000076
	1033	Chemical Oxygen Demand, COD ,,	+0.000169
	1041	Suspended Solids ,,	+0.000084
	1042	Settleable Solids ,,	+0.000124
	1047	Turbidity ,,	+0.000365
	1051	Alkalinity ,,	+0.000051*
	1052	Acidity ,,	+ n.a.
	1061	Oils and Greases ,,	+0.000012
	10951	Phenols ,,	+0.000003

* The pH factor for this industry is in the range of 4.5–10.7, with 7.0–8.0 most likely.
Sources: Philadelphia Region Input–Output Table, and Isard and Romanoff, 1967, pp. 43–44.

Table 15.3. Proposed Water Pollution Classification (WPC) Code

WPC Code	Water Related Item	Units
1000	Water Intake, Total*	1,000 Gal./$
1001	Sanitary Use	,,
1002	Production Use	,,
1003	Cooling	,,
1004	Boiler Feed	,,
1008	Irrigation	,,
1009	Other, n.e.c.	,,
1010	Water Discharge, Total	,,
1011	Sanitary Use	,,
1012	Production	,,
1013	Cooling	,,
1019	Other, n.e.c.	,,
1020	Water Consumed	,,
1031	Biochemical Oxygen Demand, BOD 5-Day	1,000 Lb./$
1032	Ultimate Oxygen Demand, UOD	,,
1033	Chemical Oxygen Demand, COD	,,
1040	Solids, Total†	,,
1041	Suspended Solids	,,
1042	Settleable Solids	,,
1047	Turbidity	,,
1048	Color	,,‡
1051	Alkalinity	,,
1052	Acidity	,,
1061	Oils and Greases	,,
1062	Surfactants	,,
1070	Pathogenic (Disease Causing) Organisms	—§
1080	Temperature	—§
1090	Other Pollutants	,,
1095	Toxic Material¶	,,
1096	Radioactive Waste	—§
1099	Not Classified	,,

* Cost of water intake is given by SIC code 4941—water supply.
† 1040 = 1041 + 1042.
‡ In addition, color should be specified by kind by its wave length.
§ No one satisfactory measure was decided upon at this time, although thermal pollution may be specified most satisfactorily in terms of millions of BTUs per dollar output.
¶ Phenols, which fall in this category, may be identified by a five-digit code such as WPC 10951.
Source: Isard and Romanoff, 1967, p. 10.

15.1, he can then set down the coefficients listed in the bottom half of Table 15.2 for petroleum refining. (For example, we explicitly list in Table 15.1 water [intake] and alkalinity.) Thus, he can take a first step in empirically linking the economic and ecologic systems. Needless to say, petroleum refining involves other noneconomic commodities, for example, air and air pollutants; and other economic activities involve still other noneconomic commodities. Accordingly, there exists a strong need to extend the classification system of noneconomic commodities further and to conduct the laborious work of obtaining the data for the development of the coefficients.

Proceeding further, the investigator may ask, What are the sources of the inputs from the ecologic system to the economic system? How are they produced? To begin to answer these questions, let us shift away from the petroleum industry to one on which much research has been conducted recently—the recreation industry. Let us also center attention on the subject of recreational planning and development.

Elsewhere [Isard, Choguill, and Kissin, 1971] a rather fine classification system of recreational activities has been developed, and so have the coefficients for a meaningful complex of these activities. One of these activities is sport fishing from boats with outboard motors. We therefore list this economic-type activity at the head of one of the columns of the left-hand part of Table 15.1 and record its appropriate coefficients in the column. One of these coefficients is, of course, fish; and in the context of a particular area of New England studied, Plymouth Bay, the chief fish is cod. It has been estimated that per 1,000 man-days of sport fishing in outboards, 6,200 pounds of cod are required in the sense of providing a satisfactory recreational outcome. Therefore, we can set down that number in the cell corresponding to the cod row and sport fishing (outboard motor) column of Table 15.1.

Clearly, for cod to be an input in an activity of the economic system, it must be yielded as an output of a process, the cod production activity, of the ecologic system. This process has been studied, and it has been found that in the context of Plymouth Bay, the cod production activity requires, among others, the inputs listed in the last column of Table 15.4. That is, the output of cod requires, as food inputs, herring, invertebrate carnivores, and small fish. In turn, herring consumes (requires as inputs) plankton; and invertebrate carnivores and small fish consume herbivorous invertebrates, which live on detritus. All these activities are part of a basic food chain in the ecologic system, and their input–output data are to be recorded in the lower right major block of Table 15.1 on Ecologic System: Interprocess Coefficients. Each of the production processes listed at the head of Table 15.4 is to be listed as a column in the right-hand part of

Table 15.4. Food Chain Requirements for Cod Production

Classification Number	Commodity	Units	Plankton Production MX 61-10	All Marine Plant Production MX 60	Detritus Production MX 6001	Production of Herbivorous Invertebrates MX 718	Herring Production MX 719	Small Fish Production MX 722	Carnivorous Invertebrates (Large Gastropods) Production MX 721	Cod Production MX 725
MX 61-10	Plankton	Lbs.	+1				−10			
MX 60	All Marine Plants	,,		+1	−1					
MX 6001	Detritus	,,			+1	−10				
MX 718	Herbivorous Invertebrates (Miscellaneous)	,,				+1		−10	−10	
MX 719	Herring	,,					+1			−1.167
MX 722	Small Fish	,,						+1		−1.167
MX 721	Carnivorous Invertebrates (Large Gastropods)	,,							+1	−8.333
MX 725	Cod	,,								+1

Source: Isard, 1968, p. 91.

Table 15.1 (which relates to ecologic processes) and every one of the commodities listed at the left-hand stub of Table 15.4 is listed among the ecologic commodities in the lower part of the left-hand stub of Table 15.1. A few of these are suggested by the plus (+) and minus (−) entries in Table 15.1.

The food chain, however, represents only one basic set of linkages in the ecologic system. The proper study of the ecologic system—and its relation to the economic system—must cover numerous other basic linkages. Biogeochemical cycles, such as the phosphorous cycle, and photosynthesis are obviously two sets of basic relationships that cannot be ignored. Consider, for example, photosynthesis. In Table 15.4 the −10 entry at the top of the herring production column indicates that 10 pounds of plankton are required per pound of herring. Now, in the Plymouth Bay setting, 1 gram of plankton may be considered as a mixture consisting of 0.86 gram of phytoplankton and 0.14 gram of zooplankton. The zooplankton grazes largely upon phytoplankton, that is, consumes phytoplankton as an input, as indicated in the last column of Table 15.5. The phytoplankton itself is produced by means of photosynthesis, as indicated in the first column of Table 15.5. Note the inputs of light in the form of incident solar radiation at the ocean surface, measured in gram calories per square centimeter per minute, and the input of dissolved phosphate in seawater, and so on. Finally, in columns 2 to 5 of Table 15.5 we take into account the fact that all the carbon fixed by phytoplankton photosynthesis is not available for consumption by zooplankton; some is used up by the phytoplankton's own respiration processes.

The foregoing empirical materials illustrate the kinds of data that can be developed to fill in the cells in three of the major blocks of Table 15.1. We now turn to the question of data to fill in the cells of the fourth major block at the upper right of Table 15.1. Here, a seemingly difficult problem is resolved once the need for an appropriate classification of commodities is recognized.

Reconsider the commodity cod. In Table 15.1 it appears as an ecologic (noneconomic) commodity in the lower half of the commodity classification system—a commodity that is yielded as an output (designated by a +) by an ecologic process and used as an input (designated by a −) by an economic process. It could, however, also be classified directly as an economic commodity or resource, just as land and labor are; and the amount of cod that is provided by the natural environment, just as the amount of land and labor, represents the stock of a resource, which behaves as a constraint on the levels of economic activities that use these resources. Likewise, the timber, or grass (for grazing purposes), or even the phosphate (basic to agricultural production) that natural production processes yield may be listed among the economic commodities in the upper half of the left-hand stub and viewed as scarce economic resources whose use cannot exceed current stocks. Given this viewpoint, then, the positive entries in the cells in the upper right quadrant of Table 15.1 would represent outputs of ecologic processes that are provided as resources to the economic system; and negative entries would represent the use of these economic resources in natural production processes themselves, such as the consumption of herring by cod, or the consumption of corn by wildlife, or the use of phosphorous in noneconomic processes in the phosphorous cycle.

However, this discussion should make clear the point that a classification of commodities often involves somewhat arbitrary decisions. Is land an economic commodity to be recorded in the upper half of the list of Table 15.1, or an ecologic commodity to be recorded in the lower half? The same can be asked with regard to water, air, fish, livestock, and so on.

Table 15.5. Plankton and Related Production Activities

Classification	Commodity	Units	PMX 61-14 Gross Phytoplankton Production by Photosynthesis	P1MX 61-15 Utilization of Phytoplankton Matter by Respiration @ 2°C	P2MX 61-15 Utilization of Phytoplankton Matter by Respiration @ 7°C	P3MX 61-15 Utilization of Phytoplankton Matter by Respiration @ 12°C	P4MX 61-15 Utilization of Phytoplankton Matter by Respiration @ 17°C	PMX 61-11 Pounds (Dummy) Unit Conversion Phytoplankton in Process	PMX 61-10 Plankton Formation	PMX 117 Zooplankton Production
MX 11	Solar Radiation	G. Cal per cm² per Min.	− 1.79							
MX 420	Below 0.55 MG. at./m³ Phosphorous as Phosphate	MG. at. per m²	− 0.06							
MX 42	Above 0.55 MG. at./m³	MG. at. per m²	− 0.00							
MX 44	Water Transparency: t = i/k		−68.68							
MX 61-11	Phytoplankton @ 3.98 g.c./m²	Pounds						+ 1.00	− 0.86	− 1.7
MX 61-12	Phytoplankton Stock	Grams Carbon per m²	± 35.54							
MX 61-13	Phytoplankton	Grams Carbon per m²		−.0201	−.0281	−.0400	−.0565			
MX 61-14	Phytoplankton— Gross Production by Photosynthesis	Grams Carbon per m² per Day	1.00					− 277		
MX 61-15	Loss of Phytoplankton Matter due to Respiration	Grams Carbon per m² per Day		+ 1.00	+ 1.00	+ 1.00	+ 1.00			
MX 61-10	Plankton	Pounds							+ 1.00	
MX 711	Zooplankton @ .68 g.c./m²	Pounds							− 0.14	+ 1.00

Source: Isard, 1968, p. 92.

But while arbitrary elements do enter any classification system, for the purposes of our conceptual framework it makes little difference how we classify commodities, provided that there is full accounting of all inputs and outputs of all commodities relevant to the problem being examined.[2] Similarly, while a classification of processes as economic and ecologic may facilitate our comprehension of a problem, basically such classification is not essential for analysis, provided all processes relevant for a problem are identified and accurately described in an empirical manner.

There is one more general issue that is to be reexamined when we attack the environmental quality problem. It is a well-known axiom in regional science that in any applied study the definition of relevant regions depends in large measure on the problems being attacked. Now, when we attack problems such as air pollution, water pollution, solid waste disposal, and sonic pollution (observe that these problems are of a very different nature than those that have plagued regional analysts over the centuries), we clearly must introduce the physical environment properly into our conceptual framework. To do so requires a drastically different set of regions than those to which we have been accustomed. In effect, it must be recognized that the regional classification system adequate for studying an economy may be grossly inadequate for studying the combination of an economic system and an ecologic system and their interrelations. Similarly, the set of regions that might be most appropriate for studying an ecologic system is very likely to be inappropriate for studying a combination of an economic system and an ecologic system and their interrelations.

Elsewhere, the senior author has suggested that there be considered at least three new major types of regions, namely, LAND, AIR, and MARINE. Each of these three major types of region is composed of subsystems; each has an economic subsystem, an ecologic subsystem, and other subsystems. In Table 15.6 these three major regions are depicted with their economic and ecologic systems. Note that this system of regional classification does not contain traditional regions such as the Philadelphia metropolitan area or New England. However, such traditional regions can be incorporated easily. Under both the economic and ecologic subsystems of the major region LAND, a subsystem region, Philadelphia, is designated. A typical column in the set of columns pertaining to the Philadelphia subsystem region would be the petroleum refining activity, and in that

---

[2] Also bear in mind the possibility that a commodity can be effectively listed twice— once in the ecologic set as an ecologic commodity, and once in the economic set as an economic commodity. In such a situation we may introduce a dummy process that, for example, uses the commodity as an ecologic commodity as an input and transforms and delivers it as an output to the economic system as an economic commodity.

Table 15.6. A Major Region Scheme for Economic and Ecologic Systems Analysis

		Land		Air		Marine	
		Economic	Ecologic	Economic	Ecologic	Economic	Ecologic
		Phila	Phila				
Land	Economic	Phila					
	Ecologic	Phila					
Air	Economic						
	Ecologic						
Marine	Economic						
	Ecologic						

Source: Isard, 1968, p. 94.

column would be listed all its input and output, some of which would be economic and noneconomic commodities that may be classified as land-type (such as crude oil, gasoline, and solid wastes); others would be commodities of marine type (such as clean water from a river system and water pollutants delivered to the marine region); and still others would be commodities of an air type (such as unpolluted air itself and particulates.)

Similarly, there can be listed other subsystem regions (with their activities) relevant for the major environmental region LAND. They can also be listed for the major environmental regions AIR and MARINE; but here the relevant subsystem regions may differ. The Philadelphia metropolitan area need not be a meaningful subsystem region for the AIR and MARINE regions.

In short, we have reached a point at which we must consider rather revolutionary changes in our conception of regions appropriate for planning purposes. In this matter the nature of the problems is compelling us to traverse unexpected ground in our effort to attack them effectively, and consequently, major changes are foreseen in the use of the input–output technique as a tool.

15.2 Standardization

While it is essential to plow entirely new ground conceptually and new areas of application, it is also important to seek new ways to achieve greatly increased productivity in regional input–output work. Perhaps the most significant step toward increased productivity would be to achieve the major scale economies available through standardization. In this section we shall discuss certain possibilities for standardization.[3]

15.2.1 Central Information Facility A first major dimension of standardization involves the establishment and maintenance of an effective central information facility. This facility should be neither understocked nor overburdened with data; that is, it should store, handle, and process an appropriate amount and mix of data. In general, it should operate as a referral center and information source on regional input–output data. More specifically, the facility should function to develop a comprehensive and accurate inventory of input–output and related efforts and to keep this inventory up to date.

Second, it should function to compile, edit, and consolidate information from particular studies to a common format, thereby facilitating access to information on past and particularly current and proposed studies. In order to perform this latter function, a questionnaire and interview procedure should be set up to absorb information on particular studies under way and/or completed. The detailed questionnaire should cover at a minimum the following points:

1. The base period for which data were or are being collected
2. The geographic area covered in the study
3. The SIC or other system employed for sectoring
4. The manner in which final demand sectors were or are being identified and estimated
5. The set of typical questionnaires and sample worksheets
6. The coverage of establishments in each sector and other relevant information on interviewing within each sector, including local sources of secondary information

[3] We draw heavily upon the memoranda issued by the Ad Hoc Committee on Regional Input–Output Studies of the Regional Science Research Institute.

7. Data problems encountered, including ways in which these were or are being met

8. Some evaluation of the quality of data in each sector

9. Disclosure problems and regulations that would have to be followed in the use of the data

10. General information concerning interview costs, time, and other expenses and effort required for the study

11. Information on the locations at which the data on each of the past and current studies are available

12. A listing of staff members of each study; these persons might be usefully contacted when detailed problems arise in new studies.

A third function of the central information facility might be to serve as an archive of input–output information, where such information is stored on microfilm, punch card, tape, and so forth. Much valuable input–output information often is lost when studies are completed and investigators move on to other activities, especially at other locations.

Thus, by having full information on past and current studies, and by effecting continuous contact with ongoing studies, the central information facility would function as a major supportive unit for those who are already in the field of input–output study and those who will be entering and who lack experience and knowledge of what has been done and how past problems have been resolved.

15.2.2 The Development of Standardized Research Procedures The second major dimension of standardization concerns the development of a set of basic research procedures that can be generally useful and hopefully adopted by most input–output studies. The need for many of these procedures has been indicated in previous chapters. We shall not repeat the many points discussed. We simply list some of the more important activities to be engaged in:

1. The development of several sector classifications, both intermediate and final demand, that may be *generally useful* for investigations (it is to be recognized that more than one standardized classification is desirable, since the size and scope of input–output studies vary so much.)

2. The development of one or more representative input–output structures for each of many sectors, with some specification of the extent of regional variation; these structures would be based on representative questionnaire returns and other quality sources of data.

3. The development of one or more consistent sets of regions usable for many studies, and suitable for effective classification and spatial disaggregation of imports and exports.

4. The integration and reintegration, at regular intervals of time, of regional input–output data with other regional and national social accounts and with the national input–output tables.

5. The specification of general input–output procedures for handling both difficult conceptual and unique accounting problems.

Beyond these basic research activities the following could also be of considerable value and might be engaged in by those connected with the central information facility or the basic research on standardization:

1. The effective presentation of the specific needs and data requirements of regional input–output studies to public agencies responsible for data collection.

2. The administration of a pool of uncommitted funds to encourage particular investigators to use standardized definitions and procedures not crucial to their work, or process and further develop their materials in ways that might be extremely useful to others. At a minimum, investigators might be encouraged to furnish the information necessary to facilitate conversion of their data and results to the standardized format.

3. The preparation of a manual on input–output procedures that would summarize succinctly the current state of the art in input–output analysis.

One final comment on standardization is in order. It is one thing to say, "Let's standardize." It is another thing to do it. Perhaps one of the best places at which to begin standardization would be with a sector that is rather common among regions, that is, one that we would expect to find in most, if not all, regions. If the common sector exhibits marked divergence in its technology, as described by coefficients of these sectors for two or more regions, then the practice of using coefficients of one region's sector to describe the technology of the same sector in another region must be seriously questioned.

In a very preliminary study, Isard and Romanoff [1968] examined the printing and publishing sectors, which are quite common among large metropolitan regions. These sectors were examined specifically for two major metropolitan regions, Boston and Philadelphia. Because of similar age, rather similar general setting and business milieu, and geographic proximity of these two regions, the investigator would expect that the technology of these sectors in these two regions would be fairly similar.

In comparing the technologies of a given sector in the two metropolitan regions, Isard and Romanoff used a similarity index, closely related to the index of relative change developed by Leontief [1953, pp. 27–31] and Carter [1967]. The similarity index was of the following form:

$$1 - \left\{ \frac{|a_{ij}^A - a_{ij}^B|}{(a_{ij}^A + a_{ij}^B)} \right\},$$

where a_{ij}^A and a_{ij}^B are the technical coefficients in regions A and B, respectively. The values for the index range from zero to unity. In the last column of Tables 15.7, 15.8, and 15.9 we present the values for the similarity index for SIC 2711, Newspapers: *Publishing, Publishing and Printing*; SIC 2731, *Books: Publishing, Publishing and Printing*; and SIC 2752, *Commercial Printing, Lithographic.* As is apparent, significant discrepancies are indicated by both the values of the technical coefficients and the similarity index. What is still more apparent, however, is the gross inadequacy of the similarity index for the purpose at hand. Technically, it is a poor measure; for example, when, say, $a_{ij}^A = 0$ and $a_{ij}^B > 0$, the similarity index will always be zero, no matter how large or how small a_{ij}^B is; and when $a_{ij}^A = a_{ij}^B$, the similarity index will always be unity, no matter how large or small these coefficients are. But even beyond its technical inadequacies, it is not an effective measure. In short, we lack effective measures and techniques whereby the investigator can test or reach conclusions on whether or not there is sufficient similarity among these two technologies to permit, for example, the Boston coefficients to be used to depict the Philadelphia sector, or the Philadelphia coefficients to depict the Boston sector.

Thus, from this one simple probe it is clear that the development of standardized definitions and procedures is no easy task. Major research effort is needed to develop the required measures and tests.

15.3 Simulation of Regional and Multiregional Economic Systems

As we bring this book to a close, we wish to identify some of the potentialities for using an input–output framework in the simulation of regional and multiregional systems. In Section 10.4 we indicated that there are several developments that now appear on the horizon. First, we may expect much more extensive and intensive collection of data relevant for regional analysis—for example, from the Census of Transportation and from the use by data-collecting agencies of multicountry units such as *functional economic areas* around which to develop a data base, particularly for the evaluation of programs.

Second, we may expect the conduct of more multiregion input–output studies now that a high degree of disaggregation, as in the Philadelphia study, has been clearly demonstrated to be feasible. Such multiregion studies may involve a pure interregional input–output model, or a Moses-Chenery-type model, or a Leontief balanced regional input–output model.

Third, we may expect certain developments with regard to the estimation of capital coefficients for regional studies and additional disaggregations and classifications that are appropriately designed for regional use.

With all these developments, it is clear that the investigator is in a position to simulate more effectively regional and multiregional economic

Table 15.7. Comparisons of Industry Coefficients: SIC 2711, Newspapers: Publishing, Publishing and Printing

4-Digit SIC Code	Philadelphia Coeff.	Rank	Boston Coeff.	Rank	Similarity Index
2298	0.000013	14	0.000598	11	0.0426
2499	—		0.000008	29	0.0
2621	0.318864	1	0.207982	1	0.7896
2641	—		0.000115	17	0.0
2649	—		0.000014	26	0.0
2652	—		0.000119	16	0.0
2653	—		0.000002	31	0.0
2711	0.000287	8	0.048177	2	0.0119
2751	0.000052	11	—		0.0
2752	0.000157	9	—		0.0
2782	—		0.000036	21	0.0
2789	0.000061	10	0.000072	19	0.9173
2791	0.000017	13	0.000766	8	0.0434
2793	0.009069	2	0.004064	4	0.6189
2794	0.001194	6	0.000036	22	0.0586
2799	0.000748	7	—		0.0
2819	—		0.000017	25	0.0
2824	—		0.000011	27	0.0
2891	—		0.000207	14	0.0
2893	0.008270	3	0.006731	3	0.9480
2911	0.000007	15	0.000788	7	0.0
2992	—		0.000037	20	0.0
3199	—		0.000076	18	0.0
3312	—		0.000245	13	0.0
3315	—		0.000378	12	0.0
3341	0.002803	5	0.000610	9	0.3575
3351	—		0.000036	23	0.0
3356	—		0.000009	28	0.0
3497	—		0.000005	30	0.0
3545	—		0.000019	24	0.0
3555	0.005768	4	0.000609	10	0.1910
3591,9	0.000050	12	—		0.1170
3861	—		0.002641	5	0.0
3951	—		0.000142	15	0.0
$\sum$ MI	0.347360		0.275355		0.8844
9842	0.021599		0.015311		0.8297
9888	0.334380		0.425367		0.8803
9899	0.296661		0.283967		0.9781
TOTAL	1.000000		1.000000		
Reported Estab.	7		6		
Reported Empl.	2,928		1,425		

Source: Isard and Romanoff, 1968, p. 43.

Table 15.8. Comparison of Industry Coefficients: SIC 2731, Books:
Publishing, Publishing and Printing

4-digit SIC Code	Philadelphia Coeff.	Rank	Boston Coeff.	Rank	Similarity Index
2241	0.002084	12	—		0.0
2621	0.080290	3	0.006970	3	0.1598
2641	0.020242	5	0.000102	10	0.0101
2653	0.000634	17	0.000685	7	0.9614
2732	0.081403	2	0.257212	1	0.4808
2711	0.008162	8	—		0.0
2751	0.004421	10	—		0.0
2752	0.002221	11	—		0.0
2753	0.000100	18	—		0.0
2789	0.100810	1	0.026406	2	0.4152
2791	0.014328	7	0.000981	6	0.1282
2793	0.022419	4	0.000335	9	0.0295
2794	0.017278	6	0.004071	4	0.3814
2799	0.000748	16	—		0.0
2893	0.004830	9	—		0.0
2911	0.001723	14	0.000452	8	0.4157
3341	0.000815	15	—		0.0
3555	0.002083	13	—		0.0
3591,9	0.000050	19	0.001935	5	0.0504
3953	—		0.000017	11	0.0
$\sum$ MI	0.364641		0.299166		0.8839
9842	0.009806		0.006335		0.7850
9888	0.244484		0.139068		0.7252
9899	0.381069		0.555431		0.8138
TOTAL	1.000000		1.000000		
Reported Estab.	4		3		
Reported Empl.	349		1065		

Source: Isard and Romanoff, 1968, p. 43.

systems. No longer is the investigator forced, in an input–output simulation, to use the coefficients of national input–output tables, adjusted here and there to reflect special knowledge about a region where such knowledge can easily be inserted into the empirical materials. At the minimum, he now has the highly disaggregated Philadelphia input–output coefficient table, the Washington State table, and a number of other tables upon which to rely for suitable empirical materials. The Philadelphia coefficients are already being used extensively to fill in gaps in the data base for different regions being studied.

Of much greater potential significance, however, are a central information facility and standardization practices. If established, these can make available a wealth of regional input–output data suitable for simulation models. One can easily imagine that with (1) several representative input–output vectors for every sector defined according to one or more

Table 15.9. Comparison of Industry Coefficients: SIC 2752, Commercial
Printing, Lithographic

4-digit SIC Code	Philadelphia Coeff.	Rank	Boston Coeff.	Rank	Similarity Index
2298	—		0.000033	27	0.0
2621	0.194193	1	0.214919	1	0.9494
2631	0.003816	11	0.000118	26	0.0600
2641	0.021577	3	0.002326	8	0.1946
2642	0.004522	9	0.001743	10	0.5564
2645	0.000160	29	0.000727	15	0.3608
2649	0.000076	30	0.000243	22	0.4765
2651	0.000624	23	0.000211	24	0.5054
2652	0.002993	13	0.000311	21	0.1883
2653	—		0.000193	25	0.0
2655	0.000307	26	—		0.0
2711	0.001580	18	—		0.0
2751	0.003750	12	—		0.0
2752	0.002723	14	0.002004	9	0.8479
2753	—		0.003003	7	0.0
2782	0.001252	20	0.000597	17	0.6458
2789	0.019742	4	0.010505	5	0.6946
2791	0.026455	2	0.012639	3	0.6466
2793	0.006495	8	0.009280	6	0.8235
2794	0.004392	10	0.000024	29	0.0109
2799	0.000748	22	—		0.0
2816	0.000454	25	—		0.0
2818	0.001295	19	0.001254	12	0.9839
2819	0.002236	15	0.000408	19	0.3086
2893	0.014668	5	0.029476	2	0.6646
2911	0.001690	17	0.000687	16	0.5781
3341	0.014316	6	0.000218	23	0.0300
3356	0.000212	28	0.001006	13	0.3481
3554	0.000541	24	—		0.0
3555	0.001816	16	0.001492	11	0.9021
3591,9	0.000050	31	0.000029	28	0.7179
3641	—		0.000462	18	0.0
3861	0.011257	7	0.010945	4	0.9860
3952	0.000228	27	0.000336	20	0.8085
3955	0.000917	21	0.000819	14	0.9436
$\sum$ MI	0.345085		0.306008		0.9400
9842	0.020183		0.017718		0.9350
9888	0.407444		0.436956		0.9651
9899	0.227288		0.239318		0.9742
TOTAL	1.000000		1.000000		
Reported Estab.	10		11		
Reported Empl.	1,083		833		

Source: Isard and Romanoff, 1968, p. 47.

standardized classification schemes and (2) a fair amount of primary data developed in ways consistent with a clearly defined set of standardized procedures, an investigator can quickly develop a regional or multi-regional input–output coefficient table that would be highly useful for studies of his region.

The investigator can go even beyond this and develop regional and multiregional input–output coefficient tables for analyzing various kinds of spatial interrelations and examining a diverse set of feedback effects. Also, as the data base improves, more sensitivity analysis can be undertaken. For example, when the investigator supplements the traditional input–output data base with air use, water use, and air, water, and solid waste pollution coefficients—as should be done for comprehensive planning purposes—he can test the sensitivity of environment quality (however defined) for any hypothetical region or set of regions to different regulatory policies. In this context, each policy may comprise one or more components relating to one or more aspects of the total environment.

In short, the promise of simulation-type models is great once the data base is considerably enhanced through a central information facility, and once proper sets of standardized procedures are defined and employed in diverse studies.

References
Carter, Anne P. (1967). "Changes in the Structure of the American Economy," *Review of Economics and Statistics*, 49: 209–224.

Isard, Walter (1968). "Some Notes on the Linkage of the Ecologic and Economic Systems," *Papers and Proceedings of the Regional Science Association*, 22: 84–96.

———, et al. (1967). "On the Linkage of Socio-Economic and Ecologic Systems," *Papers and Proceedings of the Regional Science Association*, 21: 79–99.

———, C. Choguill, J. Kissin, et al. (1971). *Ecologic and Economic Analysis for Regional Planning*. New York: The Free Press.

———, and Eliahu Romanoff (1967). *Water Use and Water Pollution Coefficients: Preliminary Report* (Technical Paper No. 6). Cambridge, Mass.: Regional Science Research Institute, November.

———, and Eliahu Romanoff (1968). *The Printing and Publishing Industries of Boston SMSA, 1963: And Comparison with the Corresponding Philadelphia Industries* (Technical Paper No. 7). Cambridge, Mass.: Regional Science Research Institute.

Leontief, W., et al. (1953). *Studies in the Structure of the American Economy*. New York: Oxford University Press.